James,

Going Out! Kill it!! Kill it!!! Oh, I'm sorry, I thought I heard a bird flush. This Book is for the deadliest 410 shooter on the Planet.

your Friend,
Web

Bond of Passion:

Living with and Training your Hunting Dog

Web Parton
Oracle, Arizona
2008

Casa Cielo Press: Oracle, Arizona
©2008

Copyright © 2008 by Web Parton
Photographs copyright © 2008 by Web Parton, except where noted

ALL RIGHTS RESERVED. No part of this work may be reproduced or used in any form, by any means- graphic, electronic, or mechanical, including photocopying, recording, taping, or any information storage and retrieval system- without written permission of the author. All requests should be addressed to:
Casa Cielo Press, P.O. Box 1296, Oracle, AZ 85623
casacielo@theriver.com

Edited by Nicole Poissant
Cover photo by Randy Babb

Published and Distributed by Casa Cielo Press
P.O. Box 1296
Oracle, AZ 85623
www.casacielopress.com

Printed in the United States of America

Portions of this book appeared previously in
The Pointing Dog Journal

Library of Congress Cataloging-in-Publication Data
Library of Congress Control Number: 2008901244
    Parton, Web
    Bond of Passion: Living with and Training your Hunting Dog/ Web Parton

    ISBN-13: 978-0-9801131-4-3
    ISBN-10: 0-9801131-4-8

Author and English setter, Musette. (Photo by Randy Babb)

Acknowledgements

A book is a major undertaking, and this one has been many years in the making. I would like to thank and acknowledge those individuals who have gone above and beyond with their generosity and assistance.

First, there is a small group of friends who I can always count on for the hard stuff, be it searching for a lost dog out on the flats or more dangerous fare. In reviewing this list, I realized that every one of these friends have held and restrained a rattlesnake for me while I defanged it: Don Prentice, Jay Smith, Cliff Russell, Mike Merry, Randy Babb, James Laws, Gil Russell, Dave Gowdey and Bob Miller.

Thank you to Glenn Seal, retired pro bird dog trainer of Marana, Arizona, who, many years ago, taught me how to snake break. In addition, much gratitude to Bill and Dee Tarrant and Gene and Cathy Hill, for their many kindnesses and their encouragement regarding writing.

I have deep appreciation for the very helpful comments of our proofreaders who were sent an advance copy of this manuscript: Kevin Carmichael, Eileen Clarke, James Gross, Brenda Jordan, Jim Jordan, Sophie Poissant, Don Prentice, Ed Rader, and Jay Smith. Proofreading a technical manuscript before the illustrations are available requires a lot of skill and imagination, which these folks have in abundance.

Sincere thanks and appreciation to Jim Jordan for his excellent foreword and Nicole Poissant for her superb editing skills. Also a special thanks to Cathy Zipperian.

Additionally, many thanks to Jason Smith, Steve Smith, and The Pointing Dog Journal, in which portions of this book were previously published.

I am very grateful to Gene Ault, DVM Retired, and Carol Rowe, DVM, who taught me how to doctor dogs and kept our string of dogs patched together while I was guiding. You are both the best in the business, willing to share your knowledge and expertise for the good of dogs everywhere.

Thanks to the many friends that I have met over the years in the industry, including: Jim Jordan, formerly of PSE and Innotek; Pi Polletta and Mark Zepp, of Tri-Tronics; Andy Bown and Ed Rader, of Innotek; Dez Young and Bob Corley of HWH Productions, producers of the Dash in the Uplands tv show; John Kirk of the International Sportsmen's Expo; Jack Brewton, Art Agent extraordinaire; and Jim Niemiec, fellow writer.

A large part of the efforts that went into producing this book were the photographs that illustrate the text. I would like to thank Nicole Poissant, Randy Babb, Jay Smith, Ron Spomer, Dee Tarrant, and Sandy McClure for permission to use their photos in these pages.

I also wish to acknowledge and heartfully thank those who have endured being in front of a camera while I was holding it: Michael Alber, Robert Arthour, Bob Bates, Bill Berlat, Tom Brown, Kevin Carmichael, Earl Carrico, Jim Charlton, Bob Ciulla, Ron Ford, Bill Gaddy, Joe Giurfa, Don Guyer, Jim Hays, Tom Huggler, Gary Hull, Larry Hull, John Hustwick, Jim Jurries, Darrell Kincade, Al Kritter, Dave Kritter, Tim Kritter, Sam Kuhns, Clinton Larson, James Laws, Mike Merry, Burt Miller, John Mullen, Wayne Meyers, Ron Olding, Tejal Parikh, Al Peevy, Don Prentice, Ed Rader, the Rice family (Matt, Laura, Jamie and Jessi), Mark Rogers, Cliff Russell, June Russell, Gil Russell, John Sherman, Bill & Carolyn Simon, Jay Smith, Harold Snyder, Tom Strunk, Bill Taylor, Linda Thomas, Bob Tinker, Dan Torrance, Martin Waldrop, Ralph Ward, and Bob Willis. I do believe your efforts paid off! And to all those others who contributed to this effort over the years, thank you!

Finally, I wish to thank my wife, Nicole, without whose help, support, encouragement, involvement, organizing efforts and patience this book would not exist.

Last but never least, my thanks and appreciation to all the dogs that have run through our lives. This book is about them.

Author doctoring an English setter, Bandita, in the field many years ago. (Photo by Bill Tarrant, used courtesy of Dee Tarrant)

TO THE MAGIC...

Table of Contents

Foreword by Jim Jordan 15

Opening Section 19
    Introduction 23
    Becky 25
    Your Dog's Primary Requirement 28
    Emma 31
    What a Trainer needs to know about Him or Herself 38

Types of Gun Dogs 47
    Dog Breed Choices 47
    Dog Breeds: Bird Dogs 55
        • Pointers 55
        • Setters 57
    Dog Breeds: Continental, Versatile Breeds 58
        • German Shorthair Pointers 58
        • German Wire-Hair Pointers (Drathauers, Griffons,
          Pudle Pointers) 59
        • Brittanies 61
        • Weimaraner/Vizslas 63
    Dog Breeds: Spaniels 64
        •Springers 64
        • Cockers/Boyken Spaniel 65
    Dog Breeds: Retrievers 66
        • Labradors 66
        •Chesapeake Bay Retrievers 67
        • Golden Retrievers 69

Training 72
    Patience: The First Thing Your Dog Needs To Learn 72
    Training Whoa or Hup: A Gun Dog's Foundation Command 73
    Place Matters: The Whoa Hook 79
    The First Two Whoa Associations 80
    Whoa Post 83

Whoa Training Guidelines by Breed	87
Putting It All Together	90
Third Whoa Association	91
Fourth Whoa Association	92
Next Step: Birds	96
Field Work	100
Flying Birds in the Field	102
Letting Go of the Check Cord	103
Learning the "Come" and "Here" Commands	105
Working with Planted Birds	108
Using Game Birds for Training	116

Transitioning into Wild Birds — 123

Flushing Breeds	123
Pointing Breeds	125
Steady to Wing and Shot	131

Retrieving — 133

Retrieving: How It Can Be Done	133
Retrieving: How It Should Be Done	141
Hard Mouth	143
The Force Breaking Table	145
Force Breaking: The Method	152
Evaluating Modified Force Breaking as an Option	157
Modified Force Breaking	158
Troubleshooting: Modified Force Breaking	159
Conventional Force Breaking	162

Information for the Field — 169

Wild Birds and Scent	169
Handling in the Field	176
Water and Heat: Keeping the Dog Running	181
Pads and Time on the Ground	186
First Aid in the Field	188

Training With Electronic Collars — 195

Electronic Training Collars	195
Using an E-Collar	204

Reactive E-Collar Use — 209
    Avoidance Training Overview — 209
    Rattlesnake Avoidance Training — 210

Training Problems — 215
    Buster and Boo — 218
    Shy: Gun, Bird, Man — 220
    Blinking — 226
    Self-Hunting — 236
    Lost Dogs — 239
    Fighting — 246
    The Broom Dance: What to Do about a Barking Dog — 249

In Closing — 257
    Saying Goodbye — 257
    A Walk In The Wind — 260
    Generations — 264

Appendix: Training Tools — 269
    Bark Collar — 270
    Beeper Collar — 271
    Bells — 272
    Belt Lead — 273
    Bird Carriers — 274
        • Bird Cages — 274
        • Bird Bucket — 275
        • Bird Pouches — 276
        • Call Back Pens — 277
    Bird Releases — 278
        • Nylon Bird Harnesses — 278
        • Mechanical Releases — 279
    Blank Pistols — 281
    Bumpers — 282
    Chain Gang — 283
    Check Cord — 286
    D-Ring Collar — 288

Dowels/Training Bucks	289
Hobbles	290
Kennel Box	291
Leather Gloves	292
Pig Tie	293
Pinch Collar	294
Tie-Out Cable	295
Training Shotguns	296
Training Tables	298
Whistle	300
Whoa Post	301
Emergency/First Aid Medical Box List	304

Index   **307**

Foreword
By Jim Jordan

I am honored to write the foreword to Web's new dog training book. I have known him for 12 years and have a great respect for his intuitive instincts in working with dogs and with people, which go hand in hand.

My first contact with Web was back in the mid-nineties when I was living in Tucson, Arizona. I had worked in the archery industry for many years and decided I needed a new hobby outside that realm. That hobby became bird dogs and shotgun shooting for me and my wife, Brenda. Our first dog, a 10-month-old German shorthair named Josey that we had just bought, was people shy, bird shy and gun shy. I had a "trainer" in Tucson tell me, "Put a bullet through her head because she will never be a hunting dog." After three hours of phone conversation with Web about his training techniques, and his various experiences with different dogs, I decided Web was the trainer that Josey needed. I could hear his love and passion for dogs through that conversation. When other folks were ready to give up on their problem dogs, Web was just beginning. He worked with our Josey to overcome her anxieties and fears.

Today, our 12-year-old Josey is a good, solid hunter. Plus, she's a great companion, gets along well with other dogs, and loves everyone she comes into contact with. She's very special and we can't imagine life without her. We're very thankful that Web brought her back for us.

During the next three years, with Web's help, Brenda and I added three more dogs to our family. They were all trained by Web. I worked with him a lot of weekends, watching and participating in their training. What I came to realize was that in addition to training our dogs, Web was also training me. I also now realize (although I couldn't see it at the time) that our "baby," Trixie (a Brittany), was so spoiled that we weren't willing to be tough enough to allow her to be her best.

The first thing that struck me when I observed Web working with his chain gang of dogs (aged one to nine years) was his patience, his connection with them and his knack of knowing exactly what the weaknesses and strengths were of each one. It didn't take long for me to figure out that his foundation for training had long term payoffs. I have witnessed this many times out in the field with my three shorthairs and one Brittany.

A unique and special trait that Web has is to recover throwaway hunting dogs from the pound and turn them into trained and vital hunting companions. He always had a couple of these dogs on the chain gang. He would figure out what piece of the puzzle was missing from each and work diligently to turn them into trained hunters. Eventually, he would sell them to hunters that he knew would "fit" with them. I witnessed one truly amazing example of this with a young female German shorthair that Web had rescued from the pound. My first contact with her was when I reached into his trailer to get her out for the chain gang, and I thought she was going to take my arm off! It was obvious that this dog had not been socialized, was very frightened and was probably abused. Eventually, with love, (he would bring these "special" cases into his home to spend time with him & his wife, Nicole) patience and training, Web made that little shorthair into a fine hunter. She became one of his main dogs for guiding quail hunts in the Arizona desert.

Emma was also amazing! She was Web's English setter that had lost a hind leg in an accident. That little girl would outhunt many dogs in open Tucson desert. I was impressed by her drive and desire to please. She was another example of Web never giving up and giving a dog every chance.

In later years, as Vice President of Sales for a company that manufactured electronic training aids for dogs, I was blessed to work with many fine dog trainers, but the early years with Web gave me insight into the wealth of knowledge that he has in working with all hunting breeds. He is very well read and can quote "scripture and verse" from many dog training books. He has put together his own individual techniques of training and is excellent at sorting through each dog's problems and how to solve them. In addition, Web can figure out the expectations of the owners and work with their dogs to bring them to that level.

I know that you will enjoy Web's book. Reading his book is like sitting and talking to him. He creates confidence that you can do the training, too. He is very intuitive with dogs and he can detour trouble before it happens. He doesn't let the dog fail and he'll teach you how to do the same. His book imparts all the wisdom he has learned about training a hunting dog, in a methodical step-by-step manner and can be used by an amateur with a first hunting dog or by an experienced dog trainer.

In the beginning Web taught me about the basics of training hunting dogs. Later, he helped me to grow as a trainer and a hunter. Ten years plus later, he taught me how to know when it was time to let our much loved shorthairs, 16-year-old Beau and 15-year-old Chrissy, go. He taught me how to "say goodbye." And yet, the wonderful days spent afield with Beau and Chris are some of mine and Brenda's best memories and will always live on in our hearts. And, by the way, our Trixie turned into a great hunting companion, too. Web was the beginning of making those great days happen.

Jim Jordan's first professional job was as a special education teacher and administrator in public schools. After eight years, he moved into the shooting sports industry in sales and marketing, where he has spent the last twenty-eight years.

The most notable of these milestones of his career are his positions as Vice President of Precision Shooting Company (archery); President of Highlander Sports (general hunting products); National Sales Manager of Beretta U.S.A (firearms); and Vice President of Innotek (electronic training aids for dogs).

He is now retired and living in East Tennessee with his three most prized companions: his wife, Brenda; shorthair, Josey, and Brittany, Trixie.

(Photo by Randy Babb)

For hunters, there is a bond of shared passion between dog and human. A drive encoded into the genes of both. A drive shaped through eons of shared memory. This drive is what nourishes hunter teams. It is the reason the dog/human bond exists, and to the extent and degree that this bond is shared and nurtured, it determines the quality of our dogs and the quality of our lives.

Introduction

Let me start with the basics: I am a professional gun dog trainer. I don't train dogs for field trials or hunting tests; instead, I train them to hunt wild birds in the field. In discussing an early draft of this book with a friend, he told me that he had found that I was different from other trainers he knew in one particular way, comparing me to an old world horse trader who would find a broken animal of little to no value and turn it into a valuable and useful horse.

I am pretty good at fixing dog problems. As a professional gun dog trainer, I spent a good deal of time fixing dog problems that would not have existed if the dog's early introductions and training had been properly handled. This book is an effort to spare the prospective gun dog trainer and his/her dog a significant measure of grief. Doing it right the first time is always so much easier than fixing a problem later.

This book is designed to assist a bird dog hunter with the training of a gun dog, starting with formal yard work and transitioning to wild birds in the field. I train in layers and have written this book in the same manner. All the layers of training required to successfully whoa/hup/sit-break a dog are clearly illustrated and described. This book focuses extensively on this essential yard work or foundation training because, typically, this is the area where the majority of novice dog trainers fail.

This critical foundational training can not be skipped nor abbreviated. To build a house without a foundation to attach to is to guarantee that the walls will buckle and collapse when the wind blows, or in this case, when the first bird flushes. Folks feel the passion and crave the magic and consequently go straight to bird introductions, neglecting the essential yard work that allows them the necessary control when a dog is on birds. In doing this, they settle for a fraction of the dog that could have been.

From the beginning, I wanted to learn how to train dogs. I was taught the old-school way as a kid, but the end results of that left a lot to be desired and the methodology was arcane. A training friend told me back then that you don't learn how to train dogs by training the easy ones, and since that time I have worked with the all the dogs that came to me. I studied and did a lot of research about dog training over the years. Eventually, what I realized was that the more I learned, the less I knew. Gun dog training is a strange mixture of mechanics and art. A trainer lays down the structured, mundane, repetitive foundation, stirs in birds, and waits for the magic to appear.

And when the magic happens...

I've observed multiple dogs when their magic moment arrives. It's never anything I can control or deliver. It always happens on wild birds, in some unique combination of chance and luck and divine intervention. A covey breaks and goes short and I come in with the dog at the instant the wind and the scent stream comingle and merge into a sort of evoked alchemy. This time the dog can smell the birds. Wild birds. This time the dog stalls in front and then locks up, certain of what lies in the grass just ahead of its nose. I walk to the side of the dog, and then step out front. I hear the commotion. Eruption. The bird clears the cover and goes horizontal with the wind. The front of the gun swings through the blurred movement of feathers, and at the report the shape puffs and slowly arcs to ground. The dog is there on the downed bird. Feathers to mouth and then to hand. The circle is complete. After the dog returns the bird to the gun, it hits the stream of scent from a second bird and then a third and each one is completed in turn and the bird returned to the gun.

From that point on, for the rest of that dog's life, he or she will hunt to complete that circle. Scent plus gun equals bird.

Each new day in the field is an attempt to conjure the magic yet again, to find it one more time...another chance to share that same passion. What drives the hunter is the same essence that drives the dog. The two feed each other and shape each other until, eventually, it's not the birds, but the magic that matters.

Kevin Carmichael stands by to gun, while Web trains a German shorthair pointer. (Photo by Tejal Parikh)

Becky

The phone call came in mid-morning. It was the local county animal control officer. He told me that she was a young German shorthair pointer. She looked to be about eight months old. Someone had turned her in as unwanted. They had had her several days in the shelter. He thought that maybe I could do something with her. They were killing her in two days.

"Well...ok."

Unlike most states, Arizona only has 15 counties. The county I live in is the size of a small eastern seaboard state. It's a two hour drive to the county shelter. That's four hours combined drive time. With training and chores, tomorrow was going to be a very long day.

I got to the shelter not knowing what to expect. I had done this before to find that their interpretation of a shorthair was some sort of shepard mix. I was led through the back room to a meager row of indoor/outdoor runs. They took me to an empty one. The concrete was unsoiled. I stepped inside and kneeled down to look through the dog door to the outside portion of the run.

She indeed looked to be an eight to nine-month-old GSP. She was clinging to the chainlink. She looked in pretty bad shape. Her eyes were sunken in and her skin hung on her. I put my hand through the door and coaxed her to me. When I got a hand on her, I tented her skin and could see that she was severely dehydrated. There was a bowl of water on the inside of the door beside me so I tried to coax her through the door opening, but she was having no part of it. I dipped my fingers in the water and she licked them. She refused the door and it was a protracted tug of war to pull her through the small opening. Once I got her inside, I put her muzzle in the water and she drank for a long time. It's probably a good guess that was the first water she drank at the facility.

Although I couldn't read much in her condition, I could tell by her color and conformation that she was old school German blood. I signed the papers, gave them money and got her out of there.

I put her on the seat beside me in the truck and she sat quietly. She looked weak. Once we got to the house, I tried to bring her in through the sun porch into the kitchen. She made it plain that she didn't do doors: didn't go through them, didn't stay by them, would not remain on the inside side of them. So, I left her outside short-tied and I went and closed off the kitchen doggy door. I then returned outside, picked her up and carried her into the kitchen, closing the door behind me.

She had no way out, so she clung to the door because it was the only way out she knew. I couldn't coax her away from it. I put bowls of food and water by her and a door mat for her to sit on. When she saw the mat she immediately went to place and then I knew that someone had been using the NAVHDA training manual very enthusiastically. I backed off and gave her several days. I didn't want to push her into more fear, so I waited for the fear she was showing to evaporate. I took her outside on a lead to void, and then carried her back in to get her back into the house. She clung to that mat.

It took about four days to get her to willingly leave the kitchen and explore the house. I introduced her to the other dogs and rolled her into the training schedule. She came around. I called her Becky.

A friend reminded me that he had been out to help me train shortly after she arrived. It was one of her first trips out to the training area on the dog trailer. I had pulled up and we had dragged out and anchored the chain gang. One by one, we returned to the trailer and brought another dog out to a spot riding the chain. He was the first to get to Becky's hole in the trailer. As he tried to pull her out through the trailer door, she attempted to remove his hand. He thought at the time that this one was beyond recovery.

Well, eventually she came on and did everything right. She made one of the best field dogs that I have ever run. She is deadly on Mearns' quail. I worked her on the string for guiding clients and she really looked impressive. She found birds. During her second season, while running on a four day booking, one of my gentlemen offered me $3,000 for her. He thought that she would be just what he needed to make a hard driving, yet at the same time careful, ruffed grouse dog. I told him I would consider it and let him know on the last day of the hunt.

I had turned down a previous offer for her of $2,000 earlier in the season; however, running dogs requires money. The situations vary, but the need for money remains the same: the dog trailer needs new springs and tires; it's annual vaccination time; I have a bird bill coming up...pick a reason to need to sell a dog. $3,000 dollars buys a lot of kibble which, by coincidence, a person needs when feeding 25 to 30 dogs.

I've never found it an easy thing to sell a dog. However, during the time I trained, I had multiple German dogs that were brought in to train out and sell. It was a condition of doing business, and for every one leaving there was another waiting to come in. I had done what I could do for Becky. She would be going to a good person and she would be hunted. She was finished, while there were others to bring in that needed help.

Since she was fully broke, I needed her to work for clients through the end of the season. I told my gentleman that I would sell her on the condition that I ran her through the end of the season and then put her on a plane in mid-February. He agreed.

I also explained to him that what he saw in her was a conditional thing. I told him that "you can't buy magic." Becky looked impressive. She was solid and dependable around me and with me handling her, but she had been a wreck when she came in. Her need for contact and proximity were being met and she responded. I didn't know how she would respond if there was a change in that proximity. I define proximity as making the dog part of my family by including her in my daily life, allowing her close access to me and my family. The dog then learns that she belongs to our family "pack" and what her position is in the family. She knows she is welcome inside our doors.

He had me ship her to a pro in the Northeast who specialized in ruffed grouse dogs. She had been running with me on desert quail and he wanted her to get some time in grouse country on grouse. He would shoot over her himself the following season.

February came around. I put her on a plane and got it done.

Months later, I got a call from Becky's new owner. He told me that the pro had struggled with her and had ultimately told him that she wasn't going to work out. The pro had told him that he could make a place for her in a put and take planted bird operation the pro ran, but she wouldn't make the grouse dog Becky's owner wanted. To my gentleman's credit, he knew what he had seen in the dog on wild birds and rather than leave her to a lesser fate, he called me and asked if I wanted the dog back.

I will always be grateful for that call. I shudder to think what the dog had cost him in training fees with the other pro, not to mention travel, vet and other related expenses, including the original purchase price. My gentleman did not ask for any reimbursement. He asked if I could put the dog back to where she was when he had seen her run on wild birds. I told him I could. He had her put on a plane at his expense.

She was a little soft for a couple of days after I picked her up at the airport. I got her back in with the other dogs and back on the chain gang during training. On day three or four we did a few laps on the whoa post. I had her in the field on birds a week after her return. It was like she had never left. It wasn't about retraining or repair, but some other thing that had been missing that caused Becky to not make the transition. I would call it proximity. There was a thing missing that she needed. You recall I told the gentleman my concern regarding Becky leaving, "You can't buy magic."

For me, with dogs, I have found that the magic is almost always there. All that is required is alchemy to make it tangible. Alchemy, and maybe a little divine intervention thrown in to boot.

Becky retrieves a male Gambel's quail.

Your Dog's Primary Requirement

I imagine it as some huge assignment board somewhere with unborn puppies waiting in line for their new postings. When dogs come to earth and into our lives they have one primary job: to look after us. While we are looking to get a new gun dog, the dog's goal is to be with us, in all our moods and actions, watching and waiting.

The old line goes that you can't make a friend out of a hunting dog. This sentiment is just plain false. The best dogs are those who have unencumbered access to their humans. They require it in order to be whole. When a dog lives with you, he is able to read your thoughts before you think them. That canine ability to gauge even the slightest nuances of body language and emotion will eclipse even the most intimate of human/

human relationships. All this translates into the sort of working relationship that will mature your dog into a superior hunting partner.

Live with your dog with this in mind. Make your life as open as is practical for the new canine that has been assigned to you. Certainly training sessions and fun time in the field qualify; but, in addition, your dog needs to lie by you when you're on the computer or talking on the phone. He needs rides to the store and shared cheap hamburgers at the fast food drive-thru. I'm not talking touchy-feely here, I'm talking shared space. Your dog needs the time and access to connect to you through osmosis. Most dog/human interactions are ultimately transferred by brain waves, not physical or verbal cues. The physical and verbal cues may help to clear up confusion or clarify intent, but if your dog isn't reading your mind the pair of you are operating with a fraction of your effectiveness and your relationship and time in the field are diminished.

I'm not necessarily talking joined at the hip here, either. Even short periods of time, ten or twenty minute chunks, are of value. If you can arrange for your dog to have three hours lying at your feet while you veg out in front of the TV or work at the computer, so much the better. In both instances, your dog is experiencing quality time. In my situation, that quality time may translate into two hours on the chain gang from 7:30 to 9:30 pm, under the parking lights in some Wal-Mart parking lot, or on a dirt strip alongside a rural motel. This after a long day on the road, guiding hunting clients. I tend to dogs and then sit down in a folding chair and eat my drive-thru Chinese dinner. Dogs may look like they are sleeping, but in actuality they are tracking everything you do, think, and feel.

You think not? Turn off the TV and try slipping out of that recliner while your dog is sleeping.

It may be that your new dog is already grown. Some of the best dogs we have had came to us not as puppies, but as older dogs. An older dog can be anywhere from 6 months to 6 or more years old. That older dog still has the primary need to bond with his human on a deep, intimate level. In the vast majority of instances, no matter what the age, a dog will connect with his human to the degree that the human will allow. This means that, regardless of the type of treatment he received prior to his new assignment, if you allow him to make a deep connection, you can bring him around.

I have seen a handful of exceptions. In working professionally with problem dogs, the hardest dogs to fix are not those that have been ill-treated or that have suffered harsh physical associations. Often, these are the dogs that really blossom once treated with patience, kindness and respect.

It is, actually, the dog which was denied human contact, shut away in a kennel with food shoved under the gate for the first months of life, which suffers the real damage. Was there mental illness, divorce, family death or suicide that made the human part of the team unavailable? Important connections can break down during the months when the puppy should have been developing the ability to bond to humans and other dogs. It can be very difficult to reach these unsocialized dogs because the very things you need to connect with don't exist. A trainer has to look for the smallest window available to begin to connect to such a dog. Depending on how complete the dearth of human interaction was, these can be dogs that are not salvageable.

Then there are the sick bastards. I had a Vizsla come in for training that had gone through some special conditioning program designed to produce wonder dogs. The Vizsla's owner had paid top dollar for this puppy, after having the gospel of "special conditioning" preached to him by the breeder. He was anticipating a wonder dog from his new puppy. That didn't happen and he ended up with a dog that was unable to cope with the everyday world. He brought the dog to me. The dog came in fearful and panicked. I isolated him in a private run and the owner left. Then the dog really came apart. He snapped at any other dog that approached the wire. He hackled up when I tried to talk with him through the fence. He clung to a wall and snapped at the air. I needed to move him and I entered the run. He panicked and came at me completely out of control with fear. He tore the end of a heavy duty cable restraint when I tried to restrain him. I called the owner and apologized for not being able to help his dog and told him to come pick him up. If my memory serves me, I think the dog was here for less than a day. Then, I sat down and did the research on this "special conditioning" to try and figure out what had happened.

Mercifully, I don't remember the name of the special program and I won't look for it to include it on this page. It is one of those facts that I don't want contaminating my mind.

However, the gist of the program was that you take a puppy at birth and torture it by submerging it in ice water at one day old, two days old, three days old. Basically, the premise of this "conditioning" is denying the newborn comfort and stability by stressing the puppy with stimuli that is harsh and jarring. This during the critical time when the puppy is learning to trust the world. You deny the newborn the basic needs of security and nurturance, and this is a good thing? The younger the age of the dog when the damage occurs, the harder it is to fix.

I used to buy dogs to train out and sell or run in our guiding string. Typically, these were dogs that hadn't worked out. Maybe the puppy was digging up the backyard or shredding mom's stuff in the garage. I discovered that it didn't matter how rocky the relationship had been between the dog and the owner, just so long as there had been a relationship. If the dog had the genetics and liked birds, he would make a gun dog. I would go by feel when I went to look at a prospective dog. Was there someone looking back when I looked in the dog's eyes? Were there kids in the house? Did the dog like the children? Kids can't help but play with a dog. I would fly a homing pigeon and see what the dog thought of it.

Folks go and spend big money for puppies, looking for something special, while "throwaway" dogs are available across the country (dogs that are killed by the tens of thousands in animal control facilities). So many angels denied.

Let me state it very clearly: along with food, water, and protection from the elements, human contact is among a dog's most basic needs. Contact with his or her human. A dog is here to share our lives, our passions, our concerns, fears and joys. Given the access to do that they will enrich and return anything you are able to share with them.

Emma, as a 4-legged puppy, pointing a wing.

Emma

There is a special moment that bonds a gunner with a new pup. As the owner holds the new arrival, the two begin their shared future. Whether it is while clearing nostrils so that a newborn can breath, or after fumbling with a very small shipping kennel door in a crowded airline terminal, this new beginning is filled with hope and promise. Into this small, delicate, uncertain bundle of fluff is transferred a dream. I suppose that each person's dream is unique. For myself, while spreading tiny paws between my finger tips, I can see the pup full grown and slamming through yellow grass. I watch as the dog slides into a head-high point, and as I come alongside, a balled up covey-rise lifts and melts towards the sunset. I believe that shared dream is the foundation of the pup's desire.

Emma was born somewhere around one in the morning. She was the third in a litter of nine. Her mother had delivered the first pup without complication, but then had clearly slipped into trouble. My wife and I got her up and walking in an attempt to try and dislodge the obstruction. One hour and fifteen minutes after the first pup's birth, while we were getting ready to make the long run into town to the emergency vet, she delivered a second pup. Shortly thereafter, "M" arrived. Emma was born ass-end first. Halfway into the world when the sack tore away, I could see a female was present. Two-thirds of the way out, I made out a large orange spot of wet fur on the top of her back. With absolute certainty, I turned to my wife and said, "There is our girl." We named her Bandita Flying Emma.

And what a girl she grew into! At five weeks, she was a strong-willed, hard-going, top-dog-in-the-pile puppy. Everywhere she went, her tail rode straight up. The other females in the litter left for their new homes at seven weeks. We had another litter due in a couple of months, and we planned to keep a tri-colored male out of that breeding. "M" and that tri-color would carry our next generation of setters.

A person who had lived much longer than I once told me that the way to make God laugh is to tell him your plans. At three months old, our adventurous trapeze artist decided to climb her way out of the puppy pen. A small bedroom in our home was set up as a whelping/puppy room. It contained a four foot high indoor puppy run connected by a doggie door to an outside kennel run. I was going away elk hunting, and because my wife, Nicole, would be away at work, I bungie corded a wire panel over the top of the puppy run as a safety precaution, to keep puppies safe in their pen. Sometime while Nicole was at work, however, Emma climbed the corner of the pen. Using my safety panel roof as a pulling point, she somehow managed to lift herself over the side of the run. On the way out she got the bungie cord wrapped around her right rear leg. With the cord cinched tight at the top of her hock, she hung with her body partly supported by the cushion of a nearby chair.

That was how Nicole found her. When she released the bungie cord tension from around Emma's leg, the small, cold, gray limb ballooned as if it had been inflated with a hundred pounds of air. Emma began to go into shock. Nicole got "M" to a vet in an adjoining rural town and he was able to stabilize her. I called home the following morning to tell Nicole that I had our year's supply of meat in the back of the pickup and I was on my way to the meat processor in Flagstaff. After hearing the news I bought some dry ice, pulled camp, and headed home. Nicole had picked up Emma from the vet's by the time I made it back, and we set out trying to save the leg.

    The steroids that the vet had prescribed brought the swelling down some, but it really looked bad. I took "M" to see our regular vet the following morning. He said that even though we didn't know how long the tourniquet had been in place nor the degree of vascular damage, there was a chance we could save the ball of the foot. His prescription was "a tincture of time and scientific neglect." His instructions were to massage the leg, continue with the pills, and under no circumstance allow her to lick her leg. The good options ended there. And so the sofa vigil began. Nicole and I took turns sitting with Emma, keeping a sock on her leg, and tending to her pill and massage schedule. Her leg, however, never regained its warmth. On the morning of the fifth day, I detected a slightly sweet odor. That afternoon, I found some green skin at the constriction site, and on the morning of the sixth day her leg began to melt.

    Up until that time, I had refused to let myself believe that Emma's leg couldn't be saved. Now we had to make a decision. We had to find a balance between our desire to hang on to her with the possibility that her needs might best be served by letting her go. I didn't know what it would be like for a pup with such a strong desire to hunt to go through life on three legs. To what degree would a dog with three legs be able to hunt? In all my dog books, there wasn't a single picture of a three-legged bird dog.

    Then, there were also the financial realities. Back then, I sold pups for two hundred and fifty dollars apiece. The accumulated vet expenses after the operation would be a few Washingtons shy of seven hundred dollars. The end result would be a dog that might or might not hunt. Arithmetic like this does not a Rockefeller make. I had a new litter due in seven weeks from which I could pick a replacement.

    Ultimately, the question distilled down to: Why do we live with dogs? I drove to the post office to check the mail and think. On the way home, a friend's wife flagged me down to ask about the pup. Word spreads in a small town. She was walking with our local school bus driver who told me not to short change a three-legged dog as a few mornings before she had seen a fat, three-legged coyote with a dead jack rabbit in its jaws standing at the side of the road. Certainly, anyone who owns gun dogs knows that it's not so they can hang onto money. I decided that we would do everything we could medically, and let Emma sort out the rest. She had the surgery that afternoon.

She came through the procedure well. The constriction site was just above her hock; however, our vet explained that because dogs can't wear prosthetics to protect the remaining part of the limb, he had to remove the leg at the hip. We kept her segregated from the other dogs for a few weeks while she healed.

"M" had always been such a dynamic personality, we didn't know how she would handle her new circumstances. It proved to be a very hard transition for her. She mostly moped. Any time a little enthusiasm broke through and she got animated, her surgery site got bumped and she would shut down. She would stand still for a long time. It looked like it really, really hurt. Dogs have a wonderful quality that humans would do well to emulate. They don't waste time dwelling on depression. The fact that Emma wasn't up to a run with them wasn't going to make our other setters feel guilty about having fun. A lot of fun. Day-in and day-out fun. A sad setter doesn't stand much of a chance in a yard full of happy ones. Besides, Emma had the top-puppy-in-the-pack position to maintain.

I used her position and sense of competition to keep her going when she would shut down during training. Yeah, that stump hurt when she banged it while looking for a thrown retrieving bumper, but it didn't hurt nearly as bad as watching her brother, Jasper, complete the retrieve if she abandoned it. Slowly she came out of it, with her top-puppy status intact.

Emma and I were covering some new ground here. Some people, when seeing "M," would tell me about a three-legged dog they remembered from a neighbor's farm when they were a kid, or one they had seen someone hunting with way back when. However, when I went back through hunting literature, no one had written about it. I had some questions that I didn't know how to answer. The only option I had was to take Emma hunting.

When our Southern Arizona weather cooled down in mid-November, I put Emma in the lineup. One hallmark of Emma's personality was that she didn't give any quarter and, by God, she wasn't going to take any. At seven-months-old she began her career as a Gambel's quail dog. I didn't know if her back leg and pad would hold up. They did. I thought I would have to make a protective leather cover for the other side. I didn't. I couldn't tell if she would still be out front at the end of a three hour loop. She was, and she had the heart for more, even though she slept very soundly afterwards.

The differences were that she was more cautious when she ran. Where the other dogs would leap through an erosion cut, Emma watched how I crossed and then followed my path through. She also had an interesting variation on a cat walk. It was something akin to step, step, skip, step, step, skip. One of my big concerns was whether she would be able to outrun trouble if she barreled into a herd of javelina or such. One late afternoon, I watched as she hunted through a mesquite thicket a hundred yards out. She drifted up to the front feet of a very large range bull, stopped to study these two strange posts sticking out of the ground, and then casually glanced up to notice a monolith standing above her. Then, the monolith blinked. She swapped ends and left the area with rocket engines attached. The javelina hadn't been born who could use her tail for dental floss.

It did change the way she looked on point. She used her tail as a rudder, to keep her balance. On uneven ground, she pointed with her tail low and held off to the side.

When Emma ran, you really couldn't tell she was missing any original equipment. She launched from the water more like a ruddy duck than a mallard, but once she got airborne Bandita Flying Emma really flew.

Visitors would come while the dogs were out running, invariably a white blur would come screeching in low and come to a stop in a gravel-strewn power slide to inspect the new arrivals. After the white blur came into focus, the standard statement was a shocked, "That dog is missing a leg!" I must admit I had a lot of fun delivering my standard response, "Yes, she was running so big, we had to do something."

I wish it could have been another way, but it wasn't. That is my perspective on it because, looking at it honestly, I really don't think it mattered to Emma. Her biggest problem with missing her rear leg was that itch on the side of her chin. It would have been easier for me if I had known how little the loss of a rear leg would impact a bird dog.

Dreams can be revisited. Now, in one of mine, after marking the sunset covey down, I turn to send the white setter after the singles. She makes scent as she enters a grass and cactus-filled pocket. She turns her head into the wind, and locks up with her head high. I move to front with shotgun at ready in anticipation of the flush. I look to the setter's eyes to tell me where the bird is waiting, and I notice that she is standing on three legs.

Emma, as a 3-legged adult, presenting a male Mearns' quail for the gun.

Rascal, a female tri-colored English setter, cooling her heels after running on scaled quail.

What a Trainer Needs to Know about Him or Herself

The relationship between a handler and a dog is very unique. Although it is more complicated than a human with human interaction, it's also in many ways much more direct.

Dogs work off of a different set of cues than we humans do. As humans, we verify and gauge our world primarily through what we see: the information that comes through our eyes. When we hear or smell something, we usually need also to see it in order to evaluate it and put it into context. For dogs, however, their primary sense is the sense of smell. If a dog sees or hears something, he needs also to smell it in order to evaluate it and put it into context.

This profound difference in how we two different beings, dogs and humans, gauge the world is key to the training process.

In a training situation, the canine trainee senses with an infinitely larger set of tools. An experienced handler can visually gauge a dog's reactions by the dog's body language and demeanor. The dog, however, in addition to these aforementioned visual cues, can also taste the air through his sense of smell. A human won't understand the most basic of dog interactions unless he watches for, and guesses at, what the dog is sensing through his nose.

During a training session, a dog identifies our moods, level of frustration, and depth of resolve through his highly evolved canine sense of smell. Dogs can smell apprehension, concern, fear, etc. They know what kind of people we are: whether we can be trusted; are honorable; or, are rageful and dangerous. Observe a dog that doesn't trust his owner. The level of the dog's apprehension is palpable. Anyone who has spent even a short period of time with dogs has experienced a dog coming up from behind and pressing his nose against the skin at the back of the knee or sniffing the inside of the wrist. That is how a dog gets a full readout of the person wearing that skin.

Now, watch a competent and experienced handler work with a dog. The handler has trained himself or herself to monitor the internal mechanisms of his or her personality and temperament, and to project positives to their canine students. An experienced handler will use strategies like breathing into a dog's nose, or spitting saliva onto a training bumper or leather glove they are wearing. The handler then places the bumper or glove into the dog's mouth, so that the dog can "taste" the person's intentions. This is done to fast track the olfactory communication process.

A dog's first impression comes through his nose.

A thought about anger: it's interesting to note that many professional trainers have had their struggles with anger. It manifests in a host of ways: alcohol, drugs, poor life choices. It seems that in many cases trainers, especially the good ones, get more out of training than they give. There are reasons why a person becomes a dog trainer.

Regarding myself, my father was a brutal man who needed to hurt things. He had a gyroscope perpetually spinning inside of him. As a child, it was necessary for me to study him closely in order to survive. Even when he was sloppy drunk, slumped in a chair, his ankle would tick and bounce his leg. The faster the tick, the closer he was to erupting, and the tighter my sister and I had to lean into the wall to feign invisibility.

Anger is an issue for me. When I was young, it was hard to control, particularly when my goal was to **not** grow up to be my father.

Life has frustrations. If you wish to heap even more frustrations onto your allotted daily pile, become a dog trainer. In order to successfully work with dogs, it is necessary to resolve any anger or rage problem you may have in your life. Anger is a necessary part of a healthy psyche, but there are appropriate and inappropriate ways to express that anger. A person doesn't deal with an anger problem by ignoring it. Try that route and you end up like my father, dying of alcoholism. I commend anyone who moves forward from that kind of a stuck life, but please don't look to dogs to save you. Take responsibility and tend to yourself first.

Thirty-something years after leaving my parents' house, followed by a failed marriage, years of on and off therapy, Adult Children of Alcoholic's meetings, and the helping grace of countless people and dogs, the anger is still there. I felt it when I was training and something happened: a youngster reared up on the chain gang when I bent down to hug her from behind, and in her exuberance I got cracked in the nose. I felt a flash of pain, followed by a flash of malice. It was that same gyroscope that was gifted to me by my father. Today, I feel it and smile. It's like finding an artifact from my beginnings under a layer of dust in a drawer. It comes up through my gut, catches in my throat, and concentrates into my lower left canine tooth. There, it stops in the soft tissue on the inside of my mouth, behind my lower lip. It belongs to me and it stays with me. When I was training professionally, some days there was a small hole there by the time I had gotten everyone through his yard work.

There is a permanent scar there that I can feel as I write these words.

I suspect this is the lesson most people learn from the process: anger doesn't go away, but it does eventually shrink into its proper perspective. Bill Tarrant and I had a conversation several years before he passed. He called and was working on a book and wanted to address the issue of anger. He asked me for my take on it. I told him that I didn't know how to address the subject in a way that a reader would hear. For better or worse, we start where we are...It's a deeply personal choice to learn to leave the past and live a different life. It requires courage. Fortunately, the world has many people of courage. The way we left the conversation was that it was probably better left unsaid. By that standard, I have said too much already.

Dogs know everything all the time. To be a successful trainer, you must be calm inside. The dog will know if you are not. Don't cheat on this. Dogs deserve better. To be less than you can be with a dog is to damage yourself, and this will serve no one, particularly yourself. Be a better person, become a better trainer, or vice versa. The two are interchangeable.

The overwhelming affect the competent and experienced handler needs to exude is confidence. This is one of the two primary components required to be successful in dog training. Confidence is the one thing, above all else, that the dog respects. Within the wild genetic memory stored in each dog's mind, he responds to a pack leader who has held his position by knowing what to do and expecting subordinates to follow that lead.

The second primary requirement is learned: a successful handler must have the ability to anticipate a dog's actions, and to short-stop a dog's actions before he does the wrong thing. This ability is a direct result of the experiences that make the trainer confident in handling dogs. The competent and experienced handler is proactive, not reactive.

For example, let's say the dog is given a command or training introduction. The dog already knows what is expected of him because it was worked out before in structured training. However, the dog's thought processes now kick in. Let's say he knows he's supposed to hold steady and point the bird, but he can smell it right there. It's inches off his nose. One short step and the bird will be in his mouth. His brain is calculating the movements required to make it happen. Depending on the handler's abilities, there are a wide range of possible responses available.

In the best case scenario, the handler reads the dog's mind and stops the dog's shift in focus with a soft "ahh" before the dog's mind finishes thinking about moving. No harm, no foul.

The next best case scenario you see is with folks who have had some dog time. The handler reads the tension in the dog's body. He sees the dog's shoulder muscle flex in preparation to transferring weight to the front foot so that he can lower his mouth to the bird. The handler sees it, utters a sharp "AHHHHHHHHH" to break the dog's focus and intent, and stops it before the dog moves. Again, no harm, no foul.

Then we get to the handler who's trying, but is not quite there yet. The dog gets through his internal mental cycling and transfers it into a lunge for the bird. The handler doesn't get a verbal brake out until after the dog has moved, but he does stop it before the dog gets his mouth around feathers. This means that the handler had to see it coming before the fact; but because of uncertainty, inexperience, inattentiveness, or botched timing, he or she wasn't quite fast enough. The damage is done because the dog now needs to be physically returned to his original location. Without this physical intervention, the dog will, from this point on, figure he can get away with a few more inches on the bird without experiencing any negative consequences for his transgression. Typically, a handler's best bet at this point is to make it a negative gain by picking up and relocating the dog to a point further away from where he originally started. This will convince the dog that there is a net loss when he moves. He learns that moving will only get him further away from the bird.

We are now at the dividing line between constructive and non-constructive handling. The above scenarios were degrees of net gain, and advanced the dog's training. There is, however, a negative possibility in this situation.

Let's say the handler doesn't see, or suspect, or it just plumb happens too fast. The dog makes his move and comes up with feathers...and then he hears his handler from the sidelines.

There are degrees of calamity here.

Maybe the dog responds to his handler's calm and soothing request to first whoa, and then gently release, the bird to hand. That's presuming there previously was structured yard work and therefore, the dog will whoa. It also presumes that the handler knows how to use his or her voice properly to avert a train wreck. The handler calmly lifts the dog and relocates him back to his pre-whoaed position, gets whatever positive he or she can out of the deal and shuts down training for the day.

Or...maybe that request isn't so calm and soothing and the dog freezes up and clamps down on the bird, crushing it and getting a start on hard mouth. The handling, following the wrestling match over the bird, doesn't help matters.

Maybe the dog takes it personally and notices that all this commotion happened while he had a bird in his mouth and decides then and there to never put one in his mouth again. Possibly, in the dog's mind, he reasons that maybe it was the flushing, or the pointing, or the bird itself that caused the problem. Then, over the next few months, the handler gets to learn about a thing called blinking.

Or...this could be a resilient kind of dog who doesn't tend to take things personally. When the howling starts from the human, he takes it as an opportunity to broaden his horizons and see some country. He's already in trouble and reasons, "In for a little, in for a lot." It's time to see the world, and the bird is already in his mouth, so it's no trouble to bring it along for the ride. He can get serious with it once he clears the county line. Once there, he resolves to find a nice shady tree. He'll lay up and chew that bird from one side to the other before he eats it. The fading profanity and whistle blasts are drowned out by the sound of air flapping in the dog's ears as he comes up to full speed. It would have been nice if the handler could have read the dog's mind and stopped the train before the wheels came off the track.

A handler should strive to anticipate a dog's improper responses before they happen, not correct them after the fact.

What does one do and where does one start if one lacks the ability to anticipate a dog's actions as well as being short on experience and confidence in handling dogs?

The short answer is: you start where you are and move forward from there. The truth is, it isn't rocket science. Your best assets are your passion for bird hunting and your enthusiasm for working with your dog. If your dog is treated with respect and kindness, he will meet you wherever you start.

Develop intentionality: be conscious of the position of your body, the use of your voice and breath, your feelings, and how you project these to the dog. One must monitor a host of things that weren't taken into account before training. It's very difficult to develop intentionality because so much of what we do is done on auto pilot. In the past, when I've worked with dog owners, this is where I see most handling problems develop. The initial failure is with the handler, not the dog.

For example, a new handler is working his dog on the whoa post for the first time. I have already done the introduction and training, and have the dog whoaing on the post. The new handler knows the drill and handling requirements because I've walked him or her through it prior to including the dog.

The new handler takes the rope and approaches the dog to release him to begin walking a circle around the post. The handler's steps are tentative and faulting. He concentrates on the dog and lets the rope fall limp, thereby losing any control over the dog. As he steps to the dog, he leans over the dog in what the dog perceives as a threatening manner. The dog stiffens. He then touches the dog on the back of the head, but miss-times the verbal command so that the dog isn't free to leave. The dog waits for the proper cue of a simultaneous touch and verbal release command, and the handler waits for the dog to move. When neither gets the proper response the owner pushes the dog forward again and the dog turns to look up at the owner, who sees the concern in the dog's eyes and responds automatically by reassuring the dog with a quick pet and a kind word which isn't the release command "hoe-on." This really confuses the dog because this is the third time that the handler has touched his head. "Does he want me to stay whoaed or to move forward, or is this a pet session?"

From the dog's perspective, all of this is done in a very unnatural manner and contrary to what the dog knows about this usually open and easily readable person. Instead: "It's kinda like when I chewed that hole in the leather sofa."

Additionally, the dog smells an acrid apprehension and an awkward kind of tension on his owner. The dog has lived with this person since seven weeks of age, but this is all new stuff. The dog wonders if he really wants to play this new game.

Do you see how quickly the process can go downhill? Now, the scenario I just described was a structured yard training session supervised by a handler, where the drill was controlled by ropes and a metal post. Imagine a dog who never received any structured yard work, but suddenly during bird season gets hauled off to a field and body slammed with the whole calamity of bird, flush and gunfire in one catastrophic episode. That is how you cause a train wreck.

So, one might ask, where is all this going and how does a handler get there?

A handler gets there any way he or she can. It takes time to learn how to train yourself to train a dog. Maybe it takes three dogs before you have a grasp on the points we have covered here. This learning process can only be improved with additional training time, and one thing is for certain: as the three-dogs-trained handler eventually graduates to thirty dogs trained and then to three hundred dogs trained, the handler will understand more clearly how to make that connection.

What is the ultimate goal? There is an ultimate means of communication that exists between dog and handler. It is a bridge formed through trust and long association. The word telepathy has a woo-woo connotation, but it's the best one I can think of to describe that connection.

Dogs can read our minds. Humans, given experience and long association, can also get close to reading their dog's thoughts. The experienced handler knows how to think a thought so that his dog hears it. It's like the bond that can develop between an old married couple whereby one starts a sentence and the other completes it, or more to the point, completes it in his/her mind without speaking additional words.

That same connection exists between a long time hunting team of handler and dog. Given adequate experience, by the time a dog reaches four to five years of age he attains a maturity level that allows him to sustain a mental connection with his human. Dogs can know what we are thinking as we think it. This is really the goal to strive for in dog handling. The ultimate goal in dog handling is not to have to handle the dog, and we can all get there if we develop experience, patience, and kindness.

Dan Torrance of Winfield, Kansas, and a tri-colored English setter take a rest break during a Mearns' quail hunt.

Web works English pointer on whoa post while excited dogs on chain gang look on. (Photo by Randy Babb)

Multiple breeds wait their turn during yard training.

Types of Gun Dogs

Dog Breed Choices

A past client and friend called me towards the end of bird season. I had trained a few shorthairs for him and another gentleman, and I can always recognize his voice when I pick up the phone. He is a West Texas native and his accent affirms that fact whenever he speaks. He currently lives in northern New Mexico, but he was calling on this day from southern Arizona. He and two old friends from West Texas had been chasing Gambel's and scaled quail. They had been at it for several days and had run themselves out of dogs. His two friends had a trailer full of Brits which didn't have any pads left. He had one shorthair that had maybe half a day left, so he called me and asked if I could meet them the following morning and bring reinforcements.

I met them near dawn at an appointed spot somewhere out in the boonies. My friend made introductions. One of the gentlemen from West Texas opened up the doors on his dog trailer and, one at a time, trotted out his string of Brits for me to have a look at. They were a good looking group of dogs that looked like they had given it their all. I could see that he was very proud of them. He told me this story:

It seems that early in their trip they had headquartered out of a motel in Wilcox, a small rural town in the Sulpher Springs valley of southeastern Arizona. Also staying at the same facility were several other freelance bird dog rigs and guide dog strings.

The storyteller got up earlier than most so he could get his Brittany chores done and have time to walk the parking area and look over the other dog trailer outfits. He approached one rig that had an assortment of dogs spread out on a chain gang in front of the trailer. There was one man tending the rig. He was preoccupied in the predawn darkness, going through his morning chores checklist. He may have had clients that were going to show up soon from breakfast and would be anxious to get out after birds.

Our storyteller greeted the man warmly with a pleasant, "Good morning." He grunted in response, but didn't make eye contact, or slow down his preparations. I would imagine that his focus was fixed on chores and getting ready. As the guide busied himself, the storyteller walked down the line of dogs. He asked as to the different types of dogs the man had clipped down the chain.

"Oh," the storyteller said, "What have you got here? Some English pointers?"

From the dark on the other side of the chain gang, "Yeah, pointers."

"And what are these dark dogs? Are they shorthairs or pudlepointers?"

"Shorthairs."

"You running some setters, too?"

"Yeah, setters."

Then, in a cheerful voice, our storyteller said, "What, no Brittanies?"

The man on the other side of the chain gang, who had been stooped over a box at the front of the trailer, suddenly jerked, then froze. He bowed his shoulders, then rose slowly and straightened like he had been hit in the gut and was taking air back in. There was a pause and then the man responded in a tired, clearly articulated voice, "Well, I have to draw the line somewhere."

Litter of six-week-old English setter puppies on the wrong side of the chain link fence.

Why a person chooses a particular breed of gun dog is often left to circumstance or pure coincidence. The dog was offered, or available, or was the type Uncle Joe had. You drive a Ford because your parents drove a Ford.

I am aware at the outset that talking about dog choice is a very touchy subject. Please don't write me letters.

I will acknowledge a personal breed preference here. Our own shooting string is mostly English setters. In addition, I always keep a couple of German shorthairs in the mix along with a retriever, either a Lab or a Chessie.

I have setters because I started with a setter thirty-odd years ago. We are now six generations in on our breeding. I know what to expect when I look at one of our puppies. I see in a dog today the same nuance, hunting style, and temperament that I saw in its grandmother and great-great-grandmother. It gives me predictability regarding training and genetics. In order to have that, a person must maintain a large group of dogs at any given time in order to have a pool of viable breeding candidates. This gets prohibitively expensive in time and money. There is, however, an intimacy created when living this close to a particular line of breeding. It's like maintaining several generations of family, or being married to the same person for multiple lifetimes.

I like all breeds of dogs. I have owned pointers, setters, Brittanies, German Shorthair Pointers (GSPs), German Wirehaired Pointers (GWPs), spaniels and retrievers. If I had a second life span to live, I would try another breed of dog so that I could share that same level of intimacy I've been able to have with our setters.

Many folks are very breed sensitive to begin with. Then, the whole issue gets muddied up further with the fact that there are some really fuzzy lines separating some of our sporting breeds today. For example, if I make a statement about German shorthairs, what exactly am I referring to?

First, there are the old school shorthairs that work fairly close and tight. Their coat is dark and grizzled, and their build is stocky. They use ground scent and are death as pickup dogs on cripples. They are methodical in their search and often very good in water. The old school shorthairs are pretty straightforward when it comes to training. They look at you and say, "What is it you want me to do?"

Then there are the field trial shorthairs who were crossed with pointers, allowing the breeder to cull the pointer lookalikes and then use the others to win field trials against old school shorthairs. These dogs train like pointers with a screw loose and have the focus of a hummingbird.

They don't want to stay in the same county with the gun, and forget about water work.

Or...am I talking about the registered "shorthairs" that are pointers with docked tails? The dogs produced by breeders who can keep a straight face while selling white dogs with pointer heads and short tails and calling them shorthairs...dogs with little to no retrieving instinct that run like all age field trial pointers because, well, they are.

There is a joke floating out there about one of these types of breeders. The story goes that the way this breeder culls a litter of puppies is to take them out into the desert when they turn six months of age and cut them loose. Whatever comes back he keeps.

There are two extremes in the world of GSPs. The ones that come from continental blood are as far away in trainability, temperament and appearance from the field trial shorthair counterfeits as white is to black.

Depending on blood, all are called German shorthair pointers, yet all are very different animals: 1) English pointer with docked tail; 2) American field trial GSP; 3) Old blood shorthair; 4) imported VDD German blood.

You see, in today's dog world it's hard to know what's in a name any more. You can spend the money for the registered dog and think that the expenditure will carry some guarantees. You can scan the pedigree and look for wins.

In previous centuries, dogs that won field trials were the dogs to breed to and those puppies were the ones to get. Today's dog novice makes the assumption that if a dog's relatives won field trials, then they must be good dogs. I've seen others put that same logic in print. When I read it, I know it's a writer who has interviewed a field trialer, not a writer who has spent any time training dogs for the public. I don't mean to denigrate field trials. I think they are a wonderful experience if a person wishes to engage in competitions. Unfortunately, they are not hunting, no matter what the intent of the organizers were originally.

Horace Lytle, gun dog columnist for <u>Field and Stream</u> in the early part of the twentieth century, wrote a great line concerning field trial dogs. Lytle said that a field trial dog is a dog that runs out of control, almost. A dog with the flash to run like a banshee and break with the style that impresses a judge is a marvelous thing if your goal is to impress a judge. If, on the other hand, you are looking for a dog to hunt for the gun, work birds intelligently, retrieve and keep within a quarter mile of you while doing it, I have found it is best to look at dogs that perform in that manner.

The problem is that a field trial dog wins on the day that he didn't run out of bounds or bust his brace mate's birds, or chase a flyer out of the county. I was picking up some gear I had bought from a retired field trialer. He had campaigned Brits for a big chunk of his life and ultimately switched over to pointers before health issues forced him to hang up his whistle. During the visit, he gave me a tour of his kennel facility and stopped at the end of a bank of chain link runs. "This was old Blaster's run," he said. He proceeded to tell me the story of one of his field trial champion Brits. He opened by telling me that the dog was insane and uncontrollable. He pointed to a polished portion of kennel floor. The kennel was covered with chain link and he described to me how the dog would run it in the manner of a squirrel cage, particularly when there was noise or the rumble of distant thunder. Floor to left panel, to ceiling panel, to right panel, to floor. The dog would go ballistic and run in place in this manner for long periods of time.

Regarding his field trial endeavors, Blaster had a very checkered track record. He was mostly uncontrollable, except for a few isolated stellar days. On those days, the judges liked what they saw and Blaster made his field trial championship. That's what the print on the pedigree said, and people came to breed their females to old Blaster. My host chuckled at the thought of other squirrel cages, holding Blaster's offspring, spread throughout the country. Enough said.

In addition, what a dog's registration papers read don't always give an accurate representation of true lineage, as one couple who brought a dog to me for training can attest. They wanted a bird dog and so they answered an ad for registered shorthair puppies. They paid their money, picked a pup and brought him home. They named their new dog, Gus.

The problem was that Gus grew into an adult shorthair that only stood a foot high at the shoulders. It turned out that Gus was half-dachshund. However, he was their boy and they loved him, so we tried to make the best of the situation. They wanted a bird dog that would serve as a pickup dog for quail and dove, if nothing else. Well, he trained out as a pretty courageous character. He liked to get birds, although he didn't have the genetics that would allow him to point. My wife affectionately referred to Gus as "the moot point" because even if we could have got him to stand his birds, a gunner would not have been able to see him above the grass.

I liked Gus. I imagined he had the same character and demeanor as his daddy, who after all, had the moxie to get his momma pregnant in the first place. Gus would swagger through the dog yard, but it was hard to get around the fact that he held his head high as he walked underneath every other dog in the yard.

Gus: registered German shorthair pointer.

So much for the issue of what's on a registration form. I have seen the same thing happen with red setters that sure looked like Brits, and Brits that sure looked like English setters, and pointing labs that sure looked like Vizsla crosses. There are English setter bloodlines that require an electric collar to keep them hunting for the gun. Within the English setter breed, there are slick-coated 50-pound desert dogs and 90-pound, woolly, slab-sided New England grouse dogs. There are Gordon setters that don't want to point. There are pointers who fold on whoa and don't like to back. It is possible to navigate these difficult waters and choose a good prospect, but it takes a lifetime's worth of experience and the cynicism of an old horse trader.

Which underlines the fundamental issue in choosing a hunting dog: genetics. A dog's breeding determines everything about what that dog will become and his physical attributes will determine the degree to which he can perfom. In truth, I mean genetics are everything. Even the subtle stuff like personality and temperament. I've seen the way a dog cocks an ear in its mother and grandmother and great-grandmother. Things such as natural retrieving and drive on birds are in that dog at birth. I have a dog that drizzles feces throughout the yard instead of leaving it in one neat pile, making clean up ten times harder: just like his mother before him and her aunt before her. It is important to remember that the phrase "dog training" is a misnomer. We do not train gun dogs. We provide introductions and associations that refine the genetic traits that were present in the dog at birth.

This means that you need to look very closely at the parents of the puppy you are considering. Go hunting with mom and dad. Look equally closely at the person selling the dog to ascertain whether you can believe what they tell you and what it says on the papers.

One final point about the importance of registration papers: some of the best dogs I've owned or seen hunt, didn't have any. I have gotten some really fine dogs as non-registered "throwaways." A novice looks to the pedigree for wins to determine the potential of a new dog. Unless you specifically want a dog that can win field trials, this can bring you a lot of grief.

Basically it comes down to this:
People who like to see a dog point have pointers.
People who like to watch dogs run have setters.
People who like precision and control go for the versatile dog breeds.
People who like lots of personality have Brits.

English pointer.

Dog Breeds: Bird Dogs

Pointers

When I was a kid, these dogs were called English pointers. At some point that changed, and they are now simply called pointers. The standard joke was that they were called English because that's where they were headed as soon as you let go of the check cord. To some degree, depending upon the individual dog's maturity and breeding, that is still true. One thing that is a constant with pointers is that they hunt hard, are extremely athletic and point like a million bucks.

Pointers are usually owned by no-nonsense kinds of folks. They are often the dogs you see filling out the strings of professional guides. They live to hunt birds and run. That's not to say that they can't get used to sleeping on the sofa, but if you leave the front door open they are going to take a few laps around the countryside.

Pointers are a good choice for the serious bird hunter. They require formal training and, as such, would not be the breed for a first time or novice bird hunter. They generally require an electric collar. Without a handler in firm control, the bird hunt will quickly convert to a dog hunt. They take training well, and are fairly straightforward about what they want, which is to run. The genetic imprint is strong and the basics like "whoa," pointing and backing come easy. Some make good retrievers. As a rule, they don't have a lot of interest in water work.

The major problem you will see in pointer bloodlines is self-hunting. In these dogs, their temperament is such that they would rather run than hunt for the gun. It may be that the dogs are not connecting with their owners because they are kennel dogs. It could be that they are kennel dogs because the owner's priority is hunting birds and, as a consequence, has a string of dogs that compete for limited bonding time. It's one of those "the chicken or the egg" deals.

Another thing I have seen in the Elhew breeding is cowering on whoa or backing. The Elhews are not soft dogs and this is not an indication of a dog folding. It is, however, a passive aggressive way of not complying. It can be tedious and frustrating to work through.

Focus on structure when you train pointers. Teach them "whoa." Really teach them "whoa." Layer the training several levels deep, creating automatic responses that will allow your handling to override the pointers' overwhelming desire to break when they have a bird in front of them. Draw a very hard line in the field and let them know what is expected of them. Trained and handled properly, these bird finding machines are a sight to behold. Handled sloppily and/or with inadequate training, they are train wrecks waiting to happen. Without adequate training, pack a sleeping bag because you will be spending the night at the truck waiting for the dog to show up again.

Setters

Field setters come in three models: English, Gordon and Irish/red. They are true bird dogs and run with their heads high to locate birds with air scent. They are softer dogs than their English pointer bird dog brethren. By that, I mean they tend to be more people oriented. A harsh look or gesture is more injurious to them than any string of profanity that could be launched upon an English pointer.

As is true with all the breeds, there isn't a standard setter body type anymore. They run from 35-pound elves to 90-pound draft horse clones. I am referring to all three breeds of setters here. They may come with delicate, small chiseled heads or large blocky noggins. They can be trim and built to run wide open or tall, slab-sided, close-working, 80-pound East coast grouse dogs.

Hair length, as it relates to the breed's ability to hunt in warm climates, is often expressed as a concern. The uninitiated refer to them as cold weather dogs. The variables of body configuration mentioned above also carry through to hair length. They can be slick coated or wooly. I hunt my English setters in the deserts of the Southwest.

Setters are a little more complicated to train than pointers. As they are people dogs, sensitive treatment is in order. They don't mature as quickly as pointers. Pointers may be coming on fairly well by the close of their second season while, with setters, you're probably going to need three seasons for them to put it all together. Many of the bloodlines are natural retrievers. Some like water, some don't.

Train with structure. Whoa break setters and give them plenty of time and encouragement. Use a lot of sugar. If a setter starts wobbling during training, don't push. Back off and give them time to come back.

As is so often the case with field trial blood lines, there are screwed up setter field trial bloodlines that self-hunt, don't like to retrieve, require an electric collar to control in the field, and stand their points looking like a million bucks. If a bird hunter is interested in one out of four, high dollar puppies are available. Again, remember to pack a sleeping bag.

Pick a well-bred puppy out of hunting stock that matches the body type of dog you want. Pick a breed that hunts the type of bird and cover you are planning to hunt. Unless you are confident of the suitability of the dog for your particular situation, hunt with the litter's parents before you make your final decision.

Opposite Page: English setter, Gordon setter, and red setter.

Continental/Versatile Breeds

German Shorthair Pointers

Old blood German shorthairs are the gold standard for the average bird hunter. They are bidable, easily trained, and generally available wherever bird dogs are found. The breed has not yet seen the wholesale genetic physical maladies brought to other breeds by irresponsible breeding. Along with that, the genetic components of hunting instinct, such as pointing, backing and retrieving are fairly solid across the breed. They rely heavily on ground scenting which makes them particularly good at recovering hard to find dead birds and running cripples.

GSPs come in all sizes. I've seen them run in weight from about 35 pounds up to 75 pounds. If my memory serves me, I think there were a few show breeding dogs that pushed 90 pounds.

GSPs take training well. They come on quickly and have a high tolerance for correction, both physical and mental. By the end of their second season, provided they have gotten into wild birds, you generally have a bird dog. It is unusual to run across a GSP that doesn't respond to structured training in a real straightforward, constructive way. They just want to get it right so they can get to the bird. Due to the GSP's willingness to cooperate, they are a very good choice for the novice upland dog owner. In addition, because they are a versatile breed, most make good warm water duck dogs, if properly introduced to water.

The negatives are that they tend to be very analytical. If someone in the dog yard is unweaving the chain link fence or opening up the gate latches, look to the German dogs first. Also, male shorthairs don't mix well with other male dogs, particularly other shorthairs. It is true of both male and female GSPs that if a dog starts a fight, the shorthairs will finish it and their opponents will be bleeding from puncture wounds. Setters can get into long, protracted, terrible-sounding brouhahas, yet the combatants will come out of them with nothing worse than wet hair and a generally disheveled look. If German dogs get into a fight, however, within a nanosecond they are going to put holes into the other dog's legs and/or ears or throat. Keep some antibiotics on hand because the puncture wounds always come up infected.

1) German shorthair pointer or GSP; 2) German wire-haired pointer or GWP.

German Wire-haired Pointers
(Drathauers, Griffons, Pudle Pointers)

German Wire-haired pointers, Drathauers, are a woollier relative of the GSP. They are harder to find and more expensive when you manage to locate an available puppy or dog. For the sake of clarity, I will include in this group both Griffons and Pudle Pointers, which, to the untrained eye, may appear to be of the same blood and have the same or similar temperament and working style. My experience is limited with Griffons as I have only had a couple in for training. Pudle Pointers are a bit more common in the Southwest, although my pool of trainees was limited to around a dozen dogs or so.

These dogs tend to be closer working and more methodical in their search than GSPs. As a rule, they are not the most stylish of bird finders on point, but when there is a cripple to be found they make the other breeds look like amateurs. Like the GSP, they use ground scent and follow a cripple until they turn it. The standard joke goes, "How do you know when a GWP is pointing? They stop moving."

GWPs respond to training with the typical Teutonic reserve characteristic of the Germanic imports. They are, as a rule, more stoic and reserved than GSPs. Like the GSPs, they take about two seasons to put it all together. Wirehairs take structured training very well. GWPs tend to be one-owner dogs more than other breeds. In a professional training situation, where the dog is trusted to a pro, there can be a bit of lag time while the pro waits for the GWP to let the new handler in. Some of the GWPs I've had in for training have been a little soft on pointing instinct, particularly dogs imported from Germany.

GWPs run from 45 to 75 pounds. Their furnishings, which refer to their wooly muzzle and coat hair, can vary significantly from nearly slick-coated to very woolly. They are known as exceptional water dogs precisely because of the extra warmth and protection their woolly coat provides them.

Some of the bloodlines can be sharp and, in a fight, a GWP will leave an opponent bleeding in very short order. If this is a problem for you, than be very careful that the puppy or dog you acquire can be left around other dogs safely. When I had customer dogs here, I had to be careful when a German dog came in for training, making sure that they could be allowed access to the communal dog yard. Due to aggressive behavior, some of the males required private runs while they were in training with us.

GWPs are a good choice for the foot hunter looking for a do-it-all one or two dog team. A friend referred to his GWP as his "old man dog." My friend had spent his hunting career on the prairie, behind high powered bird dogs and retrievers. When he attained the age of wisdom and maturity, he realized that he didn't have to beat himself up that much to enjoy the essence of what bird hunting was about. He then switched over to one calm, methodical GWP for both upland and waterfowl hunting.

Left: American Brittany.   Right: French Brittany.

Brittanies

Just as English pointer was shortened to pointer, Brittany spaniel became Brittany. With the change, Brits were again re-billed as one of the versatile hunting dog breeds. I suppose it is a good notion to reinvent a thing. Sounds American. Unfortunately, changing a name doesn't necessarily mean the thing changes as well.

Brits are not bird dogs when the term is held to the same definition that old Southerners meant when they used the term "Bird Dog." They don't run big with a head high and search for air scent. Generally speaking, they don't have the style, run, athleticism, or flash of a setter or pointer. They are spaniels. In addition, as a general rule, they really don't equal the versatile breeds in stamina and physicality, raw hunting ability, and bidability. They will make about 60% of a bird dog. Often, Brits are run in groups of 2 or 3 to match the job performed by a single bird dog or versatile dog. They are soft on pointing instinct and they don't like to back. They may or may not retrieve, depending on whether they get their way on pointing and backing. Meaning that, if you force them to back, they will get even by not retrieving.

That said, there's a legion of loyal owners out there who love their Brits. Heaven knows, I have trained a bunch of them. Brits are spaniels in the truest cocker spaniel sense of the word. Brits can be contrary and cantankerous, stubborn and manipulative. However, Brits certainly also have their charms. They are precocious and personable, and are great family dogs. When you do get a good one, you have a dog with a real go-getter hustle. I have seen several that made very good water dogs. It is said that anyone who owns a Brit, becomes a Brit fan.

Small size is the reason stated most often for going with a Brittany puppy. They can get to 45 or 50 pounds. Mostly, the average Brit comes in at around 35 to 40 pounds, depending on the amount of couch time they get. If a prospective owner's sole criteria is size, the truth is that all the mainline bird hunting breeds have puppies available that will come in around the 40 to 45 pound mark. Brits can be a bit tricky to train up as bird dogs when compared to other breeds. Keep this in mind, and don't pick your hunting companion just based on size, look at the whole picture.

For example, during training a GSP will look at you and ask, "What is it you want me to do?" Upon the trainer clarifying to the GSP what is expected, the dog will comply.

Brits, on the other hand, look at the trainer and say, "I know exactly what you want me to do and I'm not going to do it." They may then go into their avoidance mode, which generally means folding in some way, until the trainer throws up his arms in frustration and the Brits get their way...which is not to comply in the first place. At that point, the Brit is free to go about his business, which is to do what he wants when he wants to, or chew off his neighboring dog's collar, whichever will annoy the owner the most at that moment.

Even when you catch them in the act, however, it is impossible to get upset with Brits. Their enjoyment of whatever they are involved in is too contagious to get angry about.

A pair of Weimaraners.

Weimaraner/Vizslas

I have seen so few of these in for training that I wonder if it is another one of those chicken or egg deals. Which came first? Is it that there is such a small genetic pool of hunting stock left that interest among hunters has dissipated? Or, rather, that since interest has dissipated, they are not being bred for sound hunting traits?

I think the chances of finding a sound hunting Vizsla are much better than finding a sound hunting Weimaraner. Judging from the limited pool of Weimaraners that I had in for training, the show breeders have won on the breed. The dogs tend to very large sizes, and are ill-configured for field work. They have little to no pointing instinct, and no desire to range more than 20 yards or so. They do generally retrieve well. If a hunter wants a slow and ultra-close working dog and is willing to invest some time, I have gotten Weimaraners to perform adequately in the field.

I have trained only a few Vizslas, but the ones I had were at least of an athletic build. Of the few, a couple had real temperament problems. I would bet that if a person did their home work and searched nationally, a worthy Weimaraner or Vizsla prospect could be located.

Springer spaniel.

Spaniels

Springers

Springers are happy characters. Flushing dogs are not in common use as hunting dogs here in the Southwest. They predominate in parts of the country where pheasant are the principal game species. They weigh in around the 40 to 50 pound mark.

I have had only a handful in for training, so please treat my observations accordingly. I liked them. They were personable with good, solid hunting instincts. They make solid retrievers and tend to enjoy water work. They are very pleasant companions and to the degree that the genetics of the individual dogs allowed, they made good field dogs. I see many springers at Snake Safe training sessions. Just like the golden retriever breed, there are a bunch of show breed springers out there that probably make fine companion animals. However, if you want a hunting springer, be careful that you buy a puppy from proven hunting stock.

Also, there has been a fair amount of press over the last decade about a temperament issue among springers and other breeds called springer rage. It is a condition where seemingly mild-mannered dogs snap and attack their owners. Again, this seems to have originated from show breed stock. If you are considering a springer, be sure to get your puppy from a reputable breeder whose dogs don't exhibit any temperament problems.

Cockers/Boyken spaniels

My first two dogs were American cocker spaniels. I had one as a boy in Hawaii named Goldie, who used to swim with me at the beach. When we came to the mainland, my parents rented a duplex that shared a large backyard with the adjoining unit. There, we had a new cocker that matched Goldie, who had been left behind on Oahu.

In the intervening decades the breed eclipsed into a popular pet, but lost the utility for field work. There has been a renewed interest in the cocker spaniel over the last few years, and both English and American cockers are seeing field work again.

In addition, the Boyken spaniel is a proven performer in the field. Though rare, it makes a fine retriever and a good companion.

Both breeds have been gaining in popularity here in the US. I have enjoyed watching them work in the field, but have had no professional gun dog training contact with either breed except for Snake Safe training.

Retrievers

Labradors

Just as GSPs are the gold standard in the pointing breeds, Labs are the dog of choice in the retriever world. They are solid performers and take training well. There are no temperament concerns with the breed.

Their one trouble spot is genetic maladies such as bad hips, bad elbows, etc. They are one of the most popular pet breeds in the country today and because of this fact they are bred to supply a huge puppy market. At this point, genetic problems are endemic with Labs. Be sure you are dealing with a reputable hunting breeder when you acquire any Lab. If you are purchasing a puppy, make sure the parents are of hunting stock with certified hips, elbows, and eyes.

There is broad latitude in weight on Labradors. They can run from 50 to over 100 pounds. They all live for water and have strong retrieving instincts. If you are looking for a waterfowl dog, pick-up dog, or upland flush dog, it is hard to go wrong with a Lab.

Below: Labrador retriever.

Above: Chesapeake Bay retriever.

Chesapeake Bay Retrievers

Chessies are an acquired taste. They are powerful and driven, weighing in between 60 and 100 pounds. Chesapeakes are not flashy, but they are solid with the wild golden-yellow eyes of a wolf. They are dogs of a hundred years ago and really belong somewhere that offers them a heavy workload. They were bred to work seven days a week, breaking ice to retrieve dozens of birds, and they spend the time in-between retrieves guarding against anything that gets too close to their bird pile or hunter's gear. Be very, very careful of temperament with any Chesapeake you select.

We had a Chessie for 15 years, and she was a fiend on birds. We loved her dearly. Nothing hit the water like this Chessie, but, man, what a problem to live with! A friend described her going through life as a hand grenade with the pin pulled. On her first retrieve at 3 months old, she bit me when I took the bird from her. She didn't think she should have to share. She had a very clear idea of what was and was not appropriate according to her. She would give you a short sneer of a warning and then she would nail you. When she did it, she wasn't playing.

She couldn't be around other dogs because she would put a hole in them. She bit through the sinuses of a 3 1/2-month-old setter pup because it picked up her training bumper. She loved hunters and she knew the difference between hunters and non-hunters, even before they killed any birds for her. If a person wasn't a hunter and they showed any fear of her, she would try to tooth them.

She once got a toe nail caught on a piece of wire, coming out of her puppy pen as a baby, and from that point on, for the rest of her life, to touch her feet was to court dismemberment. Forget about taking her to a vet! To get a legally documented rabies shot in her, I had to hog tie her to the truck bumper in the back of the vet's building and bundle her head in a thick pillow. The sounds coming out of that pillow when the vet touched her would have made Mother Teresa question her faith.

Certainly not all Chessies are as nasty as ours was, but, in truth, they all have a piece of it in them. Even the big amiable ones, when pushed, can go off on you. My sister-in-law had a large female from different blood than ours. They had small children and this Chessie was a gentle beast with those kids. They could hang all over that dog.

One day my sister-in-law and the girls were pulled over for a routine traffic stop with the dog in the car. They were in a jeep-style vehicle with a rag top. When the officer approached the back of the vehicle, the dog went ballistic and tried to go through the fabric top to get at the police officer. The officer ran for safety and, from the safety of his patrol vehicle, waved my sister-in-law on to leave the area. I picked up that same dog at the airport and it had nearly chewed through its pet porter. I have a bunch of Chessie stories.

Perhaps the clearest indicator of Chessie temperament is how few pros will take them on for training.

Don't get me wrong, I really like Chessies, and when our current geriatric Lab passes, I may do it again. Just be aware of what you are getting yourself into. If you are not in a position to handle a problem dog you could be faced with the same difficult choice another Chessie owner friend had to make. Their adult male Chessie attacked a house guest one evening while they were standing in the kitchen getting ready to sit down to dinner. The dog really hurt their guest and my friend realized that they could not accept that problem any longer. He placed the dog in rural locations several times, but each time he got the call that it wasn't working out. They ultimately had to euthanize the dog.

Above: Golden retriever.

Goldens

When I was a kid, I used to do a lot of goose hunting. There was a warden on a federal refuge in California who had a male golden that did patrol work with him and rode around in the back of his truck. The dog was all business, surly, and would finish a fight. He was a goose fiend and a real beauty. I think that was the last time I saw an honest to goodness hunting golden in the field. That was 35 plus years ago. There are a very few field golden breeders left. Be sure of what you're getting yourself into, if you're looking for a hunting dog.

I do a lot of rattlesnake aversion training and, in that capacity, I snake break a ton of goldens. They are oversized and rife with genetic maladies. Their physical conformation for field work is gone. Many have trouble using their sense of smell. On this breed, the show breeders have won.

Above: Golden retriever.

Goldens

When I was a kid, I used to do a lot of goose hunting. There was a warden on a federal refuge in California who had a male golden that did patrol work with him and rode around in the back of his truck. The dog was all business, surly, and would finish a fight. He was a goose fiend and a real beauty. I think that was the last time I saw an honest to goodness hunting golden in the field. That was 35 plus years ago. There are a very few field golden breeders left. Be sure of what you're getting yourself into, if you're looking for a hunting dog.

I do a lot of rattlesnake aversion training and, in that capacity, I snake break a ton of goldens. They are oversized and rife with genetic maladies. Their physical conformation for field work is gone. Many have trouble using their sense of smell. On this breed, the show breeders have won.

The dog that will be worth watching, or shooting over, will be a virile, active, fiery-going dog that in puppy hood, or even in derby year, may be an impulsive, perhaps over-spirited, individual; but never a rattle-brained one. The difference between the overzealous hunter and a crazy-headed one may be more difficult to discern in the beginning but by the time a dog gets into his second year the difference should be clearly discernible. Crazy-headedness is usually an ancestral trait, and if a young dog from levelheaded mating shows signs of youthful wildness the chances are more than good that this is just the sign of a high class dog in a transitory period that, with the sobering process brought by age and judicious training, will develop into the very kind of a dog that goes to heights. Your grouse dog must develop grit, driving force, and a special sort of reckless abandon to be rated as great, but he must also be tractable, easy to handle and direct, and ready to obey promptly and gracefully. This combination of almost dual characteristics is the big obstacle that confronts the man ambitious to own a high class grouse dog. It is also the reason why so many will describe their ideal as a docile, methodical, spiritless animal that never does wrong. These are the dogs of the men who fear spirit lest it get out of hand, and hate initiative lest it become uncontrollable. But they are not the men who have great grouse dogs, just so-so ones and these are not so hard to get, should one be interested.

William Harden Forster
New England Grouse Shooting
1943

Training

Patience, the first thing your dog needs to learn.

It all begins with patience.

The first thing to teach your dog, and expect from your dog, is patience. Your dog must know how to wait. When I trained professionally, that was the first lesson any newly arrived dog learned. He learned to wait, to focus on me and what was happening around him, not on what he wanted to do. The new dog sat on the middle of the chain gang while everyone else around him got worked, until I saw that he was watching and waiting. When a hard case arrived, I short-tied him to break his willful streak. I waited to see the new arrival reach the point of boredom, and then we began. Again, this may sound small, but it is very important. If a handler begins training before this happens, the dog will fight the handler throughout the entire process.

Tri-colored English setter waiting.

English setter on whoa post.

Training Whoa or Hup
A Gun Dog's Foundation Command

In the Old South, there was a school of training referred to as the "click method." There wasn't any set method or structure to it. A dog owner just kept taking his dog hunting until it all "clicked." Often, the young dogs were run with older, experienced dogs that got them into birds and showed them how to handle them. Many dog owners today still attempt to bring on a novice dog this way. The men I trained with as a kid referred to dogs trained in this manner as "naturals." What made this possible in the old days is that there were wild birds available to put young dogs on. Nowadays, that's very hard to do no matter where a handler trains.

Pointer backed by German shorthair.

Instructing a dog properly is an intentional endeavor. It requires a conscious, structured interaction with the dog. More to the point, to say we train a gun dog is misleading. The only true training a handler does is the early yard work for whoa or hup and the obedience that goes with it. Once the training crosses over into scent, search, and birds, the dog has gone beyond a human's ability to follow.

What a gun dog trainer does is make introductions and allow the dog to refine genetic propensities that were already in him at birth. We introduce a gun dog to scent, birds, and gunfire so that his innate genetic memory can "click" in. We install the whoa, hup or sit command before this introduction so there is a way to moderate and control the dog while this is happening. With this control, we can ease the dog through the genetic frenzy of his first bird and hunting exposures and keep the dog on track as a team player working for the gun.

Teaching is easy: we can get a dog to understand what we want very quickly by effectively communicating what we want and cutting the lessons into small enough pieces. The difficult trick is getting the dog to respond and act appropriately when he would rather do something else- such as chase the bird out of the county, or carry a retrieved bird over the hill and chew it into pieces. Over the years, many clients that brought in dogs to be trained would tell me that my job was going to be easy: they had been doing yard work and the dog was already whoa broke. They meant that when he was in the training area, on a check cord, the dog would stop.

My stock response was, "define whoa broke?" I would then explain that, for hunting purposes, whoa broke refers to a dog running full bore, 150 yards out, with a bird fluttering ten feet off its nose who, when a whoa whistle cue is given, stops and freezes. "Is your dog that whoa broke?" No one ever answered yes.

How do you get a dog to there?

Let me put this in context. For pointing breeds the command is "whoa." For the flushing breeds and retrievers the command is "hup." Some retriever handlers substitute the word "sit." It all means the same thing, either standing or seated: freeze and don't move.

This is the foundation command that all gun dog work is built on. Notice I used the word "foundation." A person would be more successful trying to erect a building with no footing or slab than handling a dog with no foundational command. This is where a dog's formal training begins. You can't skip this step and expect to have a trained dog. You don't move ahead to birds and gunfire and then come back and pick this up later when you figure out how to get it done. If this training is not completed in the beginning, your dog will never be a proper, well mannered gun dog.

What must be instilled in the dog is a structure that allows a handler to require and enforce compliance. That makes for a competent dog trainer and a well-trained dog.

The command "whoa" or "hup" is introduced when a dog is mature enough to maintain the attention span necessary to accept structured training. For most dogs that age is at least ten-months-old. Essentially, it begins as an obedience command that is later modified to include a flying bird, and then a gun shot. It culminates with the dog remaining whoaed while a bird is flown, shot, and dropped to the ground. Later, it is used for backing.

Tools and associations need to be user friendly. There are a host of methods trainers have used in the past to create that structure and association for a dog. I have used many of them. I am a bird hunter, so my efforts have been to produce a dog that performs properly in the field under hunting conditions. It's hard to have a training table, or a whoa barrel, or a 30 foot check cord with you when you're hunting four miles in, perched on the side of a drainage, fighting gravity. I keep it simple and focused with the sole goal of producing a hunting dog. I adhere to some basic principles.

I follow the Rule of Three. Training takes three months and is

Whoa post

broken down into three one-month increments. I train in three day increments, two days on, one day off. This makes for a four to five day work week, depending on how the days fall. In a training session, I generally do three repetitions or drills and call it done. **The difference between an amateur and a professional is that the professional knows when to stop.**

Three is a good number. Two is too little and four is too much. Three keeps the dog fresh and wanting more. This concept works for dog training as well as chocolate donuts.

On this schedule, I train to the point of boredom, which is one of the indicators I look for on the part of the dog during training. It tells me that all the excitement and electricity that might cause the dog to move or break has evaporated and the dog is ready to move up the training ladder.

Training a dog to the point of boredom works well for a hunting dog because when he crosses over to hunting wild birds, he will again exhibit a high level of intensity. This won't, however, help a person produce the flashy dog necessary to win field trials on planted, domestic birds. Therefore, use this technique with caution with field trial dogs because if trained to boredom, they will appear lackluster on planted, domestic birds.

A tri-colored English setter receiving an introductory lift below the whoa hook.

Place Matters: The Whoa Hook

Training begins by teaching the dog the meaning of whoa, which essentially is "freeze and don't move." We teach this on one particular 36-inch circular point on the planet: the spot directly below your whoa hook.

Dogs are very place specific. They have a long memory regarding something that happens at a particular spot, particularly when it involves levitating off the ground. When returned to that spot, the association kicks in and you will get compliance. In this case, the dog associates his feet losing contact with the ground with any movement on his part after hearing the whoa command. I use a hook and rope to lift and suspend the dog above the ground during the initial introduction to whoa.

Other whoa training methods use a barrel, or wobbly platform, or table. The thought behind this is that when the dog is above ground, he is easy to handle because he is at waist level to the trainer, and tentative regarding his footing. My reason for not using these sorts of fixed training tools is that I'm not able to use them in the field. I can't carry this stuff with me when I'm hunting. I can, however, approach a non-whoaer, place my hands underneath his belly and chest and lift him straight up off the ground. With that association file tucked away in the dog's memory, the dog is right back underneath the hook suspended by a rope with his toes unable to grab the ground.

To make this association, a metal whoa hook is anchored in a beam suspended above the ground and used with a stiff twenty-foot check cord. A person can simply throw a rope over a tree limb if a tree is available in the training area, although a rope tends to slide better on a metal hook or pulley. It is important to note here that a dog should never be left unattended when he is hooked up to the hook or post.

On the dog, I fit a heavy duty D-ring collar around his withers. I prefer to use an extra wide, 2-inch collar for the withers because it's more comfortable for the dog. One of the worst dog bites I ever received was from a young female setter who panicked during her first introduction on the whoa hook because the wither's collar was biting her belly. She kicked with her back foot and twisted the rope up in a spiral, suspending herself off the ground. I scooped her up with my arms to lift her and take the tension off of the support rope, and she clamped down on my biceps. I had to use my thumb to pry her off of my arm and she then switched and tried to go through that as well. Trainers learn from experience as well as their dogs!

During whoa training I also keep the dog's everyday collar, a standard one-inch wide D-ring collar, around his neck. On the neck collar D-ring, I hang a large chain link clip or carabiner clip wide enough to allow the snap on the twenty-foot check cord to pass through easily. A dog generally looks at me real peculiarly the first time I get him rigged.

I position the dog underneath the hook, with the front of the check cord fed through the wide clip hanging from the neck collar D-ring. I then pull through and attach the check cord snap to the D-ring on the two-inch wide wither's collar near the rear of the dog. I lift the section of check cord that runs between the two D-ring contact points, along the top of the dog's back, and form the rope into an inverted v. I then raise up the point of the v and hang the rope over the metal hook. The result is that when I stand facing the front of the dog, at the end of the check cord, and pull on the rope, the dog levitates off the ground. The resulting loss of contact with the ground immediately gets the dog's full attention.

The First Two Whoa Associations

I lay out this association very gingerly, because a little goes a long way. I start by standing in front of the dog and giving him two cues or associations. I use the verbal command "whoa" and I show him the flat of my hand, like a traffic cop. I then step to the side of the dog and, while standing over him, I lift both sides of the rope and lift him off the ground like a piece of luggage. I then lower the dog and give the verbal command again, timing the word to the point where the dog's toes lose contact with the ground. I will go through this introduction three or four times. Typically, the dog will reach a point where he will turn his head up and roll his eyes at me as if to say, "OK, I get that you're trying to tell me something here."

Once I see that the dog is making the connection, I then set him up to fail. I stand alongside the dog and step off, almost like I am starting a heel command. I give the dog no cues or eye contact, and the dog takes the step with me. When he does, I turn to face him and pull the rope which levitates him off the ground. I use no voice or hand cues prior to repositioning him after he has left the ground. Remember, a little goes a long way. When you set him back up again, use a soft voice and reinforce the verbal cue, "whoa" and show him the flat of your hand. The dog will generally catch himself and give you the stare again, "OK, I get it. You don't want me to move from here."

Above: Labrador retriever learns to hup (sit).

Whoa/Hup Panel

Below: English setter learns to whoa (freeze while standing on all four feet).

When I see the dog connecting, I again bring the lesson up a notch. It may take two or three rope pulls to get to this point. I walk around the dog reinforcing with both the verbal and hand command. If the dog follows me with his eyes and tries to move with me, I step back and put tension on the rope and give the dog some air. Not much, mind you, but enough to get the dog's attention. You will have to gauge that point. Each dog is different.

When the dog is steady in spite of my moving around him, I again bring it up a notch by bumping the dog softly with my hand and my knee as I circle him. I want him to know that moving for any reason will cause him to lose his connection with the ground. The dog will tell you with his eyes that he gets it and generally this happens within one to two minutes. "OK, if you're going to be a jerk about it, I won't move."

Next, I give the dog an out. I introduce the release command which will allow the dog to move after being whoaed. Standing next to the whoaed dog, just as I did when initially setting him up for the first pull, I now put my hand on top of the dog's head and simultaneously push forward while giving the release command "hoe-on." (You can use whatever word you want to release him). It is important that the two happen together, simultaneously. Left to his own devices, a dog will quickly start anticipating the release and break early. Remember you are creating layers of associations for the long haul, and it all begins here. Those two things happen simultaneously, like two keys turned at the same time to open a single lock.

When you first release the dog, he won't believe you and will continue to stand still. Get in front of him and turn to face him. Kneel down to dog level and coax the dog to you. Milk the dog in by pulling on his collar with your hand if you have to, and when he breaks and comes to you, shower him with praise and affection. Then, lift him up and put him back on his whoa spot in the whoa position, and go through the release command again.

Finally, put the whole package together and go through each step of the drill. You won't need the rope and can leave it lying nearby. Congratulations, your dog now knows what whoa means and you can expect compliance while he's wearing the outfit and standing within this particular three-foot circle of earth. This process took about two minutes. You will now spend the next three months making that three-foot circle big enough to encompass the distractions of flushing birds, gun shots, and the great outdoors.

Whoa Post

Next we are ready to graduate the dog to the whoa post, and in the process enlarge the 36-inch whoa circle to one that is 30-feet wide.

Prior to the previously described hook session, I will have introduced the dog to the whoa post for two to three sessions. I hook the dog up to the cable and we walk three circles around the post. No commands. No expectations. I have the dog watch other dogs being worked on the post. I want the transition from hook to whoa post to be as comfortable as possible for the dog in training.

After this pre-hook break-in introduction, we begin formal whoa training and we go to the hook. During the transition period (after the first hook session) of three to four training sessions at the whoa post, we place both the neck and withers collars on the dog each time, in order to retain the associations put in place by the whoa hook.

Using a 15-foot tie-out cable, we attach the dog to a central post which is firmly anchored to the ground. Over the post I drop a large metal ring that will rotate freely and not bind. To the ring, I clip the snap on one end of the steel tie-out cable. I then attach the snap on the other end of the cable to the dog's neck collar. Standing on the outside of the circle, I attach my check cord to the same collar D-ring to which the tie-out cable is connected. Rigged properly, the post is in the center, the handler is on the outside, and the dog is sandwiched in-between, held by the check cord and the tie-out cable. By walking with a taut rope the dog is pinned in place and forced to walk in a circle like a horse on a hot walker.

During the first training session, when the dog is first introduced to the whoa hook, I move the dog directly from the hook to the whoa post. The dog will be a little tentative at this point so I move through the process slowly. The dog will have gotten the message at the hook and will be aware of an expectation when he is clipped to the cable at the whoa post.

Pick a particular spot of ground, a 36-inch circle if you will, within the arc of travel that the whoa post allows and have that be the initial stop and start point for the first two or three drills the dog goes through. Prepare a tie-off point at that spot so that you can leave the dog tied on the post, with the check cord taut and the dog held in the whoa position. The most common response for a dog when first walked on the post is that he wants to follow the handler after the whoa command. Tying him off stops him in his tracks.

With the dog rigged and clipped on the cable, step off from your

1 - 8: An example of a shorthair doing everything right and complying on whoa.

A -H: An example of a setter sitting on whoa and then balking when corrected. The dog is lifted and returned to a standing position. It doesn't look pretty, but she is standing.

starting point, and walk the dog in an arc around the post. The dog's prior exposure to the post was just doing three laps with no expectations, so begin that way now. Give him a lap or two, or three, talking softly and calming him down. When the dog gives in and walks along, focused on the movements of the handler, set up the first whoa command.

During the arc of movement around the post, approach your pre-determined start/stop point. Time your command so that the dog has three or four steps to travel before hitting the stop spot. Give a firm verbal whoa command and, as you step by the dog, show him the flat of your hand which is dangling at your side. When the dog doesn't stop, lean out with your body, and put pressure on the rope. This will pin the dog in-between the post and you, and he will be forced to stop; but, he probably won't stand. The dog may try to sit, or cower. Depending on how passive-aggressive the dog may be, he may try to roll over on his back, or turn around and face the opposite direction. This can tangle up the rope rigging, so don't let it happen, not even once. If the dog knows that he's got that out, he may learn to use it.

If you get anything short of complete compliance, then swiftly and calmly, with no vocalization on your part prior to the moment when the dog's toes lose contact with the ground, lean over the dog, grab both neck and withers collars, one with each hand, and lift the dog straight up. In the dog's mind, this will return him to that 36-inch circle under the hook where he had been a few moments before. Lower the dog back down so his feet have purchase and drop the flat of your hand in front of the dog's face, "Whoa!"

Look for the dog to make eye contact. His body should be stiff and whoaed and his eyes should say, "Oh, I understand. It means the same thing here as it did over there." If he isn't giving you that message, then pick him up again and go through the same drill until you see physical compliance. Use slow, calm repetitions. Do not move forward from this point until you get compliance because you are laying the foundation for all future whoa training.

By the same token, this is not to be a contest of wills. You are not trying to win here. You are trying to instruct the dog by giving him a positive outcome. The instant you see the dog responding properly to the whoa commands, release him by touching him on the back of the head as you say "hoe-on" and begin walking your circle again. Praise the dog. Pump him up with your voice. Let him know he did the exact right thing and you are happy to be walking that circle with him again. Do a lap or two and do the drill again. I do two or three drills per daily session for the first few days of training, moving fast and keeping it light.

Your dog may balk. It may be from the get-go, or a few days into training. There are two tools you can use to reinforce the structure you are setting down: a pinch collar and a rawhide pig tie. Both are available through sporting dog mail order catalogs. I have seen the pig ties for sale in our local feed store.

The pinch collar is a leather collar designed with a spring steel band sewn between the layers. This gives the collar a memory that forces the collar open after a pulling force draws it to close around the dog's neck. There are brass roofing nails sticking through, on the inside of the collar, so that as the collar closes on the dog's neck the nail spikes pick up the rolls of skin and pinch the dog. The collar looks a little draconian, but its appearance is worse than its actual effect. The pinching sensation gets the dog's immediate attention and has the same effect as someone sticking a pair of tweezers up your nose and grabbing hold of a bunch of nose hairs. The dog rises up on the balls of his feet and freezes, head held high: the exact position we want to see a whoaing dog in. For hupping, the handler can then step in and press the dog's rear down into a sitting position.

A rawhide pig tie is the tool that you see the rodeo cowboys use during calf roping to quick-tie an animal's feet. It looks like a small lariat that springs back into open coils once the pulling tension on it is released. This is used in whoa breaking by placing the open coil around the dog's withers, with the other end in the handler's hand. Rigged this way, when the dog and handler are working the whoa post and the dog tries to sit down, cower, or balk, the handler doesn't have to stop or lean over to adjust the dog. One quick upward snap of steady pressure and the dog raises his belly up. For the hupping dog, the handler at this point can push the dog down into the proper position.

Whoa Training Guidelines by Breed

Let me give you some guidelines by dog breed on behaviors one can expect during whoa training:

A male German dog will often go Teutonic on you and make it a battle of wills: his against yours. Don't soft pedal him. Rig him with a pinch collar and show him what you need from him. Once he is sure you're in charge, he will happily comply and both your lives will be easier for it. If a male dog is going to fight you, it is best to work it out here to

Top: A flushing breed prior to being hupped or told to sit.
Middle: A retrieving breed sitting/hupped.
Bottom: A pointing breed whoaed.

completion, in the early stages, before you get to field work and he has more opportunity to be successful in his noncompliance.

A Brit may cower and get passive-aggressive with you, trying to find a way not to comply. You will see the little guy curl up like a turtle with a belly ache on the whoa post. He will act like the weight of the world is on him and it's all your fault. He really would like to help you but, given the terrible burden that he has to endure, you are just going to have to let him do whatever he wants to do. Be ginger, but firm. Use the pig tie and force him to stand when he tries to slip down. Keep him moving during the circling and take what you can get. Take little pieces of compliance if you have to, until you get a complete drill. This can take days. Remain positive and upbeat. Be very patient and keep working until he complies all the way through. There is no partial compliance here. If a Brit thinks there's an out, you will be seeing him try to use it through the entire training process. Use the pinch collar only as a last resort. If the Brit gets resentful of the pinch collar, there can be hell to pay.

An English pointer is usually fairly straightforward. Take him deliberately through the drills and you will get compliance. The exception are the Elhew dogs. I have had them cower on the initial whoa training and then, later, on backing. Backing is an extension of whoa, so it behooves a trainer to fix any cowering early, while on the whoa post and in a structured environment, before going to the field. The Elhews are not soft dogs. They are just trying to control the situation and get what they want, which is to run without being controlled.

Take a setter one step at a time. Go easy and use a lot of praise. Err on the side of caution, and take pieces of compliance until you get the whole enchilada. A setter takes things very personally.

A Lab is very easy to get along with. Walk him through and be enthusiastic and he will get it right very quickly. You may not want to go with him first if you are training more than one dog at the same time. They learn well by watching others.

A Chessie will comply at his own pace. Don't force the issue, just stick with the repetitions and he will come around.

Tri-colored English setter on whoa post.

Putting it all together

After this first session, where the dog has been given the double whammy of hook and post, he's going to become a little tentative. Remember, this isn't a contest. Give him the time he needs to bold up. For the next few days, move along slowly. Look for compliance.

Start your daily drills from the beginning, with the full harness rigged on the dog. Give the whoa or hup command and stand above the dog, raising him off the ground by his harness. Graduate him to a whoa or hup command with a tight rope on the whoa post. Once you are getting consistent compliance, remove the harness and work with just the cable and check cord. This shouldn't take more than a few days. Training is done in repetitive layers, with each session starting with old learned activities and ending with new introductions, as in: A, AB, ABC, ABCD, ABCDE, BCDEF, CDEFG, DEFGH. If at any point you need to return the dog to A, don't hesitate.

When he is whoaing reliably with you walking alongside, on the outside of the circle, up the ante. Whoa the dog and walk in full circles around him. Gradually make the circles tighter as the sessions progress. Use the two associations, a verbal cue "whoa" and the hand signal, the flat of the hand.

As you circle the dog, bump him with your knee. Walk towards the dog and step completely over his back. Walk to the front of the dog and toe the ground like you are trying to flush a bird. Make noise and commotion. Stand over the dog and lean forward so that you shade him. Move around and stand behind the dog. If the dog uses any of this activity as a reason to move his feet, or shift his gaze to follow you, then go back and lift the dog and set him back into whoa. Use tension on the check cord to pin him between you and the whoa post. Use the pinch collar, and/or pig tie, if the dog requires it. Reinforce it all with a sharp verbal "whoaaaaaaaaa."

You are looking for boredom from the dog. When the dog whoas on cue, doesn't follow you with his eyes, and has a ho-hum look on his face, you will know you are there. This should take about a week and a half, to two weeks.

Third Whoa Association

Now it is time to introduce a third association for whoa. The dog is currently functioning with two commands: the verbal cue "whoa" and the hand signal, the flat of the hand. Now, introduce a trill whistle command. Not a sharp clarion note, but a rolling trill similar to the letter rrrrrrrrrrr in Spanish. You will need to reserve the high, sharp clarion whistle note for handling later in the field.

Go back to the very beginning. Rig the dog with his whoa hook harness and put him back under the whoa hook. The two of you are back to A. Do exactly what you did before with one exception: along with the verbal and hand whoa signal, include a trill whistle blast.

Progress from the hook to the whoa post just as you did in the beginning, using the commands "whoa," the flat of your hand, and the trill whistle in that order. Once you get to the whoa post, begin to shift the order and use the whistle first and the verbal cue last. Ultimately, omit the verbal cue altogether and just use the whistle to command whoa. The training order should go like this: voice/hand, voice/hand/whistle, voice/whistle/hand, whistle/voice/hand, whistle/voice, whistle/hand, whistle.

You are weaning the dog off of all associations save one, the whistle cue. In the process, you are preparing the dog for the time when he won't be within twenty yards of you, at the end of a rope. Instead, he will be out working birds two hundred yards away. Just a handler's physical presence and eye contact can enforce compliance when the dog is within twenty to thirty yards. Past that distance it gets dicey. He won't be there to see your eyes watching him. The only form of communication you will have available is the long range blast of a whistle.

Train as you did before. Enforce compliance on whoa using the whistle command until you get boredom from the dog. It will go much more quickly than the first go around and you should see what you need in about a week or less.

Fourth Whoa Association

Now it's time to put in the fourth and last association layer for whoa. Start by conditioning the dog to wearing an electric collar. Put the collar on the dog and let him get used to wearing it. Find the lowest level that the dog responds to by starting at the bottom and going up. On modern collars that may be the 1/2 setting. Perhaps your unit starts at 1. Look for the dog to prick his ears and tilt his head when you press the button.

" Oh, what's that?"

You are not looking for discomfort, merely recognition. On most dogs that's a very low level. On some of the German dogs, it may be a mid-level stimulation. You want the dog to feel that something is lightly touching his neck and nothing more.

Go back to the whoa hook and start at A. Both you and the dog know the drill at this point. The new inclusion on this go around will be the collar. As you weaned the dog from verbal cue to whistle cue in the previous cycle, you will now switch from whistle cue to electric stimulation cue. Everything is as before. From the hook, transfer to the post. The association chain should go like this: voice/hand/whistle, voice/hand/whistle/collar, hand/whistle/collar, whistle/collar/hand, collar/whistle/hand, collar/hand, collar.

With this layer installed, there are now four ways to tell a dog to stop in the field. The first two associations, voice and hand, are close range propositions. The third, the whistle, can carry out several hundred yards as an unenforceable request for compliance. The fourth association, the collar, has the range of the whistle and then some, and in addition, a means to force compliance. If the dog declines a polite whistle request, then it is possible to go up the ladder of the collar's stimulation levels. Whereas the level 1 is a warm fuzzy, the 2 or 3 will make him a believer.

Again, on this last association, train through to boredom. It will go more quickly than the time before, maybe a week or less. During this last training, begin to unhook the dog from the whoa post cable. Walk him

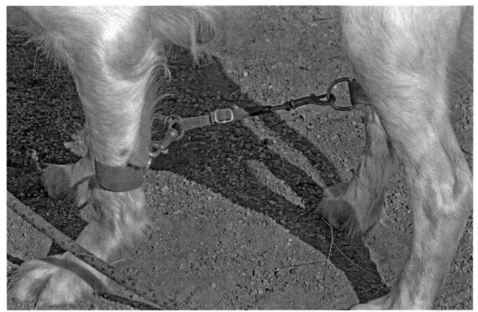
English setter wearing hobbles.

around the yard and down the road, whoaing as you go. His whoa world began with a 36-inch whoa hook circle, expanded to the 30-yard sweep of the whoa post. Now, start giving him the rest of the planet. Start with the continent you are currently standing on.

    An additional tool can be brought in at this point: a set of hobbles. These are available from the Scott's Dog Supply catalog. The hobble set is made up of three velcro cuffs with a sewn in D-ring on each cuff. In addition, there is an adjustable three-way snap made of nylon webbing and hardware. When you velcro a cuff on three of the dog's legs, and then connect the cuffs together with the set of snaps, the dog is restrained. He can move, but when he does, he pitches forward and digs a trough with his nose. A dog learns fairly quickly not to move.

    The purpose of the hobbles are to give you a portable way to anchor the dog to a particular spot. It replaces the tie-off post that you originally used when you first went to the whoa post. It drops neatly in a vest pouch, no iron spike and sledge hammer required. It can be used on the side of a mountain, six miles in from your vehicle.

    Put the individual hobbles on the dog before the the training session. Take the dog to the post, whoa him, and snap the hobbles together. Then, you will need to walk around the dog as you did before, including the bumps, commotion and distractions. For example, we have outside cats that keep the rodents down in the out buildings. They are a great draw

1) Jay Smith connects setter to whoa post cable and begins circle.

2) Smith leads setter onto a harnessed, motionless silent pigeon dropped by a helper. (Notice dogs in background)

5) On subsequent circle, Smith leads setter onto a wing-tied pigeon. Wing-tied pigeons move and make noise.

6) While bird is moving, Smith whoas setter and uses tension on the cable to enforce the command.

3) Smith whoas setter on the immobile, silent harnessed bird.

4) Smith reinforces the whoa command by lifting dog. (Notice the other dogs in image)

7) On a subsequent rotation dog is presented a bird. With a slack cable, Smith lifts dog and reinforces the whoa command.

8) Dog is now whoaed and not reacting to bird lying at her feet. The adrenalin has evaporated.

for a hobbled dog and the cats seem to enjoy strolling by when a dog can't do anything about it.

Next Step: Birds

When you see the dog doing well with the collar association and hobble introduction, then it's time to up the ante as done previously with circling, bumps, commotion and cats.

We are preparing the dog to transfer to field work on birds. I use a crate of homing pigeons. While all the dogs on the chain gang are observing, I hobble individual dogs on the whoa post and then fly individual pigeons at a distance. Over the period of four or five sessions, the pigeons get closer and closer until the birds are dizzied and lying in plain sight on the ground, in the path of the dog on the whoa post. This drill is not about pointing, although the dog may do that. It is about whoaing when told to, even with a bird on the ground in front of him. I whoa the dog, step in and toe the pigeon's wing until the head comes up and the bird wobbles around a bit. I then step at the bird and get it to fly away.

Once the dog is reliably holding, I have an assistant fire a muffled blank gun at a distance after the bird has flushed and is leaving. We let that filter in for a few sessions and then I bring it up a notch by producing a dead bird from my waist pouch after the flush and shot. I throw the bird and let the dog make a retrieve. When this additional bit of adrenaline has blended into the mix, I start compressing the layers. The bird, flap, bang, "Fetch," pieces, which initially were spread out over five minutes (with time between layers to let the adrenaline evaporate), eventually gets compressed into just a few seconds. This is all done in the whoa post circle where the structure is available to enforce compliance, including going back to A if the dog needs it.

When you see the dog doing well, unhook the whoa cable and do it off the post. Move out of the circle. Set up your drill ten, twenty, forty yards off the whoa circle. If you need to, you can take the dog right back.

When all these pieces come together, yard work is done and it's time to go to the field for bird work.

One follow up point here- did you notice how everything was done in repetitions and layers? Each segment was small and understandable for the dog. Each segment was supported by what had come before and reinforced by what came after. The entire process was accomplished inside a structured training area with the tools and infrastructure in place to enforce

Whoaed English setter eyes wing-tied pigeon.

compliance immediately when required.

Think it through when you train. Have a place to start from and a place to go to in the training process. Always be ready to step backwards to a positive interaction and end on a positive note.

1) A setter is whoaed by Jay Smith after she refuses to back a shorthair on point.

2-4) She is carried to a spot downwind from the scent cone in a position to honor the pointing dog and observe the flush.

5-8) She is positioned, whoaed and styled up. Smith is able to control the setter and enforce compliance because the dog has been whoa-broke.

9) Smith releases a pigeon from a remote launcher. Note the shorthair in the background pointing, standing in the grass and cactus.

Field Work

For field work, you will need an area that has appropriate cover for the types of birds you're going to be hunting. You will need enough ground to run dogs and fly birds.

You may be in a better position than I. When I first started training at our place in Arizona, I could shoot a shotgun behind the house. When neighbors started filling in I had to start traveling. Ideally, I like to move straight from the yard work to field work without traveling. To bridge this gap, I put in a whoa post in the field work area and transitioned new dogs with whoa post work. I also use a fold-down table in the back of my training trailer that doubles as a force break platform and allows me to transition dogs into the field from table work.

Start your initial field work by using the training layers from yard work sessions. Show the dog that the field is an extension of the yard. Begin on a whoa post and run the dog through his whoa drills. Then remove the dog from the cable and walk with him just as you did when you removed the yard whoa post cable. Whoa the dog off-post and run through the four associations: voice, hand, whistle, collar. Ultimately, once you have gone back and reinforced the connection to yard work, give the dog his legs and go for a walk. Keep the first few days in the field light. Let your dog get a feel for the place. You will have to gauge your own dog to know how much restraint to put on him. He should be wearing a check cord and his electric collar- don't let go of that check cord just yet.

When I ran customer dogs, I always included a beeper collar so that, should the dog take a flyer, I was in a better position to recover him quickly. Bear in mind that a portion of the dogs that came in for training were there specifically because they had been self-hunting on their owners, so caution on my part was the proper course of action. When I had a feeling that I might have a problem with a dog, I would also include a two foot length of very heavy anchor chain on his already heavily accessorized collar. The chain will slow the dog down and keep him honest.

Walk through the field training area and hang on to the end of the dog's check cord. Between the dog's sniffing and marking and exploring, get in two or three whoas. With the dog standing whoaed, walk in circles around him and out to the front. Make the same production of it that you did in the yard. Step up to the dog, tap him on the head to release him, and return to your walk.

1) Female English setter inspects crated pigeons. 2) Training pigeon tethered to a section of rubber hose to limit its distance during flight. 3) Hose-tethered pigeon launched from a remote launcher. 4) Lab shown a training pigeon prior to being allowed to chase the bird.

5) Lab completing a retrieve on a hose-tethered pigeon.

Jay Smith of San Manuel, Arizona, flies a homing pigeon for a Lab to build the dog's enthusiasm.

Flying Birds in the Field

Over a period of several sessions, start with rolling in the distractions that the dogs worked with in the yard: flying homing pigeons, muffled gun fire at a distance. You will notice that we haven't let go of the check cord yet...but we're getting ready.

Currently, ventilated bags and pouches for carrying birds are sold through catalogs. I used a big blue military bag that hung over my shoulder on a strap. For my training dogs, this blue bag was the fount of all happiness, because I filled it with homing pigeons in front of them before I took each dog for his whoa walk. I used the table on the back of the trailer to load the pigeons, and I positioned the chain gang off to the side so that once every few birds, I would let one fly over the length of the chain-ganged dogs. Every dog waited with anticipation for those flyers. They would jump and strain to get at the bird as it flapped overhead. Then, I would take everybody for a walk one dog at a time, and about six pigeons at a time.

A handler deals with a lot of fire when beginning bird work with a dog. This is as it should be. Don't be afraid of it. You wouldn't want a dog that doesn't light up when feathers are introduced. If done properly, this enthusiasm is controllable and moldable. Chop your introductions into small pieces that allow the adrenaline to evaporate between sessions. Do it incrementally, just as yard work was done incrementally. Essentially, the purpose of this work is to make the dog a team player who works for and to the gun. Genetics come into play, and depending on the breed and blood, there can be a wide range of responses. Just hang on, literally, and go as slow as your dog needs you to go.

Start on the whoa post with the dog strapped in and restrained by hobbles. The first couple of sessions, fly pigeons in front of him. Then, ratchet up the adrenaline and bounce the pigeons off the ground in front of the dog. Ultimately, go to the field and whoa the dog and fly birds in front of him. Just as training was done in layers on the yard whoa post, the training with pigeons is layered for the dog.

Whoa and two birds flown in succession.

Next, whoa and one bird flown and dog released to move to the end of his check cord. After the dog has calmed down and focused, milk him back in on the rope and fly the second bird out behind you.

Then, go through the drill up to the point where the dog has moved out to the front after the first flown bird. Next, with him moving freely at the end of the rope, fly the second bird. The dog comes back on his own. Maybe give him a third bird just to cement the deal.

The dog learns that he doesn't have to run out there to find birds. The birds are coming from you. He watched you load them. He knows you carry them. My dogs would swing by me and sniff at the blue bag like it was the doggy bone jar back home on the kitchen table.

Letting go of the Check Cord

When you see the dog coming back for birds, it's time to let go of the check cord. Don't, however, remove any of the dog's accessories such as the electric collar and beeper and boat chain, if you opted to use them. Be ready with your feet. When you are working a dragged check cord and you need to get a dog back under control, don't use your hands. Use your feet. Feet are much quicker and you will save yourself some bad rope burns. Step on the check cord and walk up it until you get to the dog. Then use your hands to control or reposition a whoaed dog.

You will control the dog from this point on by whoaing him if he gets farther from you than you want. It is natural for a handler to want to correct range on a dog by calling him in. You will notice, however, that we haven't done "come" or "here" in any training to date. The reason is that there is only one command that matters in handling a bird dog in the field. Yes, "come" or "here" will come later, but not now. Your dog only has one job. One command. That is to stop and stay stopped until told that he can move again. Whoa. This foundation command is 98% of successfully handling a dog in the field.

Additionally, if you are working with a pointing dog, you will notice that we haven't talked about pointing, either. We haven't incorporated it into any portion of the training to date. Pointing is a genetic trait. It is not learned, it happens independently of any training that a person can do with a dog. No amount of wings on a fly rod will change this fact. A dog may point everything at three months old, stop altogether, and not start again until a year and a half old. I had one setter that started in her second year. Yes, later in the training process there will be a time to refine the pointing instinct, to jump start it if it hasn't shown up yet, or to modify it if it isn't working right; but, as in "come" or "here," now is not the time.

We have just let go of the check cord and that is as big a bite of the apple as we want to take on right now. This is the dog's first crack at freedom. You want to give the dog a little bit of latitude. You want to let him chase departing birds and get it out of his system. On the first few he may go out a ways. I would try to hold it at around a hundred yards. The benefit of using pigeons is that they tend to circle when released. Additionally, once released, they stay airborne and leave the area. There is little chance of a dog getting his mouth on one. Once the bird gets out to a hundred yards, it is already way out front of the dog and starting to make the circle back around. This means the dog will be headed back your way shortly.

Use different methods to reel the dog back in. Fly another bird as the dog comes around to you and pull him off the bird that's leaving and over to the bird that's starting. Do this three or four times in succession and it tends to take the chase out of a dog. Done over three or four training sessions, he will learn that he can't catch them and the next one will be coming shortly, courtesy of you. Then, blow your whistle and whoa him. Go over to him and give him a hup. Release him to move and then fly another bird just off the front of his nose. Whoopee! Here we go again.

When he's coming around well and focused on you for birds, up the ante. Go back to whoa. Release a bird in front of him while he is whoaed. As you pull the release bird out of your pouch, include a fresh killed dead bird in the handful and throw both into the air at the same time. Stand on the check cord just in case. When he sees that bird tumble out of the sky, he is going to want to get to it. Keep him standing on whoa.

Stroke his back and pump him up with your voice.

"Birrrrrrrrrrrrrrddd. Dead birrrrrrrrrrrrrrrrrrrrddd." Then get a good hold of the end of the check cord and cut him loose, "Fetch!"

He may pick it up. He may maul it. He may sniff at it and look for another bird to fly over.

No matter what happens, keep it positive. If he picks it up, great! Milk him back in with the rope. Make no effort to touch or take control of the bird, just give him some affection and pump him up with praise. If he wants to give you the bird, take it from him and give it right back to him. Keep doing this until he loses interest in the bird. Then, as surreptitiously as possible, get the bird up and out of sight into your carry pouch.

If, once you get him pulled to you with the rope he doesn't feel like sharing the bird with you, great! You have no interest in the bird, anyways. Make no effort to touch the bird. As long as he wants to carry it, let him. Give him affection and praise him and then continue your walk. He can walk just fine with the bird in his mouth. At some point, he will drop the bird and shift his focus somewhere else. You can distract him at this point by flying another fly away bird for him. While he's out after that one, pick up the dead one and get it out of sight in your pouch. If he catches you doing it, give the dead bird back to him and start the process over again.

If he doesn't want to carry the bird, ignore it. Have no negative feelings or concerns regarding it. Retrieving is not the purpose of the exercise. I am not saying that I wouldn't prefer to have the dog carry at this point. I would, but retrieving will be dealt with later.

Learning the "Come" and "Here" Commands

At this point the dog is whoaing reliably. Now is the time to introduce a new whistle command for "come" or "here." Use a sharp, high, clear whistle note that carries well over a distance. I use three short blasts in rapid succession. Tooooooooooo. Tooooooooooo. Tooooooooooo. Some German dog trainers and retriever folks like to keep it to two. A handler can twist out that last note for effect when a canine's attention is needed. We want to be able to bring the dog in our direction or to us in the field. I use two different verbal cues because I need two different things to happen.

"Come" means I want the dog to move in my direction when I'm handling in the field and take a new line of travel. In this case, the dog needs to know that we are going a different way now. It's also used if the dogs are loose and I need them to load through a door or gate, or onto a trailer or vehicle. The "come" command means: "Look at me and go in the direction I need you to go." The tone is conversational and doesn't require an immediate response.

With the command "here," I am asking for a different response. "Here" literally means, "Right here, right now! I want to put my hands on you. I need you to physically come beside me immediately and stop all movement." Perhaps you see a snake or a herd of pigs in front of you, and you want to get a lead on the dog so you can walk him out of the area. Or, the dog has picked up a chunk of cholla on the side of his tail and he is flailing it like a medieval mace. You want to get him in and remove the cholla before someone else ends up wearing it.

"Here" has the effective compliance radius of about forty yards, about the furthest distance where a handler can effectively make eye contact with a dog and intimidate him with immediate physical proximity. If a dog is a hundred yards out, the "come" command, or a whistle cue, can be used to close the first sixty yards and then a sharply snapped, "Here!" finishes the distance.

One other thing I have found useful is to give myself a little wiggle room on the "here" command. "Come" is used in a conversational manner, but "here" needs to be responded to immediately and it can be difficult to be that rigid all the time. So, I modify it a little. I can be a little soft with "here" when handling, but when a dog hears me say, "Here Now!" and then sees me point to the ground at my feet, he knows that if he is not beside me in a nanosecond, I'm coming for him.

Incorporate the "come" and "here" lessons into your field training. When the dog comes back around on a fly away pigeon, or when you milk him back in after throwing dead birds, introduce the whistle cue and verbal commands.

At a distance, while the dog is swinging back on a fly away and sees you fishing in the pouch for another flyer, blow your whistle and shout, "come" to him. Since he was already on the way, you know you will get compliance. When he comes back towards you, reward him with another flyer.

When he's on the check cord and you're milking him in after throwing a dead bird, or when you know he's coming in all the way because he needs water and you have the water bowl out shout, "Here." When he gets to you, get him wet and give him affection. What canine wouldn't want that action?

Do it incrementally, step by step, with a lot of sugar. Repeat these

Attention look at me	**Attention** at extreme distance	**Attention** distance/heavy cover	**Here!** Stand at my feet I want to touch you

Twirl arm in a circular motion, blow one long sharp whistle blast	Twirl arm in a circular motion, blow one long sharp whistle blast	Twirl arm in a circular motion, blow one long sharp whistle blast	Point to the ground at your feet, blow 3 short whistle blasts

Over / Left Step off to the left	**Over / Right** Step off to the right	**Over / Left** at close range within 50 yards	**Over / Right** at close range within 50 yards

Use the vocal command "over" and give the dog a direction left	Use the vocal command "over" and give the dog a direction right	Use the vocal command "over" and give the dog a direction left	Use the vocal command "over" and give the dog a direction right

layers over several sessions and eventually the dog will respond when called. There's no reason for him not to, he's getting what he wants. There will, however, come a time when he will want to do something else and won't come when called. Don't get in a shouting match. Give your command in a civil tone once. If you honestly think the dog didn't hear you or is confused for some good reason, repeat it one more time. If the dog still doesn't respond properly, shut him down. Freeze him into whoa with a sharp whistle blast, walk over and take control of his check cord and force compliance. Do it a second time for good measure. Make him believe that if he doesn't comply with your commands, your response will be immediate every single time- no exceptions.

This is very important because, for one, you are setting a precedent for all future training. Secondly, particularly with field dogs, not handling properly and not responding when called can get a hunting dog killed. More than likely, at some point in that dog's career, his life will depend on his proper response to commands.

Working with Planted Birds

Up to now, the training has been a bit of a disjointed affair; a quilt with some big squares missing. The dog is under control and manageable in the field. He's taking directions well. The foundation of yard work is in place. It's time to start pulling the pieces together. We will start planting birds.

There are two ways to go here depending on the breed of dog you are working with. Flushing dogs such as spaniels and retrievers push their birds into the air from the ground. Pointing breeds indicate game by freezing into a point on the location of the birds they find on the ground. Both start with planted birds in the same way.

There are a bunch of different ways to go with planting birds, ranging from dizzying a bird and sticking it in a bush up to using electronic remote controlled launchers. Some of these toys are pretty pricey. Bear in mind that the more stuff you put around a bird, the more there is for a dog to smell and to realize that you are messing with him. The cleanest plant is a dizzied bird wearing nothing that the dog can smell. The drawback is that an unrestrained dizzy bird will often wake up, get up, and fly away. All at the wrong time, of course, such as before the dog arrives or at a really nonproductive moment during the training drill. With homers, at least, you will recover the bird. However, if you are planting shooters, it wastes

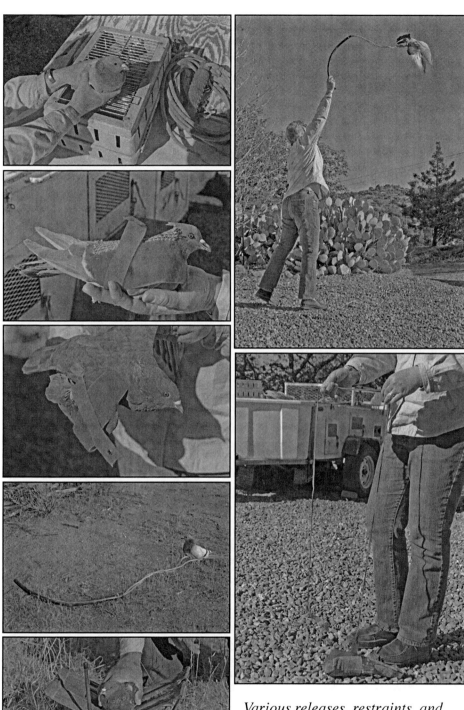

Various releases, restraints, and launchers used with planted birds in gun dog training.

Jay Smith creates a staged covey flush of five homing pigeons from a single large pheasant-sized remote launcher. Note setter and shorthair pointing in image.

money each time one flies away early.

On the other end of the scale are the electronic remote control releases. When a bird is in a release, you have complete control over what happens. A handler can dictate how high up the bird is launched by the size and strength of the launcher. On the larger units it is possible to load up the trap with three or four birds and simulate a multiple rise. A handler can load multiple traps with multiple birds and counterfeit a staggered covey flush for the dog.

The bird doesn't fly until you press the button. What also happens, however, is that the dog learns that the bird doesn't fly until you press the button and the tension and excitement that you are trying to cultivate in the dog on planted birds can disappear after just a few training sessions. I have seen this happen quickly, particularly with the smart dogs. I have seen what happens when a mature field dog, who has already run on wild birds, smells a planted bird in a metal release cage. The dog creeps up the scent trail, starts to point and then gets a look of recognition on his face. The dog then walks over, hikes his leg on the whole affair, and leaves it to go and look for the real birds: wild birds.

You can mitigate this in training by working smart with a new dog. Don't let him get too close to the plant. Try to limit his time around a release trap. Unfortunately, there is a timeline here and sooner or later the dog will figure it out. The smart ones will figure it out almost immediately. I have never been able to fool a dog for long. The best I've done is to confuse them for short periods of time. Take what you can get and then descend down the ladder. You can come back to remote control releases once you get the dog steadied and minding his manners.

After remote releases, I go to a velcro harness. The manufacturer calls them restraint harnesses. These are slick little gizmos and they only run a couple/three bucks. They come in two sizes: pigeon and quail. They are manufactured by Scott's Dog Supply and sold through their mail order catalog. They are made of fluorescent orange nylon and velcro, and each harness has a long orange nylon pullcord attached to it. The bird is held in place by means of a velcro strap.

A handler doesn't have to kneel over and fumble at ground level to release the restrained bird. It can be done quickly, with one hand, while standing erect. With a snap of the wrist, and a sharp pull on the nylon tether, the bird is flipped skyward as if it had been catapulted from a mechanical launcher. The only drawback is that you have to remember to hang on to the end of the harness cord until the bird clears it. I've lost several when the birds flew away with them. They shed them within a few hundred yards, but by that time the bird is out over the trees and there is no way to find the harness.

These nylon harnesses should keep the dog excited through most of his field training.

The next level to work with are unencumbered planted pigeons. There are a couple of options here. The standard method of planting a bird is to grasp the bird from the back with one hand covering the wings. Gently take the bird's head and twist his head back and tuck it under the wing, in what would be the bird's armpit. Lightly compress the bird's wings so that it is not able to pull its head free.

Next, dizzy the bird. Twirl the bird in fast spins like you are winding up to pitch an underhand softball. Give it a few spins, maybe six or eight. The longer you spin, the longer the bird will stay down. With a little practice, a person can learn to gauge the ratio of circles to the amount of time the bird stays put.

You can finesse the dizzying by twirling the bird the same way an eight-year-old would stage an imaginary sword fight with Zorro. Go one direction and then the other, one direction and then the other. En garde!

Wiggle the toe of your boot into the thick grass near ground level so that the vegetation forms into a small cone and then place the bird inside so that it is still compressed. Lay the bird down, wing holding head side down, so that the weight of the bird's body serves to hold the head buried under the wing. Now, however, it is no longer held with your hand but by a circular tube of vegetation. The bird should hold there for up to 20 minutes depending on how dizzy he was when he was put down.

To flush the bird, lift it with your foot and give the bird about half a minute to get oriented. The bird can come out of it before the handler brings the dog in. In such a case, the bird may take to wing and leave, or walk around and then flush as the dog comes in on it.

An alternate method is to wing-tie the pigeon. Take the bird and manipulate the bird's wings straight up over its back, as if the bird was doing a jumping jack calisthenic. With both wings fully extended, lace the wings together. Pull one wing towards the head and one wing towards the tail. Next, pull each wing simultaneously over the center line of the bird's back and let them return back to their natural position over the middle of the spine. Because they are extended over the center line of the back, when they return to center, the wings are not touching top of wing to top of wing, but rather bottom of wing to bottom of wing.

Without releasing your hold of the wings, next do the same move again, but this time reverse the wings. The wing that had originally been pulled towards the head is now pulled to the tail, and vice-versa with the second wing. Then let the wings return to center and knit the wings in a second spot, about where the primary flight feathers meet the secondary wing feathers.

A bird restrained in this manner can walk but it can't fly. It's a good method to use when you are trying to jazz up a dog and get him to point. He can see the bird moving in front of him, but the bird can't just up and leave on him. Be sure, however, that your dog is steady or restrained on a check cord or both, because this is a good way to get a dog thinking that he can catch a bird on the ground.

The way a handler releases a wing-tied bird is by whoaing the dog and walking to the bird. The handler has to lean over and twist the upper of the two wing-ties free. Step back and leave the bird, it will unravel the rest pretty quickly. The bird may fumble a bit, but it should be off the ground in less than a minute.

Another alternate method to dizzying is to hang something off the bird to slow it down and restrict the distance that it flies when it's flushed. I've seen it done three ways: with a length of rubber hose, a piece of cardboard, or attaching the bird to the end of a fishing pole. In my training, the rubber hose works best for me. On rare occasions, I've used the fishing pole.

With the rubber hose, I keep several set up and ready to use. I cut an old garden hose into 24-inch lengths and then cut a notch on one end, as if I were making a whistle. Next, I take a length of nylon cord, maybe a foot and a half, and tie cinching knots on both ends. I use hangsman's nooses so that they can be tightened and untightened multiple times during training sessions. I take the cord with the knots tied and fold it in half so that both knots are on one end. I then push the cord's other end through the notch in the hose, pull the cord through the end of the hose, pass the knot end through the newly formed loop and then cinch it down tight. Done properly, both knots are at an equal length and dangle down on several inches of cord.

In use, an otherwise unencumbered pigeon is fitted with the knots pulled snug, one on each leg. I dizzy the bird slightly and plant it for the dog. During the flush, the dog points, or is whoaed, and I step in and lift the end of the hose and flip the bird into the air. Wearing a hose set-up, a pigeon is not able to flush from the ground. It must be set aloft manually. Upon gaining altitude the bird tries to fly away, but is encumbered by the drag and weight of the length of hose. They can fly, but not well and not for long. The distance that the bird can travel is variable and determined by how high it was initially tossed at the flush, and the individual strength of the pigeon. Some birds are bigger than others and can go farther.

Regarding hose length, an individual handler can experiment and find what works the best for his particular situation. I've tried shorter and longer lengths. I've used short lengths that I weighted down with lead. I found that at 24 inches, I had a good handle length and that drag alone would pull the bird back down at a good distance for the dog to come in and point or locate for a second or third flush. After a couple/three flights, the birds get tired and it's best to swap them out for a fresh bird on the next dog.

Cardboard works on the same principle. If a piece is tied behind a flushed bird, the drag pulls the bird back down. In my experience, cardboard is cumbersome and not as portable as a length of hose. The hose fits nicely with a bundled bird in a carry pouch and also drags clean if the dog is allowed to fetch the bird. Cardboard tends to hang up on vegetation and the dog's feet.

Another option is to use a fishing pole: a long, thick, stout, deep-sea kind of fishing pole. The outfit will need to include a large spinning reel. Rig a double noose nylon cord set up, like that which has been used with the hose, except omit the hose. Tie a mountaineer's hitch in the center of the harness. Tie the bird to the end of the fishing line via the center loop of the nylon harness which is attached to the bird's legs. Thread out about twenty or thirty yards of fishing line and set the bird out in the open. A second person will be needed to work the pole. This setup works well for pumping up a dog on birds. The dog will come in and see the bird standing on the ground. Unlike a hose set, with the pole the bird is able to flush from the ground with no assistance from the handler. The dog gets too close and boom, the bird is gone.

The pole comes into play when the bird has gotten out far enough and the assistant, who has been holding the rod through the flush, now flips the bale on the reel. The bird runs out of free spooling line and comes back to earth like a bungee jumper with the cord just a shade too long. The dog then hunts up the bird on the second go-around and points, or is whoaed or hupped. While the handler works with the dog, the assistant comes along cranking up the line back onto the reel and gets into position for the next flight. This method can work well in open grass, but if there are trees or brush to contend with it gets complicated with line tangles.

Finally, the cleanest method of working birds is just to spread a bunch of them in the training area and bring a dog through. By spread, I mean very lightly planted. Tuck the head under a wing and lay it wing side down so that you have just enough time to move away without flushing it. The bird will wiggle out and flip itself right and start walking around. Some will leave immediately. Keep them spaced far enough apart so that the one leaving doesn't take the next as it flies over. I had the luxury of a coop full of homers so that I could put multiple birds out for several dogs. Spreading birds in this manner means that many will be gone before you get back with the dog, but it is also the closest that the dog will get to wild birds while being trained with pigeons. The contacts are random and the handler has as much knowledge as the dog about where the next bird is going to be.

1) A strip of velcro positioned as a reusable hobble for planting game birds. Note surveyor's tape used as a flag on the hobble to facilitate readily locating the planted bird.
2) Chuckar partridge used in gun dog training.

Using Game Birds for Training

Up until now I have only been referring to pigeons, but upland game birds such as bobwhite quail, chuckar, and pheasant also allow a handler to get close to simulating wild bird contact during training. I prefer pigeons for a dog's initial introduction to feathers and for most of its field work because, in a training situation, they get up and leave. They make a few circles over the dog's head, where the dog can see them, and then they take off for the horizon. No amount of chasing by the dog will put that bird in his mouth, something the dog learns quickly.

A twice-flushed quail will take to wing, go out 40 to 80 yards, and then pitch back to the ground. The dog watches the bird go back in and wants to follow, figuring he's got a shot at getting his mouth on that bird and, unless the trainer is careful, his wishes will come true. We need the dog to become a team player and realize that his best shot at getting feathers is to work for the gun and mind his manners. The dog needs to believe that the sound of the shot will produce a bird on the ground that he can get in his mouth. Pigeons are more likely to make a dog a true believer.

Pigeons are also an easy keep. They can be kept in a loft as homers that return after being flown in a training session. They reproduce like, well, like pigeons.

Pigeons for shooting are easily trapped from feral populations found world wide, or can be purchased from pigeon trappers for a reasonable fee.

Finally, they are the safest bird to use for training because they are pigeons, not the type of bird that a gun dog will be asked to hunt in the wild. If anything bad happens during training, if the dog picks up any bad associations, they will be related to pigeons and not to birds that matter for hunting.

Working with upland game birds is a little more complicated. To be useful for training they need to be reared and kept in a large flight pen, which is more than most folks can do. When a person starts down that road, they end up spending more time tending to birds than training dogs. If they are kept in a small pen, by contrast, upland game birds won't fly strongly enough to convince the dog that the bird is gone. As a consequence, if a trainer wants to use game birds for training, he or she will have to buy them per session unless they are reared and kept in a large flight pen.

Game birds are expensive. Training requires multiple layered associations, which translates to a chunk of birds over the span of a dog's training. That chunk of birds will add up to serious money.

There is a way to cut the cost. Upland game birds such as quail, chuckar, and pheasant can be handled in all the ways that were mentioned previously regarding pigeons. In addition, they have a covey instinct which causes them to recall back to the group. They return like homing pigeons and thereby cut a handler's bird costs down significantly.

Recall pens come in varying sizes ranging from small hand-held hardware cloth cages to shed-sized buildings. The fundamental component in the design is a small wire cone positioned at ground level and tilted upwards as it enters the enclosure. The cone starts wide at the bottom and narrows at the top. The diameter of the cone is tailored to the type of bird that will be housed in the cage: small for quail; medium for chuckar; larger for pheasant. The interior portion on smaller recall pen designs is partitioned into two equal sections to retain a group of birds inside the pen while the second group is liberated for training. In larger pens, there is one large communal interior area, and only a portion of birds held inside it are released.

The purpose of retaining birds is to provide a covey to return to for the liberated birds. The retained birds will call to liberated birds who then attempt to regroup and join the covey. As the singles straggle in, they circle the outside of the cage until they get to the open cone. The bird enters the cone, climbs towards the narrow constriction at the top, and ultimately enters into the interior of the cage. Because the interior opening is elevated

Below: Domestically reared bobwhite quail raised for gun dog training.

Wing-Tying a Pigeon

• *Separate wings*

• *Cross wings at base*

• *Pull rear wing foward and cross again above first cross*

• *Pigeon is now restrained and unable to fly or right himself*

• *To release, undo upper cross with your fingers and the pigeon can do the rest*

Dizzying and Planting a Pigeon

1) Restrain pigeon by hand
2) Fold head under wing
3) Grip bird firmly
4) Spin bird in a circular motion
5) Open a boot-sized hole in the grass
6) Place pigeon gently and move away

(it is above floor level inside the cage) birds don't have the option of leaving through it. In addition, because the cone's diameter constricts as it narrows, a bird which has entered the cone does not have the option of backing up and can only move forward into confinement.

Recall pens can be used as mobile devices and hauled with dogs to different training areas. They can also be set up as stationary affairs and built into a particular piece of ground. The ideal situation is to have a cover area that contains the birds and keeps them confined to the recall pen site: a grass field or a piece of agricultural land that the birds don't want to leave, until the point that they recall and re-enter the pen. Such a recall pen site is called a johnny house in the South. Trainers with the luxury of contiguous tracks of quail ground position their johnny houses on a loop, separated by an appropriate distance, and the dogs can follow the course and go from fresh contact to fresh contact, thereby simulating running on wild birds.

Most of us aren't going to have the option of large tracts of land and multiple johnny houses and, therefore, the recall pen provides an opportunity to create a covey at an available training site. If you have developed a training area, you can position a recall pen on site and plant or control the surrounding cover to hold birds and maximize the training options.

My situation was a little different. I trained in southern Arizona where there is little in the way of private land. The cover is restricted to one single vegetation type: former Sonoran desert grassland. There are no breaks, but rather one monotonous type of contiguous cover that goes on mile after mile. When I released birds they would recall if I didn't push them too hard. However, if the dogs flushed them a time or two and they got a ways out from the recall pen, I think the birds simply got lost and couldn't find their way back. I used recall pens for several years with varying degrees of success. I tried a medium-sized unit I left in place. What worked best for me, ultimately, was a smaller mobile affair that fit on top of the dog trailer. I could set it up before training at dawn, use it to work dogs and then return at dusk that evening to pick it up. Often, I would use it at the trailer and take birds from it as I worked each dog. After I had completed my dogs for the day, I would then place the recall pen as a pickup device to recover birds that hadn't been shot in training.

As I stated before, my preference is to use pigeons during training, but towards the end of a dog's schooling, running on quail or chuckar can up the amperage for a dog that is going soft on pigeons. With some of the "smart" dogs, it is the only option a trainer has available. It is also a nice transition for the average dog: to show them domestically reared game birds in preparation for running them on wild birds.

I did find that game birds can be difficult to contain once they are planted in an area. They can be dizzied and planted, but once they come out of it, they tend to start walking and walk right on out. If the dog doesn't get there in time, the bird will be gone. The birds can be contained in traps. I also had success using little velcro cuffs that I made from cutting a strip of velcro into short lengths and outfitting planted birds with a small set of leg hobbles. Birds, restricted in this way, tend to stay put until the dog comes in. They are still able to stand and take to wing, they just can't run. I used the devices with bobs and chuckar. For the bobs, I cut a chuckar hobble in half lengthwise which gave the smaller birds a little more flexibility to stand and push themselves up into flight.

In reality, chuckar are a more effective bird to train with because they flush stronger and fly farther than domestic bobs. Again, as stated before, if the bobs have been held in a flight pen they can offer an acceptable alternative for simulating the flush of a wild quail. However, they can also flutter up and pitch back in at forty yards and, in the process, entice a dog to break and chase, and by consequence, undo weeks of training.

Hunter connects on a straight-away shot on a flushing Mearns' quail. A setter and shorthair rush in to make the retrieve.

Transitioning into Wild Birds

Using planted pigeons begins the process of sorting the layers of the dog's previous training into proper order, so that the dog can ultimately transition on to hunting wild birds. Start the dog on planted birds. As mentioned earlier, there are two types of gun dogs: those that flush their birds, and those that point them. The type of dog that is being worked will determine how a handler proceeds.

Flushing Breeds

With the flushing breeds, it's a fairly straightforward affair once you reach a certain point in training: the dog is hupping reliably on command and he is returning when called. When you fly a bird, you can stop him with a whistle and expect him to remain hupped until released to pick up the dead bird you threw with the flyaway bird. In effect, he is operating in manual mode. When you provide the proper cue, he operates as programmed. Now is the time to move the dog from manual to automatic. He needs to be given the controls and learn to operate himself.

Remote control launchers work well to start a flushing dog. They get the bird up in the air quickly and at a distance before the dog can make any mistakes. The advantage is that you control the flush at the transmitter. A dog doesn't have to find and follow up the bird's scent stream to push the bird into the air. A handler can watch the dog working and, when he sees that the dog has made scent, he can flush the bird while there is still distance between the dog and the bird. This is the same as would be expected with a wild bird. The distance keeps the dog honest. He is not trying to catch a bird that is right off his nose. Instead, he is focusing on his manners so that the handler will release him to hunt up another bird. There will be plenty of time later to try and catch wild birds, when it's more of a fair fight.

In lieu of launchers, plant birds in a course throughout the training area. Make the plants at least a hundred yards apart, initially, and place only one bird per plant. The difficulty here is that the plants need to be very soft in order to allow the birds to flush quickly before the dog can get ahold of them. It's a fine line, and even when done well, many of the birds will up and leave before the dog gets anywhere near them. Done improperly, the incoherent birds are unable to respond to the approaching dog, and the dog goes from pick-up to pick-up.

Here is a method for getting birds in front of a flushing dog that has worked for me. Walk the course with the dog working in front of you (no birds have yet been planted in the field). Carry the birds you are going to use with you, in your bird pouch. When the dog quarters to one side and you are out of his line of vision, angle in the other direction and quickly throw a bird deep into the vegetation at your feet. It takes a little bit of practice to get the snap of your wrist just right to do this. Essentially, what you want to do is flip the bird into the vegetation and leave him a little disoriented or a little annoyed. Either way, in a minute or two, the bird will fly out of there. The dog, however, will be cutting right back to you on his quarter, and the bird will still be there to flush when he approaches.

Cut this drill up into pieces in the same manner as all the dog's previous training has been conducted. Set up the test and run through it for three or four sessions. We're just looking for simple compliance here. The expectation is that the dog will travel through a field and a bird will flush in front of him. Upon seeing the bird come up, the dog is to hup and stay put until released to find the next bird. Don't pump up the adrenaline on this. Keep the lesson at three flushes, one bird per flush. Don't add any pick-up birds to the mix.

The dog may anticipate the hup command and begin stopping on his own. Sometimes, they figure it out. More than likely, however, you will need to phase it in for him. The whistle cue has been stopping him in the field until now. There are three other associations that the dog equates with hup: voice "hup," flat of the hand, and a light electrical stimulation. Layer these if you need to get compliance. Ultimately, use the electrical stimulation without any other cues if the dog struggles with hupping on his own. As a last recourse, you can gingerly go up in stimulation level until the dog complies. Do this only after you are certain that the dog understands the expectation and is deliberately defying the command. Be very careful using electricity as a compliance tool on birds.

Once you see compliance, then start upping the ante. Kill a bird after the dog has flushed and hupped. It may be wise, for the first few shot birds, to return to the structure that was introduced in the yard (such as hobbles and physical restraint). When the dog hups, move in and kneel down and keep the dog in place while an assistant kills a second bird that he has flown. Release the dog to retrieve.

Next, kill birds that the dog has flushed, being careful to force compliance on the dog.

Later, add multiple birds flushed and shot at each individual plant.

This exercise is intended to evaporate any adrenaline out of the dog which would cause him to break and not mind his manners. Just as you did on the post, we are looking for something akin to boredom. It won't be the yawning that we pushed to during yard work, but it will be a certain level of maturity or a businesslike affect, if you will. Once you see this, we have what we need and can move on to polishing up anything that needs attention.

Pointing Breeds

The second type of dog that needs to be covered here is the pointing breeds. This process isn't as straightforward because pointing gets stirred into the mix. This can get interesting.

Pointing is a genetic trait. It is not trained. It appears of its own volition, in many different manifestations. Most pointing dog puppies will freeze on a wing, but when they hit about five months of age they start chasing, trying to catch, and the pointing instinct submerges. Most dogs that start training at ten months of age won't stand their birds.

Ideally, we want to see pointing show up about the time you start planting birds for the dog in the field. It may have shown up earlier, when the dog was first introduced to pigeons while strapped in on the whoa post. At any rate, when a pointing dog comes upon a bird in the field, his natural instinct tells him to stop and smell the bird before it flies away. During the smelling, something kicks in for the dog causing instinct to take over and he freezes into point. He is pointing the bird to freeze it in place so he can remain in the scent stream.

Therefore, when a handler begins planting birds, he or she is waiting for point to come floating up from below the surface. The earlier training encouraged the dog to chase birds. With any luck, pieces of pointing have already shown up during the process of encouraging the dog to chase. What a dog learns from chasing is that he can't smell the bird when it is flying away. Secondly, he won't get it in his mouth if it flies away. When a little chasing doesn't accomplish either of these things the dog goes to Plan B, which is to chase harder. Depending on how clever the dog is, he may go through a good portion of the alphabet thinking harder and faster will get it done.

At some point in this process, however, a handler will see a dog start thinking. The dog comes into the scent stream and instead of a burst of speed, he will creep in closer, ostensibly to get a few steps closer to the prize before it flushes. Perhaps the dog reasons that if he can close the distance it will get him close enough to catch the bird. In the process of creeping the dog freezes, as a prelude to creeping closer yet again. This is how pointing reappears: stop...catwalk...stop...flash point...stop...point.

Since the dog has been whoa broken the handler can intervene and jump start the process. The dog's structured yard work allows the handler to whoa the dog in the scent stream. Hobbles can enforce compliance. It is choppy and mechanical to maneuver a dog on birds, but it's a necessary bridge if the dog isn't offering to point his birds on his own.

Readers of this book are going to experience a broad range of responses from their dogs during training. Depending on breed choice and genetics, some dogs are born on point, it seems, and some aren't.

Pointers (English) in particular are hard-wired to point. English setters are almost as good a bet. They start later and are slower to mature, but it's almost always there. I have only had two Gordon setters in for training, not exactly a valid statistical sample, so take it for what it's worth. Both these Gordons were small field trial dogs and neither dog wanted to point. It was there, but they just wanted to run more than they wanted to point. They really wanted to run. I have had several red setters in and none of them were pointing. In the case of the red dogs, my take is that it is weak genetics and not much can be done. Any dog can be taught to stand his birds, but it isn't too pretty to do so.

Crossing over to the versatile breeds: German shorthairs are almost always a good bet for pointing. If my memory serves me, I had trouble with one male GSP that was from show blood. In addition, some of the imported German dogs are stronger on tracking and retrieving than pointing, but a handler can get them to point. Ditto for the German wire hairs. The GWP's are, as a rule, not the most stylish of pointers, but they get the job done. Again, with GWP's, dogs that are imported from Europe can be stronger on tracking than pointing, but it is almost always there. Some of the other versatile breeds are a hodge podge of instinct. The Weimaraners are a genetic mess. They are the red setters of the versatile dog world. I don't think I have had but a handful of pure blood Vizslas in for training, which says something in and of itself.

Brittanies are going to do what they want to do, when they want to do it. That generally includes pointing of a sort. Don't expect a lot of style or cooperation from the little guys.

Hopefully, most trainers will not have to struggle with the issue of pointing. Your dog will point of his own volition. Unfortunately, the law of

Author, in the early days, hauls in a wayward German shorthair to relocate him on a planted bird.

Musette, a female English setter.

averages dictates that if a person trains a good number of dogs, a portion of that number are going to be soft on point. It is important for a handler to keep in mind that this is not the sign of a dog that won't eventually develop into a bird dog, and it is not a reason to wash out a dog as untrainable. It just means that it will take a little more time. The dog may have to be dragged, or in this case, whoaed, through the entire training process. I had an English setter of our blood that didn't start until I crossed her over on wild birds. If it's any consolation, it's not the easy dogs that teach a person how to train dogs, it's the hard ones.

 Let's assume this pointing dog is now whoaing and coming when called. As we have done with all previous training, cut the planted bird introduction into pieces. Remote release traps work well for the initial planted birds if the handler has some available. As previously stated, these are expensive toys and a person can use string release traps that are available at a much lower cost. These units are the same as those used with the remote releases, they are just sold minus the electronics. Before I had commercially made releases, I used string release traps that I made of wood, steel and canvas. They weren't flashy, but they got the job done. Ultimately, the dog will learn to smell the release trap and at that point I cross over to Velcro and nylon restraints.

 The important component for the dog to understand is that if he gets too close to the bird, the bird is going to flush and leave. This is accomplished by planting a bird for the dog- a bird whose leaving can be controlled by the handler. Take the dog for a flyaway bird loop. Fly a bird or two and whoa the dog. Revisit yard work for the dog by whoaing him and going through his drills. Circle. Step over. Kick the grass to the front of the dog and run through the four whoa associations: voice, hand, whistle, and low electrical stimulation.

Next, bring the dog into the general area of the planted bird. Be conscious of the wind direction and watch the dog to observe when he makes the scent cone of the planted bird. If the dog is already pointing, he may lock up and stand the bird. If so, go to the dog and hobble him. Pick him up and move him back so that he is twenty yards off the bird. Circle the standing dog and go through the four whoa associations. Then move to the front of the dog and kick the grass as if you are trying to flush a bird (This can be done in pieces if the dog is paying more attention to you than to the location of the bird). Do it over several planted birds until you get everything in and the dog still has his attention on the location of the bird.

If the dog is not pointing, it may be necessary to whoa the dog and stop him from following up the scent to the location of the planted bird. Once the dog is whoaed, hobble and pick him up. Move him back off the bird. It may be necessary to move him quite a ways off to dilute some of the excess adrenaline. Then, go through the aforementioned theatrics: circle while running through the four whoa associations and then move to the front of the dog and attempt to kick flush an imaginary bird into the air.

When the dog is focused on your grass kicking performance, release the bird. Since the dog has been moved off his original location, the planted bird is now far out in front of where you are kicking. Depending on the type of restraint device that contains the bird, it may be as simple as pushing a button. It may require that you pull a string. Keep it as natural and hidden as the situation allows, and try to keep the dog fooled as long as possible. At best, the dog will figure it out in a few sessions, but buy as much time as you can.

When the bird flies, the dog is going to launch after him. Stay out of his way. The dog is wearing hobbles. He won't get far. Typically, a dog will make one great leap and arc back to earth. In the process, upon his return, he digs a trench with his muzzle. Don't react to the break. Use no verbal cues. Calmly pick up the dog and reposition him about five feet further back than his original launching pad. Set him up and whoa him. Go through the whoa associations and kick some grass. When you see the dog calm down get a firm hold of his check cord, tap his head, and release him and walk him away from the area of the launcher and on to the next planted bird.

Look for a repeat performance over the next several training sessions. Don't react and don't intervene. The goal of these repeated introductions is evaporation. The handler is waiting for the time when the dog will choose to stop digging muzzle trenches. Depending on the dog, it may take three or four birds, or four or five days, but it will happen. The dog will get a look of recognition on his face the same as with earlier training epiphanies. He'll hear the bird flushing and flex his muscles to spring and then think, "Well, maybe I should just watch this one."

When this happens, up the ante and allow the dog to come incrementally closer to the bird as it flushes. At the same time, move closer to the bird during the kicking performance until you reach the time that the bird is actually rising beside you. As the dog's level of compliance permits, roll in other temptations. A fired shot. A dead bird produced from your or an assistant's game pouch and thrown off to the side after the shot. Next, during the shot. Next, exchange the dead bird for a live flying shooter. Have an assistant fly and shoot the bird. Next, you fly the bird from the front of the dog and have the assistant shoot it. Finally, you both fly and shoot the bird while standing to the front of the dog. This is after he has calmed down from the excitement of the flush and is standing whoaed.

When this is successfully stirred into the mix, crank up the voltage. Point or whoa. Step in. Flush and shoot the planted bird. Place a second release behind the first, and flush staggered birds for the dog. Then include a dead bird with the flyer in the second release. The dog will track the departing birds and see one of them fall back to earth. When he's ready, let him retrieve the down birds.

Add multiple birds to each release and get him used to groups of birds going in staggered succession, then in quick succession, then all at once.

This is all incremental and designed to allow the dog to eat a rather large enchilada in small, manageable portions. If at any point the dog needs it, don't hesitate to go back to "A." I have found it useful even during later training to roll training dogs in with new arrivals on the chain gang and take them through a yard session or two at the post. I did it to benefit the new recruits, but the more experienced dogs gain from it as well.

At the end of this, we want to see a dog minding his manners. A dog that has solid yard work in place so he has a solid foundation. A dog that exhibits a level of maturity that allows him to be reliable in the field on planted birds. It would be my hope that at this level the dog is pointing. If that isn't the case, ignore it and keep whoaing the rascal. We will continue to wait for it to kick in.

Handler holds a pair of dogs steady to flush on a pair of flushing homing pigeons.

Steady to Wing and Shot

One constant in my training days was finishing the dog steady to wing and shot. I found that for me, two months wasn't quite long enough to get it done with most dogs. The dogs weren't absolutely reliable by that point. As far as the benefits of fully breaking a shooting dog, it is a judgment call. Most field dogs aren't steady. In truth, I don't want my string dogs to hold at shot. In my part of the world, we lose too many birds if the dogs aren't allowed to break and get to a downed bird immediately.

Once a dog crosses over onto wild birds, it is very hard to maintain a steady dog. It requires that the hunter not carry a gun, but handle dogs instead. Most shooters aren't willing to do that. They are ultimately there for the shooting and are not willing to give it up. I found with my training clients that they might profess a desire to have a fully broke dog, but in practice they would not maintain it once the dog went home. That is fine with me. It is a pain in the rear to be that rigid, and ultimately it can get in the way of the dog doing his job on wild birds.

Having said that, I do think it is very important to finish fully breaking the dog during training. I found that it took the chase out of the dog and it had a maturing effect. It was kinda like a college education: information that may not be used in the real world, but required as a rite of passage. At the end of two months of training, all the tools and training are effectively in place. To finish breaking a dog, a handler just needs to stay on most dogs one or two weeks longer.

Retrieving

Retrieving: How it can be done

In a perfect world, field dogs retrieve naturally to hand with no training involved. Genetics provide everything. All the handler needs to do is take the dog to the birds and knock one from the sky. The dog will do the rest.

This is not a perfect world.

Some of the most bizarre, unexplainable behaviors I've seen dogs act out have been around retrieving birds. This is a charged issue for the canines because this is their payoff for being a team player. They tolerate our idiosyncrasies and odd requirements so that they can get the bird. Dogs hunt to get a bird in their mouths and then we want them to give it to us? You can see how some dogs may have a problem with the human take on this issue.

If a person studies gun dog training and goes back through and reads all the literature, he might be left with the erroneous impression that there are certain mechanics to compelling a dog to retrieve: that done properly, retrieving training will yield a certain and predictable result and that structured training methods like the force break table provide the safety net that allow a trainer to compel even the most adamant non-retriever to get with the program and bring in the birds.

Let me tell you some stories.

Rose was precocious as a pup, and a driven fiend at retrieving.

She was raised with two other litter mates: another orange and white English setter female named Belle, and their looker of a sister, a full masked tri-colored named Kate. The three were brought along to retrieve naturally and they responded. All carried from the time they were little puppies.

Rose was especially wild for carrying. While just a little thing she took to retrieving from water with a passion and it was her mission to not allow her sisters to best her, a situation I used to best advantage. I used all the principles of developing natural retrieving on these three setters to ensure that we got good, solid retrievers.

And we did...Rose retrieved to hand for her first two seasons. Then, she decided she wasn't going to do it anymore. I guess the obvious question is: why? I still don't really know to this day. However, we had

Rosie as a young puppy pointing a quail wing.

lost Kate at the beginning of their third season, while hunting, to a car on the highway. Rose was always the intuitive sort. Was that a piece of it?

After Kate's death, I hunted the two remaining sisters together and they worked out an accommodation. Belle retrieved and Rose didn't. Belle was the dominant personality, but it wasn't like she had Rose cowed. They were pretty much equals. It's more like Belle was the responsible one and claimed retrieving and Rose wasn't and didn't.

Now, I wouldn't lose a bird with her. If Belle wasn't there at the shot, or if I hunted Rose alone, she would charge the downed bird and locate it. If the bird had some run left, she would gather it up and carry it to the nearest shade at the front of my line of travel and wait there for me to come fetch it. If the bird was dead when she found it, she may have mouthed it a bit to make sure it was anchored, and then looked to see that I saw her and the location of the bird. Once she saw me coming, she went on hunting. I could pick up my own birds.

So, going into her fourth season, I set out to fix it. We went to the force table and went through the drills. She didn't like it much, but she didn't fight it too hard, either. She performed on the table, but shut down once we went to ground. I could force the issue and get compliance, but it was like a compass needle returning to true north. She understood what the expectation was, and she would humor me if I made a point of it. However, she just wasn't interested in retrieving to hand.

That's the way it remained for the rest of her life. Rose was an exceptional bird finder. If you put her on the ground she would go into this Winnie-the-Pooh, Eeyore-esque kind of walking trance when she came across the slightest bit of covey scent. She would start slow walking with her nose up in the air. It could take a quarter mile, but she would take you into the birds. She had this habit of stopping at the end of these long walks. She would stand on one side of a rise and wait for me to catch up. When I got to her, she would stalk slowly over the hill and point the covey on the other side. She was a hell of a dog.

I tried to push the retrieving with her, and heaven knows, I can be persistent. She never took it personally, but at the end of the day she just wasn't interested. So, I put together Plan B. I had a Chessie that was steady and trained as a pickup dog. I figured I'd kill two birds with one stone. The Chessie could get some exercise and pick up birds at the same time. I took the two of them out.

Rose hunted out in front and the Chessie walked alongside. It was afternoon and, if my memory serves me, we killed seven or eight birds. Some history is required at this point. The Chessie herself was a difficult beast. She didn't like other dogs and the rest of the canine world reciprocated, Rose included. So, when I shot a bird, Rose had no interest in letting the Chessie retrieve it. Every bird I killed was quickly and neatly delivered to hand by Miss Rose herself and the Chessie remained hupped beside me. Clearly, she had learned her lessons on the force table. I hoped we had turned a corner and that the switch had finally turned on. I tried her alone the next day. Foolish me.

Consequently, Rose became my premiere training dog. She worked well with youngsters because she didn't intimidate or compete with them for downed birds. She patiently waited for them and watched them. She would take youngsters into wild birds and teach them the ropes, and then let them make the retrieves. She lived here during a time when there were eighteen to twenty string dogs and then around ten customer dogs in for training. We had lots of dogs for retrieving, but we only had her for starting young bird dogs. She died here at fourteen as the reigning grande dame. She survived all her siblings and some of her children. She enjoyed life to the absolute end. Maybe she knew better than I why she was here.

Then there was Beau, a four-years-oldish, big burly boy GSP. The customer was a big game guide here in the Southwest, and he wanted a dog to take clients bird hunting in the event that they filled their big game tag early. The guide had a family and Beau had been raised with kids and socialized well. It wasn't that Beau had been mistreated in any way. It's just that Beau seemed angry to me. I'm guessing that he spent a lot of time waiting in the backyard, a small urban housing tract backyard.

Beau was a bird dog. The owner wasn't a bird hunter and he really didn't know how to go about training a bird dog. I'm guessing he had gotten the puppy and figured it would somehow all put itself together. Sometimes it works, but in Beau's case the owner needed a little help and he brought him in. The owner didn't want anything fancy, just a straight-forward shooting dog. Yes, he wanted him to retrieve.

We started training. Beau was a mature, four-year-old male short-hair, with all that implies. He took to his lessons well, but he was never warm and cuddly. He was a bit stoic and reserved. I liked Beau, and he made one hell of a dog. He would point birds forty yards out and go into a low-down, stylish point. He liked birds. I got him under control and steadied in two months. The problem came when we got to retrieving. He wasn't interested in giving me a bird. More to the point, that anger that he carried bled out and he was adamant that he wasn't going to give me a bird. He would run to the bird when it went down and if there was some wiggle, he would administer the Teutonic coup de grace. You wouldn't lose a bird with him, but that was as far as he was willing to go.

I put him on the table and we went through the drills. He got all of it, with one exception: he would not lower his head to pick up a buck or bird. I could apply a nerve hitch and force him to comply, but that anger would well up and I could see the look in his eyes. I didn't know what was on the other side of that look. In surveying how far we had gotten, it seemed to me that on the whole we had the makings of a great dog. I didn't think it was worth the risk to push the issue of retrieving and risk losing all we had achieved.

I called the owner and told him so. We were at the two month mark and I offered to go another month if he felt that he wanted to pursue retrieving. I told the customer to come and take a look at where we were, and that I thought he might feel that we were done. We set up a meeting time.

I put out two bobs and flagged the release sites. Beau did every-thing right. He came in, caught scent and froze in a picture book point.

Beau leads the parade out on the flats while pointing a scaled quail.

I walked in, flushed the bird, and killed it. Beau held like a rock. I then walked back to the owner who was standing near Beau.

"Here is where we have the problem," I said.

I tapped Beau on the head to release him to retrieve. He charged out and found the dead bird. He nosed it a bit and then went to leave it. I blew a whoa whistle and stopped him. I ordered him to fetch. Nothing. I walked over to him, tapped his toes with my boot and snapped "Fetch." His stance and jaw muscles went rigid. I kneeled down and touched his two inside toes and commanded fetch. Beau lowered his head and scooped up the bird. I walked back to the owner, leaving Beau standing in position. Once I got beside the client I ordered Beau, "Fetch." He ran back, came to my side, and presented the bird.

Then we switched off and I had the owner handle. Beau found the second bird and pointed. I walked in, flushed and killed it. The owner then took over. He released Beau to retrieve. Beau ran out, snapped up that bird and delivered it to his owner's hand like he had done it a thousand times. After releasing the bird to his owner, Beau looked over at me with a look that said, "You and the horse you rode in on."

He never retrieved another bird for that man.

I got a call a couple of years later from Beau's owner. He was focusing on the big game and Beau just wasn't getting much use. Did I want him?

"You bet!"

I picked him up and let him settle in. After a few days he and I went out to see where we were...it was like he had never left, including the retrieving. I polished him out a bit and called a friend who needed a dog. I told him the history and added that I thought he would retrieve given the right circumstances. Beau went to a new home where he got daily contact and training from folks he bonded to, and the company of a couple other bird dogs. The anger went away. He started retrieving a month later. He's an old dog now. He lives with his new family in the South and hunts there and in the prairie states. He remains a solid retriever.

Finally, the story of George and Ladybug, a pair of Brittanies. Their owner was a retired military non-com. He hunted most days during the season and they got a lot of time on the ground. He had bought the pair as babies from a backyard breeding. They were probably a little too young to leave mom, and their blood line wasn't of the best breeding. They worked close and dusted up anything within shotgun range. They suited his needs.

Neither dog retrieved, which can be a problem with desert quail. Either the cripples run out and are lost, or the dead birds fall into a jumble of cover and are not recovered. He regularly hunted with another gentleman who ran a setter, and the little Brits had no manners regarding backing another dog. He wanted these things fixed.

He brought in the pair and we ran them through yard work and gave them some manners regarding honoring another dog's point. When we switched to retrieving, things got dicey. Neither dog had any interest. I spoke to the owner and had about the same conversation as I had with Beau's owner. Unlike Beau's owner, he was very definite. One of them needed to retrieve. He didn't care which.

I went back to the force table and pushed. Ladybug balked, shattered and imploded. George merely folded, so he was our guy. I spoke with the owner again. He was adamant, "I need one to retrieve."

I got it done, but it wasn't pretty. Brits have a drama mode they go into when they don't get their way, and George played it for all it was worth. He wasn't reliable with a toe/nerve hitch, so I had to condition him to an electric collar. When he was given a fetch command and balked it, electric stimulation was the association used to complete the retrieve. He would roach up and tiptoe out to the bird, pick it up and tiptoe back. That was the most George's owner would let him get away with, and it was painful to watch. George didn't want to do it, but he did retrieve.

George and his owner spent the next several years in this debilitating dance. Around eight years old, the dog unraveled mentally and his owner put him down. Or...the argument could be made that George's decline was the result of his required retrieving.

A friend once told me that when a person tells you something, you should listen to him. I think the same applies to dogs.

Sometimes, no matter how well you train or how good you are, it ain't gonna happen.

So, at the offset, it is important to remember that there is a Rubik's cube component when you compel a dog to do something that he doesn't want to do. The law of unintended consequences. That isn't a reason not to train to retrieve. It's a warning or a boundary. Just be aware as you work with your dog that you may not like what you think you want to get once you get it.

George and Ladybug taking a rest during a desert quail hunt.

Retrieving: How it Should be Done

Retriever training starts when a puppy is very young. It begins as a game in the puppy pen before the little ones are weaned off their mother. One of the pups finds a particularly nice piece of shredded paper from the mounds of shredded bedding lying on the floor of the whelping box. He grabs it up and then, out of nowhere, gets blindsided by the puppy next to him who grabs up the prize and starts out towards the other side of mom mountain. Before the second pup gets ten inches away, a third pup clamps down on the second pup's tail with little needle daggers masquerading as teeth. The little guy yowls and expels the prize which is quickly mouthed and brought back into play by a new operator.

That's how dogs learn to carry, before they have any contact with a trainer. This is the natural component of retriever training. When the puppy leaves mom and goes to live at his new home, it's important that the game continues through play and nurture.

To do this, set up a confined area, like a hallway, where the puppy has to get by you to get away with the prize. Use something you don't mind throwing away later, because the retrieved object is going to get slobbered on, battered and chewed. A short piece of soft rope or a sock- let's call it his binky- is a good thing to start with because part of the play process for young dogs is tug of war. The puppy can't play tug of war with you unless they bring the thing to you. Hence begins the cooperation of the dog/hunter team.

In this game, the little one grabs his binky, lowers his head and gives you the look: the "I got it and you can't have it" look. The chase is on! Scoop up the little guy and jostle and wrestle him until he drops the binky. Don't take it from his mouth and don't touch it while it's in his mouth unless you are playing tug of war. When you get control of it, toss it down the hall, so that the puppy has to come back by you to get away. The game will be learned quickly. Expand out to other areas of the house. The little guy will start finding his binky on command or presenting it unsolicited when he wants attention. When this happens, be sure you drop everything else and interact with the pup enthusiastically.

Around two and a half to three months old, move the game outside. You might add some feathers or scent to the binky. Maybe switch over to a ball or a little bumper. I made my puppy bumpers out of a short piece of cut garden hose. I would put a hole on one end for tying a throwing string. In addition, I stuffed a little ball of cotton up inside the hose so I could apply some commercially produced bird scent, or push some feathers up the inside of the tube.

At this point, I start putting the binky up between sessions. You will find that little ones at this age, left to their own devices, can buzz-saw through binkys in short order.

As the puppy gets older, say four to five months, broaden out the youngster's horizons. Add grass cover and shallow water to the retrieving game. At this point, the two of you should be past tug of war, and the dog should surrender the bumper in anticipation of watching another throw and going for another retrieve. That's about as much as a trainer needs to accomplish before the puppy reaches around one year old and begins formal training on birds in the field. This is the foundation of natural retrieving.

The way this translates to birds is that the dog has a history to fall back on. He always got his binky back at the next play session and he will expect the same when he starts retrieving birds. I don't take birds away from a dog when we begin with birds. I keep giving it back to the dog until he shifts his focus elsewhere. Then I pick up the bird and get it out of sight in a pouch and make sure that the dog has another focus, like the bird I just flew for him.

Your dog may balk at turning over the bird. When he does, kneel down to his level and milk him in with the check cord. Don't attempt to touch the bird or remove it from his mouth. Pet him and try to distract his interest from it. If the dog won't fall for it, then go for a walk while you keep him close by at the end of the rope. When he eventually lets go of the bird, give it right back to him, and then continue the walk. At some point, the dog will lose interest in the bird. Leave him certain that you are not going to take this bird away from him. When he eventually loses interest or is willing to trade it for a new bird, secretly pick the old bird up and get it hidden. Then go back to your training drill.

Some trainers may express a concern that by allowing the dog to drop the bird you are laying a bad foundation and teaching the dog to drop birds. I agree with half of that: the dog is being taught to drop birds. With dog training, you get compliance in increments. The important piece to start with, regarding retrieving, is that the dog picks up and carries the bird. I want to be sure that chunk is in place, and to my way of thinking, I'm not willing to risk it by trying to get more.

If a dog has been set up to retrieve naturally during early puppy work, or the genetics are in place to let it happen naturally, then the dog may zoom in with the bird and release it to hand graciously. It does happen. If that is not the case and the dog continues to drop short, or is sloppy about presenting birds to hand, the time to address it is later in the training process on the force break table. A handler is courting hard mouth to do otherwise.

I saw some very adamant looks on a training dog's face when he finally got a bird in his mouth for the first time. He had been waiting all his life for that moment and there was no way in hell that he was giving it up to anybody, particularly me. That rascal was coming home with him. Don't pick a fight with this dog. There can be a very steep price for winning and you may be dealing with the fall out for the rest of the dog's life.

Now, let's say that the dog won't carry the bird. This makes things considerably tougher. Before a trainer can do any retrieving work, the dog has to carry the bird. The dog finally has the opportunity to get a bird in his mouth and he balks at it. Some dogs have no interest in carrying a bird and the trainer will have to make a judgment call as to how to proceed. It may be possible to jump start the dog. Take him back to the early puppy associations. Play him against other dogs that are retrieving. Throw some treasure in the communal dog yard and see if you can't get a game of keep away started and see if the hold out doesn't want a piece of the action. Train him with a dog that is retrieving. Throw a bird and let the other guy get it several times. Next, go through the same drill, but short stop the retrieving dog with a check cord and let the non-retriever get to the bird first. See if he doesn't pick it up and carry it away so that his buddy can't get it. When he starts carrying, build from there. Getting this dog to retrieve reliably may require time on the force break table.

Hard Mouth

I touched briefly on hard mouth earlier, but it deserves a thorough explanation. It is a general term describing a dog that bites, chews, eats, or otherwise takes unacceptable liberties with the birds he gets in his mouth. This can be a tough one to fix. It's one of those things that's best avoided before the fact. The methods for doing so have been covered previously. Unfortunately, this proactive avoidance of hard mouth won't help a trainer who gets a year-old dog that chomps birds.

Many times it's just a dog new to picking up birds who may get rough with them. The dog, amped up with excitement and adrenaline, gets carried away and goes too far. Be careful not to jump in too quickly on this and get it fixed. Remember the adage: be careful what you call a fault, for fear that you will feel compelled to fix it and then really screw up the dog. The rule of unintended consequences applies.

I have found that with young dogs, the best initial course of action is just to try to evaporate the behavior. If the cause is inexperience and adrenaline, then the cure is a bunch of retrieves to give the dog the necessary experience and to dilute the adrenaline. He may hit the first few pretty hard, but by the time the dog gets his fortieth bird in his mouth it just won't be as important. Try it and see what result it produces. If that doesn't work then go to Plan B. Put the dog on the force break table and see if you can get to it there. There can be a genetic component and it may not be completely fixable. You should be able to mitigate it to some degree, but it might be one of those things you either have to learn to live with or make other choices.

Hard mouth often shows up in the German dogs. They want to grab something and throttle it and bite it to kill it. I had an adult male GWP come in for training to fix hard mouth. His name was Gator. I think in literature they refer to that as foreshadowing. Gator was hunted mostly on quail and dove, both small birds that don't take well to rough handling. If Gator had been used exclusively for large, sturdy birds like pheasant, his hard mouth wouldn't have been a concern. Unfortunately, the small birds he brought to hand were compressed and mangled, so it was a fault that needed to be fixed. I went the full gambit with Gator. I put him on the table and force broke him. I went back through the old books and got draconian with him by making little spiked harnesses to put on the birds so that if he bit down, the bird bit back. That addressed the problem except for one important unenforceable contingency: I couldn't figure out a way to get wild birds to put the harnesses on before we shot them. I got Gator to the point where he carried a bird back like he was delivering a delicate egg. The one thing I couldn't change was the genetic imprint he had to bite a bird when he first picked it up. It was but a nano-second of movement when the bird first entered his mouth; but with small birds, it was all it took for them to look like they had been staple punched.

I had a Chessie, one of our own dogs, who would bite every bird she picked up. It started with a teal she retrieved as a youngster. The duck was very much alive when she got to it. It was dead when she delivered it to me a couple of minutes later. There were some gymnastics during the two minute lag time. Over the course of her career she retrieved thousands of dove. A dove may be the most delicate bird a gun dog is ever asked to handle. She never made a hole, but when she gave me the bird the spine was always severed underneath the skin, below the wings. It happened at the back of her mouth, at the instant that she picked up the bird. I guess that would have made her hard mouth by definition, but she found a way to make it a non-issue.

With genetic hard mouth that may be how you have to make peace with it.

Up through the end of a dog's second month of training, perhaps two months and a week, I am happy just to see the dog carrying. I will take the bird if the dog offers it, but I don't push it. At the end of this time period, if the dog is dropping short, chewing birds, sloppy on delivery, or not carrying altogether, it needs to be addressed.

I then transfer training to the force break table.

The Force Breaking Table

There are a couple of different configurations of this training platform used in the gun dog training world. The wood design generally used by bird dog and retriever trainers is two-foot wide by sixteen-foot long. The practical reason for this is that when you cut a four by eight foot plywood panel in half lengthwise, you get two eight-foot long by two-foot wide panels. When those same panels are butted together lengthwise they become a surface sixteen-foot long by two-foot wide. This is not a portable affair. Most times it is permanent and sturdy and installed into the infrastructure of the training area. Often I've seen them built onto the side of a building. There will be an overhead cable that runs the length of the training surface and some kind of pole or eye bolt to anchor the dog. My table has a pole on both sides so I can work two dogs at once.

The versatile hunting dog folks have modified this design as follows: They cut one of the eight-foot long by two-foot wide sections in half and configure the table so that there is a four-foot ramp or wing on either side of the eight-foot long by two-foot long central training surface. The two wings are hinged so that the table folds flat into a two-foot by eight-foot traveling unit. When the table is in use, the wood training surface is supported by two folding saw horses. I've seen tables that are carpeted or have wood slats on the surface to allow a dog to grip the surface of the table more efficiently. There are no overhead cables or pulleys or anchor points. The dog walks up one ramp, is trained on the mid-section and then walks down the other. In addition to force breaking, this design is used for whoa work, bird introductions, and general obedience commands.

Force breaking can be very effective. It allows a handler the means to compel a dog to do something that he wouldn't ordinarily do. Basically, this training utilizes opposite techniques from positive reinforcement.

1) Jay Smith rigs dog properly prior to placing him on the table. Smith uses both a neck and withers band to control the dog's movement.

2) Here Smith shows the two attachment points used to restrain a dog on the table.

3) Smith lifts the dog onto the table to begin the training session.

4) Smith orients the dog so that the dog's head is pointing towards the end of the table and his head lines up beside the cable pipe. The dog's head will initially be bound to this pipe.

5) Smith allows the dog time to become comfortable on the table. Smith leaves the dog standing fully rigged and restrained until the dog relaxes. That may take 20 minutes of time or more. Smith allows the dog all the time that the dog needs to reach a relaxed state. It can take a day or two for some dogs to soften.

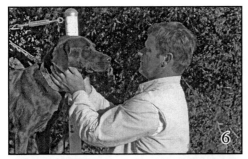

6) Smith makes eye contact and tells the dog to hold. Initially "hold" means maintain eye contact with me and don't move your head. Later, it will mean hold an object in your mouth and do not drop it.

7) Smith also uses his breath to reinforce his connection to the dog in this training. When the dog is focused, maintaining eye contact and waiting for Smith to release him from "hold" before moving his eyes, he is ready to go to the next step.

8) Smith introduces his fingers into the dog's mouth and instructs the dog to "hold." Smith then tickles the dog's tongue while his fingers are in the dog's mouth and teaches the "release" command. Smith follows up by replacing his fingers with a dowel. He instructs the dog to "hold" the dowel.

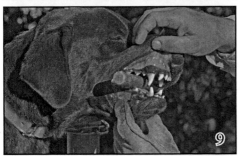

9) As a note of caution, always make sure that the dog's lips are not caught between his teeth and the dowel.

10) Here, Smith attempts to put it all together. "Hold it," "Release," "Hold it," "Release." Note that Smith has his thumb positioned under the dog's jaw and he keeps pressure upwards on the bottom of the dog's tongue so that the dog can not drop his jaw and spit out the dowel before Smith instructs him to.

11) Next, Smith puts some distance between the dog's jaw and his hand. He expects the dog to hold the dowel independently of any contact from Smith. Ultimately, Smith will walk away and expect the dog to hold the dowel for 2 to 3 minutes at a time.

12) Smith continues to reinforce "Hold it," "Release," " Hold it," "Release." The training described in these panels can take up to 2 to 3 weeks, depending on the pupil.

13) When finished, the dog will not drop the dowel until instructed to do so. Depending on the dog, the trainer may be able to accomplish this with little to no "force." Or, the dog may require a conventional force breaking program.

14) "Hold it."

15) "Release."

16) An additional 1 to 2 weeks is spent with bumpers, followed by frozen birds, followed by fresh-killed birds, followed by live harnessed birds. The dog is allowed to travel the length of the table to complete retrieves and is ultimately transferred to the ground to complete the training. These panels are a very abbreviated illustration of a very involved process.

Above: Image shows proper rigging placement. Below: Hopefully, the ultimate result.

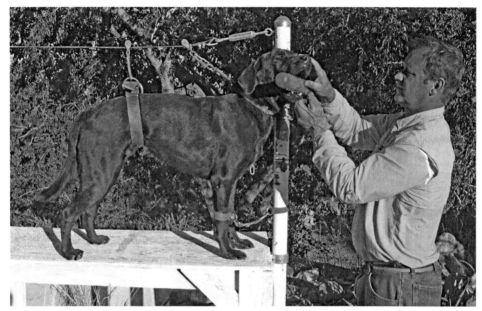

Jay Smith places a bumper into the mouth of a Lab going through a modified force breaking program. The dog will be expected to hold the bumper until instructed to release it to drop into the handler's hand.

A common force break table design. This table is constructed of one 4 X 8 foot plywood sheet. The single sheet is ripped up the center into two 2 x 8 sheets. The allows for a 16 foot table top run to do the training on. At this 16 foot length two dogs can be worked at the same time. One is actively trained while the other watches while restrained at the other end of the table.

The handler inflicts a negative stimulus on the dog until the dog complies and then the handler terminates the negative stimulus. That is a politically correct way of saying, "You hurt the dog until the dog does what you want and then you stop hurting the dog."

The basic tenant of force breaking is that the ball is in the dog's court. He controls what happens to him. If he follows the program, the negatives are kept to a minimum. If he fights, a consequence is introduced which is sufficient to force the dog to comply. Depending on how tough the dog is, the process can get pretty grim.

I have an old book from the early days of the last century that has a drawing of a force breaking device. It looks like a sort of paddle with a handle on one end. The paddle end had holes cut in it and a type of strap or harness running through the holes. The apparatus was placed over the dog's head and tension was applied through the harness. Then, the paddle was twisted as the negative stimulus for the dog. I just looked at the drawing again. I still can't figure it out, and that's probably just as well.

Today, there are generally two methods in use for applying the negative stimuli. The bird dog trainers use a toe pinch or a nerve hitch. The retriever and versatile dog trainers tend to favor the ear pinch.

The toe pinch or nerve hitch was first popularized in Bill Tarrant's book: *The Best Way to Train Your Gun Dog, The Delmar Smith Method.* The way Tarrant explained it to me, Smith had been an MP during World War II. The MP's were issued billy clubs that had a small stub or dowel projecting out of the hilt on the handle of the club. One of the methods used at the time to control rowdy or drunk servicemen was to grab them by the hand and place the dowel on the billy club between the pinky and third finger of the serviceman's hand. To control even the most rancorous of individuals, all the MP had to do was squeeze the fingers of the serviceman's hand together so that he felt his pinky finger bending over the dowel and being squeezed towards his third finger. All struggling stopped and the serviceman could be uneventfully led out to the paddy wagon.

The other thing Smith noticed was that when that particular hand pressure was applied, servicemen always opened their mouths as if to say, "Ahhhhhhhhhhhhhhh."

Upon returning home he incorporated this into dog training. He found that if you squeezed the two middle toes of a dog's foot together he opened his mouth, and this allowed Smith to pop in a dowel or retrieving buck during force breaking.

Versatile and retriever trainers use the ear because it makes more sense for them. Much of the work they do is with the dog standing at the trainer's side or walking at heel, with the ear within easy reach. In addition, the versatile dogs spend a lot of time on the table where the trainer has ready access to the dog's ears. Also, for the retriever folks, their dogs are seated besides them on the casting line when the need comes to enforce compliance on a retrieve. Later, during a trial, there isn't a way to gracefully bend over and squeeze a dog's toes and not have the judge notice it. However, the trainer's hand is dangling down at his side right next to the dog's ear, where the association is the strongest.

Force Breaking: The Method

Begin force breaking by introducing the dog to the table. As has been done with all previous training, work incrementally and let the new dog wade into the process. In the beginning, I use two or three introduction sessions where I place the dog on the table and let him move around freely. Depending on the dog, the first session may be limited to letting the dog watch other dogs being worked on the table as he sits clipped on the chain gang nearby. Next, I confine the dog to the post and let him get comfortable. I show him the tools that we will be using: the dowels and collars and the lengths of chain with snaps. I make some noise by snapping the snaps and rattling the chains. I give him the opportunity to smell everything thoroughly. Then I strap him in and leave him for a few minutes. This could be while I work another dog at the opposite end of the post.

My table is rigged with an overhead cable that has four pulleys riding it. To the pulleys I clip a length of chain. Each length has a snap on each end. One snap is to attach the chain to the pulley so that it can travel the length of the overhead cable. The other snap is to attach the chain to the dog, so that the dog's route of travel while he is on the table is restricted to running the length of the table's surface.

I use a very structured approach for bringing the dog to the table. I do not vary this approach in any way, at any point, during the training. I never allow a dog to jump from the table. I want him to learn that I lift him onto the table and I lift him off the table and place him on the ground when I deem the session done.

We begin while he is on the chain gang. I attach a check cord to his neck collar and buckle in a D-ring collar around his withers, the same collar that he wore during the early stages of whoa training. I then unsnap him from the chain and walk him over to the side of the table. I whoa

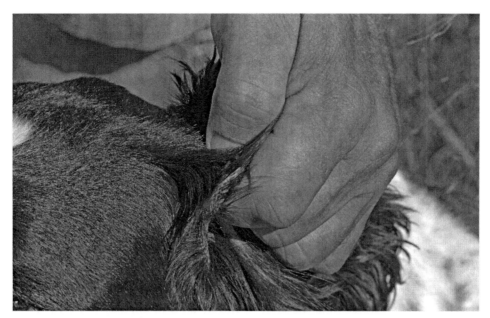

The ear pinch method often used by retriever trainers. When a retriever is cast from the handler's side, the handler's hand is positioned beside the dog's ear and this makes for a strong association. Some handlers pinch against the dog's collar to get a more immediate result.

The toe pinch method is often used by bird dog trainers. This approach requires that a length of cord is wrapped around the dog's two middle toes. When the cord is pulled, a nerve pinch develops from the pressure on the toes and this causes the dog to open his mouth and accept the dowel. The dog learns that holding the dowel stops the pressure.

the dog, and while he is whoaed, I lift him from the ground to the table. I place him at an end post with his neck at the post and his tail pointed towards the middle of the table. I attach a chain to the withers collar and make it snug enough that the dog's hind legs are restricted to the centerline of the table. I then attach a snap at the neck post so that the dog's neck is snugged down to the post. Near his front feet, I have a hobble tied off to the post so that I can also hobble him and limit the movement of his front feet. When the snapping and velcro-ing is done, the dog can't do much but wiggle his tail and turn his head.

Next, I move to the front of the dog and breath into his nose and tell him to "hold it." As I say the words, I cup his face with my hands and restrain him from moving his head from side to side. I look for compliance in the form of unbroken eye contact. I want the dog to freeze any movement of his head and maintain eye contact with me. Some dogs will fight you for a while on this, but it is important that a trainer stay with it until the dog folds. A precedent is being set in this contest and if you don't win here when it's a tiny request, you will be in trouble later when you ask for big stuff from the dog. When the dog freezes and looks to you for what you want next, you may progress to the next step. It may take a few sessions to get him there.

Notice that we used the same collar for the dog's withers. Also, that we whoaed him before lifting him onto the top of the table. In addition, he was strapped in while he was whoaed. We are back to the same ABC approach that the dog learned when he was introduced to the whoa command. Also, as in the whoa command, the table training is layered so that each session travels up a ladder of A, AB, ABC, ABCD.

The next rung up is to escalate the "hold it" request by placing two fingers of your gloved hand into the dog's mouth while he is standing with his head held still. Slide them in and hold them there until any struggle or movement on the dog's part to expel the fingers ceases. Use your other hand to control the dog's muzzle and keep it closed around your fingers.

When the dog stops fighting and holds your fingers in his mouth, introduce a second command, "Release." Please feel free to pick a word of your choosing. I have heard handlers use "give," "drop," "here," the dog's name, etc. Now that the dog is willingly holding the fingers in his mouth, we are commanding him to expel them.

The dog is going to look at you funny, like he is wondering when you are going to make up your mind. He will probably hold still and ignore the request because he's not quite sure what you are asking and you just made such a big point of keeping the fingers in his mouth.

Give the command "release" again and as you say the word tickle the surface of his tongue with the two fingers that he is holding in his mouth. He will promptly spit out the two fingers. Run the drills on this over several sessions. "Hold it." "Release." "Hold it." "Release." "Hold it." "Release." Dogs generally get this cemented in quickly. Make the hold time longer as you progress through the sessions.

At this point, the dog has been on the table for maybe a week and is ready for the next level. We are going to substitute an eight-inch dowel for your two fingers. Pieces of old broom handle work well if you don't want to have to track down some hardwood dowel stock. Place the dowel in his mouth and have a strategically positioned back-up dowel handy to pop in place should, or I should say when, he spits the first one out.

Go back and cup his head with your hands. Remember A,B,C. Place the dowel in his mouth and position a finger below his muzzle to keep his lower jaw from opening to drop the dowel. Use the other hand to restrain his head and keep the dowel in place. Cut the drill up into pieces as needed until you get compliance. Just as before with the "hold it" "release" drill on fingers, now do the same with the dowel in position.

Try to anticipate the dog dropping the dowel before the fact by interrupting him with a verbal "Ahhhhhhhhhhhhhh." This verbalization on the trainer's part interrupts the dog's thought process and freezes him from dropping the dummy. If he does drop the dowel, don't fumble for it. Instantly grab the strategically positioned back-up dowel and pop it into place. Stay on the dog until he maintains eye contact and can be released to drop the dowel in your hand. When he starts looking stoic standing there on the table with the dowel in his mouth, step back away from the table. Incrementally increase the time and distance that you are away from the table.

Step back to the dog and set him up to fail just as was done on the whoa post by bumping a whoaed dog with a knee or leg. Tap the dowel lightly with your hand. Flick it with your finger. Wave your hand underneath the dog's muzzle as if you are waiting to catch the dowel when he drops it. When the dog twitches his jaw muscle to begin to open his mouth to drop the dowel, shut him down with an "Ahhhhhhhhhhhhhhhh." Teach him that the only time he can drop a bird is when your hand is in position to catch it, and he hears the "release" command. These two cues must be given simultaneously to allow him to act. Either done independently of the other has no effect. Again, we go back to the whoa post. As on the post, where the only time he was free to move off of whoa was when he was given two simultaneous cues: a push on the head, and a verbal hoe-on; he now needs two simultaneous cues to release a dowel.

This will need to be layered for a while. Maybe a week. Maybe more, depending on the dog. Incrementally give the dog more latitude to act independently by physically moving further and further from the table. Ultimately, step around a building and remove yourself from the dog's sight for a short period of time. Give him the opportunity to screw up and see what happens.

Now may be the time to introduce the nerve hitch. Some dogs persist in dropping the dowel when the handler moves away from the table. This is the point at which willfulness may make force necessary. Is the dog acting willfully? Is his conduct an act of defiance? Does the dog have the personality and psychological make up to withstand a force breaking program? Is the trainer capable of making the dog believe that he or she is willing and able to get this thing done? We have been placing the dowel in the dog's mouth up until now. We want to start transitioning the dog to grabbing the dowel of his own volition, hence the introduction of the nerve hitch.

This is a crossroads of sorts and a judgment call is in order. Many of today's trainers, including myself, view the nerve hitch or ear pinch as a last resort if there is no other way to get the dog to come around. The term I've heard used for sidestepping the force part of force breaking is "Modified Force Breaking." Using pain creates resentments that are sure to surface in other ways, in future components of the training process.

If a handler is to use some component of pain while working with a dog, then that person must always remember that pain does not instruct.

The **fear** of pain instructs.

The dog complies to avoid feeling pain. He responds at the threat, before a level of pain is introduced. To use pain, and not the threat of pain, as an integral component of a handler's training routine is to destroy trust, destroy the dog, and ultimately for the handler to destroy himself.

With a stubborn, willful dog the contest can degenerate down into who is going to give up first, and this sort of exchange just gets ugly quick. Ideally in force breaking, the handler introduces a short, brief pain caused by pressure at the toe or ear and the dog goes, "Yow!" He takes the dowel and holds it and he doesn't ever want to go through that again. To take the dog back again, to that level of sensation, desensitizes and angers the dog. The dog's angry and feeling violated. He took it twice and survived. The dog responds as if to say, "Is that the best that you can do? Bring it on." That stubborn and willful streak may be genetic, but more than likely it was man-made and could have been avoided by using pain very judiciously. It is a terribly powerful tool and must be used as carefully and deliberately as a diamond cutter would use a sledge hammer. The future relationship of the dog and handler depend on it.

I've seen dogs come in for training that were preconditioned to be defiant on the table. The field trial washout is sold to a foot hunter at six-months-old because the dog won't make it on the circuit. It's hard to imagine what associations were laid down for that dog during his first six months of life, while he was getting his washout status. I put the dog on the table and he sets his jaw and glares at me.

"Give it your best shot, buddy. You can't hurt me. Bigger jerks have tried." Where does a trainer go from there?

Evaluating Modified Force Breaking as an Option

In many instances, something other than the threat of pain can be used to motivate the dog to open his mouth and reach out and grab the object to be retrieved. The variable is how much natural retrieve is in the dog as compared to the owner's expectations.

The following are examples of modified force breaking techniques. For example, a handler may be able to go straight to a fresh killed pigeon at the post. This is something the dog wants. He may be willing to reach out and grab it of his own volition. Another dog can be put at the other end of the table to retrieve the pigeon first if the training dog is on the fence about picking the bird up. Live velcro-harnessed pigeons are an even bigger draw. It may be that the dog isn't so keen on pigeons, but a new bird, like a quail or chuckar, will have the dog pulling at the post to get the bird. It may require that the handler jumps forward a few steps and gives the dog the freedom to run the table after a bird set down at the other end. I have gone straight to the ground at this point and gotten the dog to pick up and carry a bird. Once he has a bird in his mouth, then the "hold it" and "release" drill can be used to clean up any presentation problems.

There is a great deal of trust involved in doing modified force breaking. Things may not happen quickly. A handler gives up the structure and control that step by step force breaking allows. He or she, and the dog, work as a team and create a working accommodation. It may take continuing work through the dog's first wild bird season for it to finally all come together. The trade off for the extra time is, almost without exception, a happier dog in the field and on birds. A pro with a fixed three month window doesn't have the option to modify his training when working on a fixed schedule.

About halfway through my professional training years, I stopped pushing dogs on the table if I felt that it would not benefit them and we could do it another way, and if the owner was in agreement. It meant that the dog was going to go home without a solid resolution on retrieving. I did this in particular with English setters, as they seem to mature more slowly and don't take pressure well. My experience taught me that if we didn't push them on the table, but instead let it sit until they got onto wild birds during their first hunting season, they put it together naturally.

Certainly, it varies from dog to dog, but it is possible to make some generalizations. The German dogs and pointers (English) are genetically imprinted to the table, it seems. They flourish with the control and structure. Setters as a rule don't like it and it can be counterproductive with some of them. Some field trial setter bloodlines may require force breaking if they are to retrieve at all. The choice with the field trial dogs may be to just forego them retrieving altogether. If retrieving is important to you, don't buy those field trial English setter bloodlines. The other versatile breeds have a broad response range and should be judged on a dog by dog basis. The Brits generally don't do well with anything that requires them to work within a controlled structure. They may bend on the table, but there will be consequences later. A handler doesn't get a hundred percent with a Brit.

Modified Force Breaking

If the decision is made to go with modified force breaking, then look to see what will motivate the dog to pick something up on his own without the use of force. This means finding some form of a bird that the dog wants. Many times a fresh killed pigeon will do the trick. The easiest is a frozen bird. I have used frozen quail successfully in the past with some dogs. Wing-tied or wing-pulled live pigeons, or pigeons in restraint harnesses can also be the trick for motivating a dog.

While the dog is on the table, clipped to the post, offer a bird and see if he doesn't open his mouth and reach out and take it. When he does, praise him lavishly and tell him to hold it. Step away from the table. Come back to it. Wave your hand under the dog's muzzle and tap the bird lightly just as you did with the dowel. Order the dog to release. When the dog drops the bird in your hand, you're on your way.

Move quickly through the training by removing restraints that are on the dog. Let him run the table and carry the bird. Place the bird on the far end of the table and send the dog to fetch it. Take the dog off the table and go to the ground with the fetch drills. Do all of this over a period of several sessions, always taking care to keep the dog excited about the bird. Move as quickly as is possible to the ground so you can start shooting birds for the dog.

When the dog is picking up and carrying on his own, the only thing left to shape is the manner in which the dog presents the bird to the handler at the end of the retrieve. "Hold it" and "release" is in place, and "whoa" is in place. When the dog comes back from a pick up, whoa him when he gets in front of you. Walk around him and do your whoa drill, then stand beside the dog. Put your hand below the dog's muzzle and command him to release.

Next, after the dog is whoaed, stand beside the dog and release him to walk with you. Travel in a soft bending arc until you end up facing in the opposite direction from where you started. At that point, command the dog to release and take the bird. Layer this in.

Once this is going well, don't whoa the approaching dog, simply take the last few steps with him and bend him back around. Stop him with the flat of your hand and tell him to release. Take the bird.

Finally, see if he hasn't put the pieces together. As he approaches, motion him around and see if he doesn't come to your side and present the bird and wait for you to give him the release command.

Troubleshooting: Modified Force Breaking

What I just described was a perfect world. Sometimes you get this from a dog, but mostly there are hitches along the way. I mentioned that trust was an important component of modified force breaking. When the glitch hits, take a step back and work through it. If you can't get the piece that way, then wait and see if it doesn't come later when you start shooting birds for the dog, or when you go to wild birds.

The most common problem a handler will experience is that the dog will start dropping the bird somewhere in the process. Generally, this shows up when the dog is asked to present the bird or the dog is whoaed before being asked to release. One thing that can help is to use a live bird that will walk away if the dog lets go of it. If the dog is concerned that the bird will leave if he releases it, he is much less likely to allow it to fall from his grip. If you continue to have a problem, turn a second dog loose

The essence of modified force breaking is that jealousy and envy trumps force.
1) Setter pulling feathers off a pigeon instead of retrieving it.

3) The setter immediately picks up the bird and turns towards the handler to prevent the shorthair from having a chance at the bird.

2) A shorthair is released to persuade the setter to carry the bird.

4) The setter delivers the bird to the handler and ends the retrieve as a positive training interaction.

as the retrieving dog approaches the handler. He is not going to want his buddy to get ahold of the bird and he will hang on tightly until told to release. Have an assistant hold the end of the second dog's check cord so that when the retrieving dog is beside the handler, the second dog can be reeled back out of the picture.

There are a wide range of associated behaviors that potentially can show up with a modified force breaking. It may be that at some point in the process the handler will wish to incorporate conventional force break training methods, and that option is always available if the trainer deems it beneficial. Perhaps the dog gets willful or defiant. Perhaps after working with the dog, the handler feels that the structure of the table might communicate what the handler is trying to get across to the dog more effectively. A handler can choose the level of negatives he or she employs and moderate the training to suit the individual needs of a particular dog. The strength of dog training is that there is always a Plan B.

Conventional Force Breaking

Now we can look at the second option. If the decision is made to go with a conventional force breaking, then the dog is motivated to open his mouth and reach out to grab an object through the use of a nerve hitch or ear pinch. This is used when the dog will not grab something (such as a bird) willingly and on his own. The handler applies a negative stimulation (pain) until the dog opens his mouth to yowl. At the instant that the dog's mouth opens, the handler pops in a dowel and ceases applying the negative pressure (the handler stops applying the pain). When the dog opens his mouth to expel the dowel, the negative pressure immediately returns until the dog once again has the dowel in his mouth. The dog quickly learns that he is in control of the pain. If the dowel is not in his mouth: pain. If the dowel is in his mouth: no pain. The dog says, "OK, I'll keep this dowel in my mouth. Just don't pull on that cord or pinch my ear."

The cord the dog's referring to is loosely snugged at the top of his ankle above the foot. The cord then trails down and is wrapped in a loop around the two middle toes of the dog. When the end of the cord is pulled by the handler, it forces the knuckles of the two middle toes together and pinches a nerve, which hurts the dog. The pain is sharp but causes no lasting physical effect. When the pressure on the cord is released, then the pressure on the nerve is released, and the pain the dog is sensing comes to an end.

The ear pinch is done with the handler's thumb and finger. The dog's ear is gripped by the handler in the same way you would shoot a marble, with the difference being that the dog's ear takes the place of the marble. A handler uses his or her thumbnail and pinches the soft part of the base of the dog's ear, squeezing the tissue between his or her thumbnail and adjoining finger. I have heard stories about pros on the retriever circuit using other tools to pinch the dog's ear, which I won't repeat here. Suffice it to say that there are reasons why many trainers have turned away from force breaking.

The dog learns to comply quickly. When it is clear that the dog isn't fighting it anymore, then go for the next piece. With the dog strapped in at the post, hold the dowel an inch from the dog's mouth and apply pressure. The dog will yowl. If he touches the dowel with his mouth while yowling, meet him half-way and let him take the dowel and cease the pressure.

The dog may be defiant and refuse to go near the dowel. Some dogs will not relinquish control and refuse to take the initiative to stop the negative pressure by proactively grabbing the dowel from the handler. I have seen some fairly stubborn dogs over the years. They set their jaw and glare at you. This is a fight you have to win. Unless you get compliance from the dog, you can not move forward. As I stated before, force breaking can be a grim business. Push forward until the dog takes the dowel. Once you get compliance, give him some decompression time. Stay at that level for a couple of sessions until you see the dog lighten up. You need to be sure that there is something left when you win the war.

When the dog is reliably taking a dowel held an inch away from his mouth, increase the distance to three inches, then six inches, then nine inches. Release the dog from the snap on the post so that he has the mobility to extend his body a couple of feet in either direction. Undo the hobbles so that he can go up or down. Ultimately, turn him around on the table so that he is facing the center of the table and is in a position to begin traveling down the table three feet, six feet, nine feet, to get to the dowel and to put it in his mouth.

The next hurdle comes when the dowel is laid on the surface of the force break table and is not held in the handler's hand. This is consistently the point where a break occurs. For some reason, many dogs will not extend themselves to lower their head and pick something up from the ground.

For this situation, the dowel will need to be modified by including four short legs on each end. A dowel thus modified is referred to as a training buck. The legs hold the buck above the surface of the table and allow the dog to get the round dowel into his mouth easily.

Start with short distances. Lay the buck a couple of feet in front of the dog and give the fetch command. If the dog doesn't go for the buck, then apply pressure and compel the dog to get the buck in his mouth. When the dog is reliably going to the buck and picking it up, start extending the distance until the dog is running the length of the table to get to the buck.

Insist that when the dog returns to the handler to deliver the buck, he presents the buck properly. Instruct the dog to hold it and then to release once the handler has his hand in position to catch the falling bird. When the dog is running the length of the table and minding his manners on delivery, then begin rolling in additional items to be retrieved. Use a retrieving bumper, a glove, a fresh killed pigeon. When the dog is working reliably, switch the dog to the ground.

The transition to the ground is another consistent trouble spot for dogs in force breaking. Just as they don't want to lower their head to pick up a buck off the surface of the table, they don't want to transfer what they did on the table to the ground. I try to smooth the way by having them initially run their drills on the ground beside the table so that the association is still strong, but it is generally a struggle. Just as we expanded a dog's sphere of association with the whoa command by going from whoa hook, to whoa post, to the training yard, to the field, the dog must now do the same with retrieving.

If your dog does fight you once on the ground, stir in a bit of modified force breaking to see if that will get him over the hump. Give him a fresh killed pigeon, or up the ante and make it a live pigeon, quail or chuckar. Anything to get him to forego the force and to choose to pick it up because he wants to, not because he is compelled.

The big stumbling block for the handler during the transition to ground is that the dog is no longer located at waist level. If the handler is using an ear pinch as the force association, then the change of height doesn't alter the training significantly. The handler can still get ahold of the ear while the dog is walking alongside.

If the association point is a toe hitch, then the handler has to rethink the way he or she physically interacts with the dog. The problem is that a handler needs to get right down on the ground to get his or her hands near the dog's foot to apply pressure for the force association. With a little practice, the handler can learn to apply toe pressure by running the toe cord under the sole of his or her boot and pulling the cord upward along the line of his or her leg. Some dogs will respond simply to the handler touching the dog's toe with the toe of his or her boot. In reality, I find that during this transition time I often have to kneel down on the dog's level, get his foot in my hand and apply the association in order for him to scramble to get the bird in his mouth.

Regarding the choice of which association point to use in training: ear or toe? I use a toe because that is what I was taught. I have tried using the ear on retrieving breeds, but I don't like the thought of hurting a dog with my hand. I know that probably doesn't make a lot of sense and, looking at it rationally, I don't guess that to the dog there is much of a distinction. An ouch is an ouch. However, it is fair to say that the toe seems to be more tolerable to the softer dogs, such as setters.

At this point in the training process, I have also brought in an electric collar stimulation association as an additional cue for dogs that are resisting retrieving and may be a long term problem. I have found that an e-collar is much more practical for compelling a dog to complete a retrieve while hunting in the field. Just as a matter of expediency, the working dog cannot wear a toe cord while running on birds. The cord gets caught up in vegetation. Also, the handler must get to the dog in order to place the cord on the dog's foot or use his or her fingers to make the correction. All of this takes time, and by the time these prerequisites are completed, the moment is waning. Any portion of time that the dog can stall the inevitable consequence of refusing a retrieve is a window of time where the dog can feel he's winning. If he can stall and maintain some physical distance from the handler, then he buys even more time. If the offending dog is wearing an electric collar, then the consequence of not responding to a retrieving command is instantaneous at whatever distance the dog is from the handler. By using an electric collar stimulation, the dog is much less likely to continue balking retrieves.

Continue on the ground with the dog. Roll in new components like grass, distance, additional dogs and new types of birds. See if it isn't possible to develop some enthusiasm on the part of the dog for the process. Ultimately, what the dog has learned through retrieving training will need to transfer to hunting wild birds. The level of adrenaline that a dog experiences with wild birds should mitigate the mechanical and forced affect that the dog exhibited on the force table. The desired outcome is a dog that enjoys retrieving and presenting the bird. A dog that retrieves because he wants to and has the training to do it properly.

Look, I've gone back and reread this section on force breaking and it sounds way too easy. I don't know what to do about that. If it's any consolation, this is the way it's supposed to work. It's the way it does work on rare occasions.

I remember when I was trying to learn how to force break and I went through the chapter on force breaking in Tarrant's book: _Best Way to Train Your Gun Dog, The Delmar Smith Method_. I took notes. I made step by step index cards. Tarrant's writing was well articulated and organized succinctly. It described the way training is supposed to be. I've since learned that it's the way it works on rare occasions.

The problem is that much of this is internal and is predicated on the determination and psychological make-up of the two parties involved in the contest. The dog is probably figuring the odds in his head as to just how far he thinks the trainer is willing to go. The trainer may have real problems pushing when that is what is required to force compliance. I hope for the trainer's sake that he or she does have qualms about using the level of pain that is sometimes necessary to force compliance on an obstinate dog. Force breaking is more diplomacy than science.

I know someone who described an interaction he had with a German dog. I know the person. I hunted with the dog. I believe the story.

He bought the dog young and had him shipped in from out of state. The dog was advertised as started. This person had the dog for the entire length of the dog's life. Over the course of the dog's fourteen year hunting career, he retrieved untold numbers of quail and dove. However, his first season he was real flighty on retrieving. He didn't want to carry birds. He gave the owner fits until it came to a head one day while hunting. The owner had knocked down a bird which fell in plain sight. The dog went by and acknowledged the dead bird, but refused to retrieve it. The owner called the dog to him and sent him back to retrieve. The dog balked.

Then, the owner told the dog with absolute and complete sincerity, "You son of a bitch, if you don't retrieve that bird I'm going to shoot you in the head and end it right here and now."

The dog thought about it, went over and picked up the bird, and completed the retrieve. He was a solid retriever for the rest of his life.

I'm not condoning the methodology, but it is the essence of force breaking. The dog believed him and because he believed him, he retrieved the bird. I hope this helps.

opposite page: modified force broke trained setter delivers sharptail grouse to hand.

Information for the Field

Wild Birds and Scent

The dog has now completed the first three months on his training calendar. All the raw materials are in place. He is a college graduate with a piece of paper and no real world experience. The dog must be crossed over onto hunting wild birds. This may mean a few months off until the season rolls around. I have always viewed the first season after a gun dog completes his formal training as the most critical time of the dog's working life. Before, training was structured and predictable. The surprises were kept to a minimum. It gets wilder in the field on wild birds. For the most part, the handler is just along for the ride. The dog has moved beyond us and is relying on a nose that senses things we humans will never be able to understand nor comprehend.

The handler looks to provide that golden moment for a new field dog where he makes scent, steps in and points a bird, the handler flushes and kills the bird, and the dog retrieves it. If a handler can make that happen for a dog and then cement it into place by repeating it in rapid order a couple of times more, the dog is made for life. I mean that literally. All the experiences that the dog had during training will fall into place and the dog will never look back.

Using scent is the determining factor and this is something which, as humans, we can't understand or help a dog develop. The phone call goes something like this: "There's something wrong with my dog. He ran right through a covey of birds and didn't even know they were there. His nose doesn't work!"

Since the time that the first human followed a canine on the trail of game we have worried and wondered about a dog's nose. We humans weren't bestowed with the ability to scent game and so we live unable to understand what a dog is sensing when he moves into a bird's scent cone.

My ex-father-in-law, Joe, was an old timer from Arkansas who ran bird dogs and shorthairs back when there were wild birds in the South. As a young kid, I trained with him way before I thought about marrying his daughter. This was before electric collars. His preference was eight shot to turn a ranging dog. He gave them about 70 yards.

He instructed me that scent comes in two varieties: ground scent and air scent. Ground scent originates from the bird's physical contact with the ground and vegetation as it moves to elude the approaching dog. Ultimately, the source of the scent is body and feces oriented and clings or lies along the bird's travel path. While searching ground scent, a dog is attempting to run his nose up against a bird's rectum. As an experiment, next time you are holding a freshly killed bird allow a dog to smell it and see where the nose goes. In short order, it will be buried under the bird's tail.

Air scent, on the other hand, floats in the air about high nose level on a pointing dog. Air scent is the warm breath that is being expelled from the bird's lungs caught by the breeze and floating upwards. It travels with the air in currents like water moving in a river channel. The more birds in the group expelling breath, the easier for a dog to smell and pin the group. Hence, a traveling pointer can nail a feeding covey at forty yards with complete confidence, atmosphere permitting, and then, five minutes later, look tentative when pointing a holding single at three feet. The little feathered rascal is holding his breath and has his nether regions puckered. That was the gospel according to Joe.

Once the two primary sources have been identified, ground and air, then other stuff needs to be factored in, the atmospheric stuff I mentioned earlier. Popular wisdom says that scent is composed of free floating molecules that attach to water molecules (humidity) floating in the air. This would lead someone to reason that the more humidity in the air and on the ground, the greater the carrying capacity for scent molecules (up to the point, of course, where the sky opens up and washes everything clean). I don't know where that point is, but I am certain there is a continuum and that some days a dog's nose works much better than others.

Hence, it would follow that on days of cold, humidity-laden air, on moist ground, your dog is going to be a bird finding machine. It sounds simple enough, doesn't it?

I am reminded of the cartoon where a group of scientists are standing at a blackboard covered with a scrawled, long rambling equation that ends with "+ a miracle =."

Years back, I used to keep shooting journals where I wrote copious notes on temperature, wind, moisture and the like. I was going to figure this scent thing out. I wanted to be able to predict with certainty how the dogs would do on birds. There were a lot more birds back then, so the number of my contacts regarding the mystery of scent were amplified. I had my assumptions and I looked to unravel the secret of scent.

Those dogs are all long dead and I eventually stopped writing in journals. The more I studied, the less I knew.

This is what I'm left with. Scent is an ephemeral thing. It is inconsistent and erratic. It comes in windows and while I think that moisture in the soil and air may help a dog to detect birds, it is not a consistent piece of the equation. It may last a morning. It may last for five minutes. Or, it may not come at all.

In the warm Southwest where I live, scent is generally present in the morning and the evening, with the middle of the day scentless or at least scent diminished. The last hour to hour and a half of the day is often when my dogs can use scent most effectively. Maybe the warmth of the sun's rays heating the ground and the air makes air scent more consistent, but I'm just guessing on this.

Contrary to the above scenario, in the Southwest's higher elevation Mearns' quail country, we don't get any scent early and late. The ground is shaded and covered to a greater or lesser extent with grass and oak trees. The birds are found in tight canyons that mitigate the movement of a strong wind. Our window for working Mearns' is from about 10:00 a.m.

to about 3:00 p.m. Does that have to do with the birds only moving and generating scent during that time period and holing up on slopes the rest of the time? Maybe? I'm guessing again.

What about wind and cover? I can give you my opinions. Wind does affect a dog's ability to pin birds. If it is a strong wind your singles work will evaporate, but on some of those days when the wind howls my dogs pin coveys at 40 to 50 yards and the birds don't have a clue that the dog has them until I walk in for the flush. Are there some consistent and predictable traits that I see either with wind or the lack of it? No, there aren't.

Cover is also something that consistently influences a dog's ability to smell birds. There is the obvious reason which is that cover provides a place for birds to hold in, thereby allowing them to be available to be scented. Cover creates micro-climates that foster the thermal shelter and insect protein that sustain bird populations. Additionally, cover holds moisture in soil and plants and in the air. I repeat, popular wisdom says that scent is composed of free floating molecules that attach to water molecules (humidity) floating in the air.

I would agree that scent is tied to moisture on some days. However, I would guess that on any given day there are multiple conditions affecting scenting conditions. In the West, where early season days are dry and hot, I just go hunting and sometimes I'm pleasantly surprised and I have a good 30 to 45 minute run on days when I shouldn't. The dogs are able to turn birds over points. Sometimes, the bird hunting gods smile!

We humans will never be able to understand with certainty the environment's influences over scenting conditions, so we should look to the other two players in this triangle for predictability and clarification: the dogs (smellers) and the birds (smellies).

The dog who is actually doing the deciphering of available scent has much to do with how successful the two of you will be in finding birds. If scent is available, an older, mature and experienced dog can work with minute whiffs of it and follow the jigsaw puzzle to a successful contact. A youngster, on the other hand, can get those same minute indicators and not have a clue that a bird is anywhere in the area.

Hence the phone call that opened this chapter. As much as we would like to have a dog that is going to read scent consistently, a hundred percent of the time, it just isn't going to happen. As dogs get older and more experienced, they learn to read scent trails in pieces. They walk through the voids waiting to pick up the next bit of clue, like a bow hunter following an intermittent blood trail. If you have done some following of

Becky, a German shorthair, pointing Elegant quail in Sinaloa, Mexico.

blood trails you learn that you often travel by instinct in the spaces between blood.

    Where does this kind of confidence come from? Maturity and experience? It is the same with a bird dog. They get good because they've done good. I love that look in an old dog's eyes when he comes to a stop and raises his nose to air scent. He turns his face to you and you can see him think, "It's here somewhere."

    So, how do we get a dog to that point? We don't have a nose with which to second guess him. All we humans are left with is to do the necessary early training, and then take him hunting and stay out of his way. Give him the time and allow him the mistakes to gain confidence.

    The issue of false or unproductive points is relevant here. I have

Jim Jurries and Jasper, an English setter, anticipate a Gambel's quail flush on the flats.

spent so much time and energy over the years trying to get customers' dogs to point that the thought of faulting a dog for pointing, even if the bird is gone, seems dangerous to me. Pointing is behavior to encourage, not discourage. If a dog is pointing and nothing is there, it almost always means something was there and the dog is doing everything right. With more experience, he will get better at deciphering the clues he is sifting out of the air. Young dogs will stop pointing song birds when they realize what they are really after. Regarding German dogs on mice and rabbits, get used to it. It's genetic. As a dog gets older and smarter, he gets more cautious around birds, yet will continue to false point on some days. He is doing it because he is trying to produce birds for the gun. This is a good thing. The minute that we humans look at a dog on point and dismiss it as unproductive is the minute that we see a bird get up and fly away.

Get your dog into as many wild birds as possible. Dead wild birds make a bird dog.

I've often heard bird hunters comment on how good a particular dog's nose is. Some will worry about whether or not a new puppy will have a good nose. The truth is that a canine's nose is so infinitely superior to ours that, compared to a human's, the difference is exponential. This assumes that the ability to smell is the determining factor, which it isn't. It's how the dog uses the information and works birds. For example, let's say that a particular dog's nose is an 8.9 instead of a 9.7. How helpful would such information be to your hunt? There are no magic pills or cure-all treatments that could change the dog's nose. To my way of thinking, it is an irrelevant issue. It ain't what you got, it's how you use it. Dead wild birds make a bird dog. There are no other substitutes. Always trust that the dog is doing the best job he can and stay out of his way.

We've looked at the bird dog's job, which is to find the bird. Let's now address the bird's job, which is to not to let himself be found. This is something that wild birds do amazingly well, and is perhaps the thing that humans understand the least. Birds control scent. During nesting season, they release no scent at all, which is how ground nesting birds survive to bring off subsequent generations. As the months progress into autumn and the hunting seasons, that ability to mask scent completely tapers off and birds are left with a patchwork quilt of scent manipulation. Sometimes they can hide from a dog's nose, and sometimes they can't. If your dog is dealing with a group of birds, it is never the straightforward interaction that we humans would like to think it is. Birds use scent as a tool to mislead and confuse, and this can take many forms.

For example, your dog comes in and points on a feeding covey of Western quail. The covey of thirty-five birds moves off when they hear the heavy footfalls of the gun approaching. They run fifty yards and burrow in. They stop breathing and pucker up. Half a dozen of their number angle off and leave a solid walking scent trail for the dog to follow. First the dog and then the gun walks right through the holding covey, thinking that the entire group is running ahead. The half-dozen decoy birds peel off and hold, leaving no scent until two hundred yards later when the trail dries up and the pursuers are left wondering: where did everybody go?

Or, on prairie grouse, a single flushes and gets hit hard. The bird tumbles in with no operating flight gear, but legs that are working just fine. The bird runs to the first clump of heavy stuff and leaves solid scent. He then immediately hot foots it to the next clump and the next, all the time leaving scent. The dog comes screeching in for the pickup and finds the bird gone. He trails to the first clump and locks up solid. When you walk in, you don't know if it's the cripple or a fresh bird. As you come even with the dog, you can see the doubt in his eyes. His tail starts a slow, low tick and you release the dog, who then runs a short distance and slams down on the next clump of grass. He only holds half as long this time when, as you approach, you see the slow tick of his tail start again. By the time you get to the fourth scent decoy station, that bird has left the county. In the process, he's also bought his buddies an extra 10 minutes and a hundred and fifty yards in which to evaporate, as well.

While hunting Elegant quail in Sinaloa, Mexico, you push several coveys along a open buffle grass field/heavy thorn forest jungle edge. A shorthair locks up where a point of jungle pushes into the grassland. The dog can smell the bird just fine and when you release the dog to flush, the dog burrows into the thick mat of grass and creepers and vines. The bird will not flush and continues to entice the dog to gopher through the thick matt of vegetation, her tail twirling like a mechanical gyroscope at grass level. You call for a gun to circle around through the jungle growth and come up on the other side. As the shooter enters the thick growth, he catches the rest of the birds running out of the field and into the safety of the heavy growth. Although there were two experienced dogs on the ground, the only bird they were able to smell was the one single pulling them off of the escaping group.

All of these examples illustrate how little we humans can do to assist or instruct our canine hunting companions. Once we get into the field we are fish out of water and we need to turn over the scenting duties to our bird dogs.

A dog's relationship to scent is sporadic and imperfect. Given the difficulty of its work, it is impressive how good dogs can sometimes be at turning birds. Be grateful when it's working. Be persistent when it isn't. Dead wild birds make a bird dog. There are no other substitutes. Always trust the dog.

Handling in the Field

Once a dog is transferred to the field he will have to be handled there. I have seen this turn into an elaborate production and it really shouldn't be. The less a handler uses to communicate his intentions to a dog, the stronger the bond between the dog and the handler will become. The ultimate goal of dog handling is not to have to handle the dog.

I use a hierarchy of cues to talk to a working dog. The first and least on the level of impact is a low whistle that I produce by pursing my lips and blowing lightly. I use this soft whistle probably eighty-five percent of the time in the field when I need to tell a dog something. I'll call it a check whistle for lack of a better term. I use it to get a dog's attention when I'm about to do something that will be obvious to the dog if he is watching what I am doing:

I'm turning and going this way now.
Do you want some of this water?
Since when did you start thinking about chasing rabbits?

The dog hears the whistle and gets diverted from whatever was running through his mind, makes eye contact and says, "Oh yeah, boss, right away. I'm on it."

I can use a check whistle as an attention getting device at close to moderate range, when I need the dog to see a hand signal. I do this by blowing a very short sharp chirp. It is especially effective when the dog and I are standing in the middle of a busted covey of birds and I want to give the bird the least amount of information about our location. I might need the dog to understand a myriad of things at a moment like that:

We're going to go this way.

I saw the bird go into this bush.

Pay attention, this flat of the hand means whoa. You have a dog on point in front of you. Mind your manners.

I also use the check whistle to release a whoaed dog to flush a bird that he has been pointing in thick cover. If I go in to flush the bird, I'll end up standing in the middle of a jungle and be unable to take the shot. So, I get into optimum shooting position and give a light check whistle to the dog. He then jumps in and flushes the bird.

The next cue up the scale is my voice. I use voice cues maybe 5% of the time, reserved for short range handling generally within thirty yards of the dog. I don't yell at dogs and I don't give a command multiple times. I reserve my voice for the times that I can enforce compliance. My dogs don't hear me give a voice command very often, so when they hear it, it has the weight of authority for them.

I may address my dog in a conversational tone to check on him or to ask him to stay and rest when we stop for a shade break. I might admonish the dog if he is wriggling around when I have him over on his back and I'm trying to get cactus out of his feet. I don't perceive these as commands and I don't think the dogs do, either.

Next, I go to whistle cues. By that, I mean the sound of a whistle emanating from a whistle on a lanyard around my neck. I use the hard whistle about 10% of the time. There is no need for some mega superwhistle, just a simple coach's or dog whistle will do nicely. There are good selections available in several of the outdoor/dog related catalogs. They come in plastic and metal. Metal holds up better, but a handler wouldn't want to touch one to the lips in temperature extremes on either side of zero degrees.

When a dog hears me blow a whistle, he believes it! I have three whistle commands I use in the field. There is also a hand signal component for each of the commands that I use in conjunction with the whistle cues.

When it is necessary to get compliance on whoa, come, and over, I blast the whistle.

"Whoa" is a trill whistle blast, blown until the dog complies and freezes. The accompanying hand signal is a flat hand pointed at the dog.

"Come" is a very short, single attention chirp followed by three strong blasts blown in rapid succession. I may put some feeling into the third and last whistle blast if some coercion is necessary. The accompanying hand signal is the attention signal of a hand held straight up in the air over my head. Once the dog spots the raised hand, I add movement to the signal by twirling my arm in a cone shape over my shoulder, sort of like a desperate elementary school student signaling his teacher that he really needs to use the restroom, now! I can extend this hand signal, if the dog is working out at a range, by holding a shotgun to extend the height of my arm. For extreme range, or when the bulk of my silhouette is obscured by brush, I can place a hat on top of the gun barrel to provide more movement to the twirling motion. When the dog closes to within thirty or so yards, I follow up with a hand signal or voice cue. It may be that I ultimately give the dog the "here" command and point to the ground at my feet where I want the dog to plant himself.

The hand signal may give the dog a new line of travel as in "over," the third handling command that I use. As the dog approaches, I motion with my hand and point in the direction of the new line of travel. I may give a verbal cue, "over." I then angle my body and step off in that direction. I give dogs straight lines to follow so that they can keep track of my line of travel while we are in the field.

Finally, I have the whoa association of an electric collar stimulation. If I have to, I can at any point stop a dog and declare a time out by whoaing him. If a train wreck needs to be averted, we can shut down and start over. I use it on rare occasions, maybe once or twice during a week's worth of hunting. Maybe one of the older dogs is crowding a younger dog who found the birds first, and the senior dog doesn't want to honor the young upstart's point. When this happens, it may be appropriate to "touch" the dog lightly with enough stimulation from a collar to break through the adrenaline. I may "touch" the older dog to remind him of his manners. I may "touch" a younger dog who doesn't stop when whoaed.

Attention look at me	Attention at extreme distance	Attention distance/heavy cover	Here! Stand at my feet I want to touch you

Twirl arm in a circular motion, blow one long sharp whistle blast	Twirl arm in a circular motion, blow one long sharp whistle blast	Twirl arm in a circular motion, blow one long sharp whistle blast	Point to the ground at your feet, blow 3 short whistle blasts

Over / Left Step off to the left	Over / Right Step off to the right	Over / Left at close range within 50 yards	Over / Right at close range within 50 yards

Use the vocal command "over" and give the dog a direction left	Use the vocal command "over" and give the dog a direction right	Use the vocal command "over" and give the dog a direction left	Use the vocal command "over" and give the dog a direction right

Photo by Sandy McClure

Water and Heat: Keeping the Dog Running

I once had a bad morning when I was training, with a guy who had bought way too much dog for himself. He was a brand new bird dog owner/bird hunter. He had brought the dog to me for training and it was the checkup morning to see how the dog was coming along. His brother-in-law, bird dog expert, came along to assess my performance. I'm guessing he was the same expert who had advised him that he needed an Elhew to be the complete bird dog owner/bird hunter.

It was during a typical Sonoran desert summer and I had asked him to meet me at dawn while we still had some coolness to work the dog. He refused. He had something else going that morning. He liked the sound of 10:00 am better. He had his two youngsters, a boy and girl, in tow when he and the dog expert arrived. They had shown up earlier than our appointed time and, since they had some time to kill, he taught his son how to throw rocks and break the beer bottles that someone had left in a pile right where my clients air out their dogs. Upon arrival, I was greeted to a long line of rocks and glistening glass shards...he and his son had been very thorough. I get quiet when I'm angry. I was real quiet that morning. My one consolation, after seeing the busted glass, was the certainty that the dog was going home today.

There were several low points that morning that stick in my memory, but a particular one applies here. At one point, the owner addressed me with an exasperated tone in his voice, "The dog isn't doing well. He isn't smelling birds." The temperature was pushing 100 at this point, and the dog's tongue was dragging at his feet. I was watering him frequently to keep him going.

The owner stated, "There are mornings that I hunt during the beginning of the season when it gets to 105." I think he wanted to impress me with the fact that this "hot" thing with the dog was unacceptable. The brother-in-law/bird dog expert looked on over his shoulder, knowingly. I guess I should have done a better job training the dog to handle the heat. I don't remember responding to his comment, but I had an extra forty-five minutes to reflect on it, after they left with the dog. It took me that long to pick up all the broken glass.

Dogs and hot don't mix. Dogs don't have the ability to cool their bodies like humans. They don't sweat through their skin. They have only their tongues and the pads of their feet to regulate their body temperature. The tongue acts like a radiator to vent heat out of the body. The dog's lungs pant air across the tongue and thereby facilitate cooling.

Dogs cool through their bellies. Here, a warm pointer gets his belly spritzed down to help him cool off.

The early bird season can get too hot to safely run a dog. This isn't just a condition of the Southwest. I remember a day of hunting in September, in South Dakota, when the temperature climbed to 107 and the humidity in the air was thick enough to swim through. We were running on sharptails and we had a dog go down hard. The humidity seemed to compound the heat and cause trouble for the dog. I have seen the same effect running dogs in Sinaloa, Mexico, where it can feel very tropical at midday, even as early in the year as February.

The heat builds up in a dog's body until it reaches the point that the dog can't control it. It is more than his body can do to expel the heat and maintain a proper core body temperature. He looks disoriented. He stumbles. His eyes glaze over. Once a dog gets to the point of visible distress, it may be too late to stop the spiral. The dog is in danger of dying. He will fall over, go into convulsions and expire. The handler must act immediately to stop the cycle and cool down the dog's internal body temperature. There can be long term consequences even if the dog lives- systemic failures, or infarctions of internal organs. For the rest of the dog's life, he can have stamina problems. I speak from experience when I say that you do not want to watch your dog die of convulsions.

The antidote for heat is water. A dog can be run in moderate heat for reasonable periods of time, but they must be kept wet and they must be watched closely. They must not be allowed to get too warm or the handler

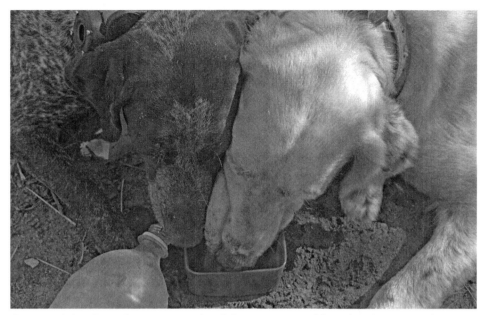

Setter and shorthair sharing a waterbowl during a tropical hunt for elegant quail in Sinaloa, Mexico .

will not be able to reverse the effects of heat prostration. When a dog starts hunting shade instead of birds, or digging holes in cool earth and flopping his belly down into it, it's time to shut down and head back to the truck. Give him shade breaks as you travel and rest until he stops panting before heading back in.

It can be easy to ignore the early signs, and a bird dog will run because his instinct tells him to run. He will run past the point of no return, and therefore it is imperative that the handler be on top of things and not let it get that far.

The quickest way to cool a dog is to submerge him in water and get his belly and the insides of his legs wet. If a body of water is available, get the dog to it and get him in it. A steel livestock drinker tank will work fine if no running water or dirt tanks are close at hand. Just pick the dog up and drop him in. A dog that has gotten too hot will splay his back legs and belly down in shallow water for five or ten minutes. They may take on a lot of water and then regurgitate it all back up. Let him do whatever he needs to do to get the heat out of him.

When I'm running dogs in the field, I water them regularly. During hot days, at the water breaks, I grab a dog by the two inside legs and pull the feet out from under him. This causes the dog to roll over on his back where I can get at his belly and pour and rub water onto the exposed skin of his stomach and inside his thighs. This works like an evaporative cooler

During a break while running on scaled quail, these two setters enjoy a dip. When a dog can get his belly wet, a handler can get another half hour run out of him.

to help get the hot out of the dog.

    The best things I have found for carrying water are clear plastic throwaway water and soda bottles. They come in graduated sizes. They are clear so it's easy to see how much water is inside. You can't beat the price and they are nearly indestructible. I've had them last for three or four seasons of hard use before they spring a leak. The long tube-like shape allows them to be carried easily by laying them in the bottom of the carrying pouch of a game vest. Depending on the intensity of the day's heat, the number of dogs, and the time I anticipate being out, I carry two or three of these water bottles with me to provide water for the dogs.

    I also have a clip-on water dish that hangs from a snap at the front of my game vest. Sitting up front like that, it is easy to get to. After use, it drains to the great outdoors and not the inside of a pouch. I don't have to fish around by feel in the bottom of my game bag to find it. By using the dish, I can easily control how much water the dog is getting. Unlike the squirt bottles that are in use with some handlers, I know that what I poured into the dish had to go into the dog, because if he hadn't drunk it, it would still be in the bowl. It cuts wasted water to an absolute minimum. Any undrunk water in the bowl gets poured onto the dog's stomach.

    Typically, when the dogs and I start a run I will water them heavily two or three times within the first twenty or thirty minutes. This seems to get them started properly. After that, I'm more judicious with the water and make it last. I ration the water so that we don't run out and when I see that we are getting low, we begin the circle back in. I don't run out of water in the field. If I can use available surface water to keep the dogs wet during the hunt then that is less water I have to carry, but I never count on it being there. I always have some water on board.

There is a condition called hypoglycemia that can cause the bottom to drop out of a running dog. The condition involves the dog's insulin and glucose levels. When the dog's blood sugar level crashes, the dog does the same. This condition can start slow and a handler may see early signs of it in a young dog. It might make its first appearance two or three years into the dog's hunting career. It could be a random rare occurrence or become a chronic condition that could ultimately kill the dog. Either way, a handler should always be prepared with a sugar bump in case a dog gets in trouble. Even if it is just a case of heat prostration, I give the sugar.

In my dog first aid box I have a bottle of Karo syrup and a large needle-less plastic syringe that I can fill with syrup and squirt into the back of the dog's mouth so that he is not able to spit it up. A dog that is incapacitated is not going to offer much in the way of assistance when it comes to getting something into his system.

Also, I sometimes carry honey packets in my vest as a more immediate low tech way of getting the dog a glucose bump. The honey is thick and sticky enough that if you can get it in the dog's mouth, most will get into the dog's system.

While running in the field, I give the dog some protein to keep his insulin from stripping glucose. I do this at about the two hour mark. Somewhere around three to three and a half hours in, they will need another snack. I used to use little cans of gourmet kitty food. I still carry them at times, but now I most often use the high energy protein bars that are marked for endurance runners. They are much easier to carry in a vest pocket without the danger of a messy leak. I chew up a bite of the stiff bar and soften it for the dog. Then I give it to him during a water break. It really makes the difference in keeping a dog going, healthily.

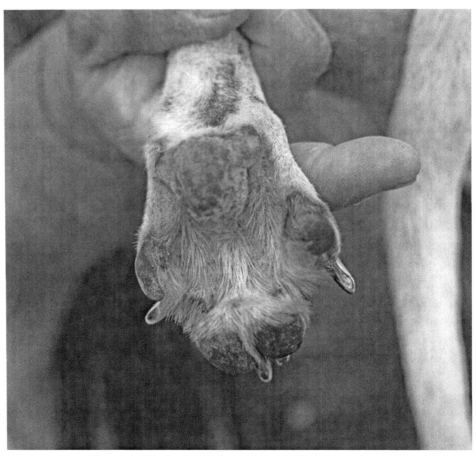

Blown-out pad on a Kansas pointer.

Pads and Time on the Ground

Depending on the physical condition of a dog, the most that a handler can expect is about five hours to five and a half hours of go time. I have pushed dogs past that to over six hours when I have been guiding clients in the field and, after a dry run, we finally got into birds. It's doable if the dog is in extremely good condition, but it's not advisable. When a handler does this, he is literally right at the end of the dog's rope. There is no next wind coming. When the dog stops, he will have to be carried out.

Anything past four hours means that the dog will be down for a couple of days for required rest. If, on the other hand, a handler restricts time on the ground per day to three or three and a half hour blocks, the dog should be able to perform for a three or four day stretch.

At the start of a new season, what goes first are the pads on a dog's

Picture of Western volcanic Malpai rock. In some areas, these rocks litter the ground. It is like walking on a layer of soft balls or, as one gentleman said, "cantaloupe fields."

feet. Soft pads can literally separate at the outer layer and slough off. If a handler watches periodically during the dog's first runs, he will see the edges feathering and separating. If a handler moderates the dog's run time and keeps the runs short, he or she can avoid pad problems by letting the dog's feet gradually toughen up.

    Slipped pads are extremely painful for the dog. He won't feel it while he's running, but once he stops he will get extremely ginger with his feet and hobble around with each step. There may be worn bloody patches the equivalent of a human blister. When a dog loses a pad, he is going to be down for a while. In extreme cases, it could be a week and a half to two weeks before the feet recover and the dog is ready to go again. The good news is that when the pads come back in, they come back hard and the dog is good to go for the rest of the season.

    Different types of ground are going to affect the dog's feet differently. If the dog is running on soft, leafed-over forest loam this may not be an issue. In the Western deserts of North America, the ground is mostly varying degrees of rock. Some areas are volcanic cinders referred to locally as "malpai" bastardized from the Spanish "mal pais" which literally means bad ground. Running a dog on this type of surface just plain chews up a dog's feet. Even late in the season, when my dogs' feet are conditioned, I have to limit their time on malpai if I want to keep pads on them.

    Over the years, I've tried conditioning and a product called "tough foot." All our kennel floors are gravel to help keep the occupants' feet in the best condition possible. None of this seems to make a difference for the abrasive type of ground we run on locally. All our dogs lose their pads to varying degrees at the beginning of the season. We can't run our dogs consistently during the summer because of heat and snakes, so when the season rolls around their pads are soft. Handlers in other areas may have the option to run their dogs on a consistent year-round schedule and this keeps the dogs' feet in shape.

First Aid in the Field

While we're on the topic of caring for a dog while running, a handler should be prepared for other types of health emergencies in the field. I have a large medical box that I keep in the truck when I have a dog running. This is for emergency care once I get the dog back to the vehicle. Size and weight preclude carrying it while hunting, so I have just a few standard items that I always have with me when I leave the vehicle.

I keep a small roll of vet wrap in the pocket of my hunting vest. It is a type of elastic bandage that is frequently used by horse folks for wrapping the legs of horses when tendon problems occur. It is available anywhere equine products are sold. It has a latex rubber backing that sticks to itself, so it is the ideal material for dealing with punctures and tears on a dog in the field. It can be used to keep pressure on a bleeding wound and hold the dog together until he can be cleaned up and stitched or stapled back at the truck. It comes in a jazzy array of colors including fluorescent orange, if a person wants to use it to mark individual dogs.

Along with the vet wrap, I carry a small supply of toilet paper: a quarter roll is a good size. In addition to the obvious reasons, I can use the paper as bandaging if a dog comes in with a bleeding wound. Wadded up toilet tissue under vet wrap makes a pretty good impromptu pressure bandage.

Also, I wear a couple of whistles hanging from lanyards around my neck for handling the dogs. If I need a tourniquet for any reason, these lanyards can be pressed into service.

The other tools I have with me are a pair of needle-nosed pliers and a small medical needle suture puller, similar to a clamping forceps device. I keep both of these together in a leather sheath on the front of my game vest, so they are always easily available. I use them for pulling things off a dog that shouldn't be there. In our part of the world, this generally means

Dogs and porcupines don't mix well together.

some form of sticker from cactus and cholla, but it could be porcupine quills or some metal relic from past farming or ranching activity.

In addition, I have a Swiss army knife on my belt that covers just about any other possibility. In particular, I often find the small pair of tweezers provided with the knife the perfect tool for getting the small stuff.

For handling and restraining dogs, I have a couple of snap-on leads hanging from my belt- I never go into the field without them. I carry two leads because much of the time I have two dogs running simultaneously. If I'm going to take out three dogs, I also throw a short check cord into the back of my vest.

There will be times while hunting when an emergency situation develops and a dog must be kept under control and/or led away from the area. It could be that you run into the local version of a nasty critter, be it a snake, pig, skunk, lion, or grizzly bear. It may be that you pop out unexpectedly from heavy cover onto a farm road, and vehicles are approaching in the distance. Most of the time, there isn't much forewarning when one of these situations crops up and the leads need to be readily available to snap on the dog, to be certain of complete control.

That's about it, with the exception of a small flashlight for an evening hunt and a cell phone if there is reception available in the area. I keep things at a bare minimum because once I load on the collar, vest and camera and get the water bottle stowed in the game pouch, I have about as much weight on me as I want to deal with. The number and type of items have evolved and changed over the years, with the current bare bones collection having held constant for about the last five years. In that five year time frame, I have always gotten everyone back to the truck in at least repairable condition.

Meanwhile, back at the truck is a behemoth of an old metal ice chest that serves as a catchall for anything that may be needed in the advent of any type of medical emergency. I'm going to winnow down the contents list here to the necessary items. If a person wishes to add, they can always go to a bigger container.

Probably the most common serious injury that occurs to a dog in the field is some sort of skin puncture or tear. Given the speed and momentum that a field dog develops while running, some of the wounds can be a little unsettling. The current veterinary wisdom is that soft tissue wounds should be irrigated and left open to heal. Certainly, there is a line where the wound, because of its size or severity, will need to be stitched or stapled. I used to close up even moderately-sized wounds, but anymore they need to be pretty severe before I will intercede and close them. We do almost all of our own doctoring. The exception would be if the wound was very invasive or there was pronounced blood loss. I get nervous when I look in and see working parts. We load up that dog and go see the vet.

To treat a soft tissue wound, I keep a couple of large cans of contact lens saline solution in the truck medical box. These saline containers are under pressure and squirt a stream of sterile saline that is the perfect solution for cleaning and irrigating a skin tear or puncture. A vet will typically clip the hair away from the wound site before beginning any course of treatment. I have found with my dogs that it just leaves the site more exposed and vulnerable, in addition to adding cut hair to the exposed wound site. I may, on rare occasions, cut back some of the longer hair so that it stays clear of the wound when the dog is licking it, but mostly I just leave it alone.

Dog saliva has stuff in it that keeps the wound clear of infection and facilitates healing. I use saline to get foreign objects and dirt out and, providing that the wound isn't severe, I let the dog do the rest. I will check it daily for any signs of a developing infection. I also start the dog on a course of Amoxicillin. One 250 mg pill twice a day for four to eight days, depending on the condition of the wound. Punctures can be prone to infection and so I err on the side of caution and give the dog a six to ten day run at the above mentioned levels. I may also use Panalog, which is a topical antibiotic cream sold through the veterinary industry. There is a tube, stored in a plastic zip lock bag, in the dog medical box.

What you will see is that, along with the injured dog, other dogs in the group will also lick and doctor the site. I don't discourage any of it. The more dog saliva, the better. Someday, they may discover a way to synthesize and bottle the stuff.

If the wound is too large, say the size of a golf ball, then it will need to be closed. For this, I have both sutures and medical skin staple guns in the box.

I remember as a kid I had a girlfriend whose father ran hounds on bobcats. He would bring those dogs in after a day of running, just shredded. He would lay them out on a table and start sewing. He sprinkled some wound powder in and sewed some more. It is amazing what a dog will tolerate. My dogs will let me sew them back up. Some are better at it than others, but we get it done. Sutures should be removed in seven to ten days.

What works much better for long runs of torn skin is a medical staple gun. These devices are made out of plastic and use a stainless steel clip or staple to hold the skin together. They are packaged with about a thirty staple capacity and are disposable once the sterile seal is broken and/or the complement of staples is used up. In a medical procedure, the stapler can not be reused, even if most of the staples are still in the unit unused. Surgeons that I have trained for and friends in the medical profession have been able to get these used staple guns for me and I keep several in the medical box.

If staples are used to close a tear, they can't be simply removed at the appointed seven to ten day period of time. They are metal and don't snip with scissors. What's needed to remove them is a small hand-held type of specialty pliers. They grasp the middle of the metal band and, when squeezed, they apply pressure that curls the points of the staple back up and out of the healed wound. A pair of these will be necessary if staples are used. Mine were provided by the folks that procured the staple gun for me. As is always the case with any doctoring: if a person isn't comfortable doing this sort of repair work, it is best to pay a vet to perform the procedure.

In the same bin with the staple removal pliers, I have an odd collection of differently-shaped stainless steel surgical scissors, forceps, long and short tweezers, sharp sterile scalpels for when I have to make a hole to get something out, and a neat little pair of grabbing forceps that only move at the tip for getting out foxtails and seed heads from the nostrils and ear channels of dogs. I also include a pair of welder's tweezers designed for

Author de-cholla cactuses Musette's rear foot. (Photo by Sandy McClure)

removing tiny slivers of metal. They are just the ticket for the really small stuff that the Swiss army knife tweezers can't get. Also included is a length of small diameter surgical tubing for a proper tourniquet; and, some disposable plastic razors in case I have to clean up the hair around a wound site. Lastly, a spoon. You never know when one will come in handy.

Another very important set of items is a coat brush and stripper for getting seed heads and burrs out of a dog's coat.

Also, you will need a stout, high quality set of dog nail cutters. These are needed for probably the most common injury dogs experience in the field: broken toe nails. These can be very painful for a dog, and a handler may need to intercede and cut the nail off if the break is bad. Don't skimp on these. Buy the best set you can afford.

I also keep wound powder in case I have to sew someone up, a bottle of Betadine and an assortment of Band-Aids, sterile surgical bandage packs, a roll of gauze, vet wrap, and some white medical tape.

I also have a lighted scope for looking into a dog's ear channel or nostril for foreign objects. It is an inexpensive plastic model I bought through a drug store. I would imagine that there are much pricier models available, but I wouldn't go overboard on this item. For the limited use it will receive, plastic works fine.

I include a little electronic thermometer, inexpensive and available through a drug store. You can gauge what's happening in a dog by its temperature. It should run about 102 degrees. If the temp runs hot, then you know that it's probably an infection. You may want to see a vet.

I have a stethoscope for listening to what's happening in the dog's lungs.

There are several bottles of medications in my kit. I carry antibiotics: Amoxicillin for internal stuff and Tetracycline for skin-related ailments. I have Prednisone as a steroid for allergic reactions and swelling. There is a bottle of Dramamine for motion sickness and Benadryl to calm a dog. I include a bottle of aspirin to address soreness and stiffness after running. I also have some horse doctoring stuff: Cut Heal, and Wound-Kote blue lotion.

For glucose related problems, I have my large needle-less syringe and a bottle of Karo syrup. I include honey packets and several packets of water soluble electrolyte powder.

Next, there are an odd assortment of orphaned socks. Socks make great covers for injured feet, tails and ears.

Finally, I include one book: *Dog Owner's Home Veterinary Handbook*, Delbart G. Carlson, D.V.M., and James M. Griffin, M.D., Howell Book House, New York, N. Y., ISBN 0-87605-537-4.

Training with Electric Collars

Electric Training Collars

Electric collars were originally developed in the 1960's by the forerunners of what eventually came to be called the Tri-Tronics Company. Those original units were used on hounds running lions and bears. Since that time, these electronic training devices have been incorporated into all segments of the dog training world.

These are incredible training tools when used properly. They allow the handler to have an immediate response and association while standing hundreds of yards away from a dog. They allow pros to complete yard and preliminary field work in a three month period of time for their training customers. Having said that, their effectiveness can also destroy a dog as quickly as they shape positives. Using a collar doesn't eliminate the need for training. Instead, it makes it an imperative that the dog is thoroughly trained before the collar is used, and that the dog understands completely what associations the handler is making by using electrical stimulation.

The explosion of technological development associated with all things electric has also accelerated the evolution of e-collar design. They bear little resemblance to the antiquated units of even a few short years ago. Along with the explosion in collar design has been an expansion of companies producing e-collars. Tri-Tronics was the only manufacturer for decades. In the early 1990's, Innotek took over a portion of the market share. Today, there are five collar companies selling e-collar product lines.

These are still expensive toys, but the market is responding to competition and as the innovation and quality increases, the suggested retail price creeps steadily lower.

Whether or not to purchase and use an e-collar for training and handling is a question many dog owners vacillate over. This uncertainty, experienced by a novice trainer, gives many people pause. Unless a handler has very strong feelings for non-use, I would recommend that they take the plunge. They really are an incredible tool for training and for later handling in the field. In addition, purchased with a remote beeper collar capability, they provide an additional margin of safety that can provide just the necessary tool, at just the critical time, for locating a lost or injured dog in the field. I never release a dog in the field unless they are wearing an e-collar/beeper unit.

The concern inexperienced e-collar users have is that, as a result of their inexperience, they may damage the dog. Some dog owners I've worked with have told me candidly that when they get angry they are afraid they will get carried away and use this tool punitively. These are both valid concerns.

So, let's talk about how an e-collar works and how to use one properly. First, e-collars are products designed to sell in a competitive mar-

Early day Tri-tronics training system using separate stimulation level plugs to control stimulation levels delivered by the collar.

Below: image illustrating the variety of present day collar designs.

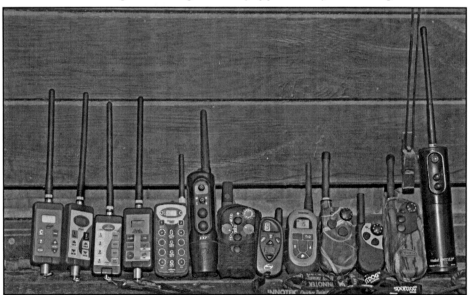

ketplace. Range and features determine price. They are advertised with certain bells and whistles. Some of these features are useful and some have a limited benefit.

Let's begin with stimulation levels and types. There are typically up to four types of stimulation modes built into collar units. The standard and most useful means of stimulation is "continuous." This means that the dog feels something as long as the button is held down. As a safety measure, collar units are designed with an override function that shuts off the collar stimulation after a period of continuous use. The length of time varies with the different manufacturers, but it is typically about ten seconds. This protects a dog from prolonged accidental stimulation.

In addition, collar designs are often equipped with "momentary" stimulation. This is one of the additional functions listed on the box of the medium to higher priced units. "Momentary" means that as long as you hold the button down, no matter how long you hold the button down, the electrical design will only apply a fraction of a second's worth of stimulation. This feature is incorporated into collar design and marketing strategies to appeal to folks who are inexperienced with collar use and are concerned that they will over apply stimulation. This design feature serves as a stimulation duration governor.

I personally view the momentary stimulation feature as unnecessary. Even an e-collar novice will quickly learn to operate a collar's continuous button as a momentary button. When one acquires his first e-collar, he should hold the collar's receiver unit in the palm of his hand and set it on the lowest level he can feel. The electrical contacts should be held inward against the skin. With the other hand manipulating the continuous stimulation button, the operator can practice applying corrections. In this way, one will quickly learn how to time and apply a correction, and how to use a continuous button as a momentary button. The handler substitutes brain and muscle interaction for the electrical circuit cutoff switch. When using a collar, I apply a correction and then wait to see a response from the dog. Then I discontinue stimulation. In my experience, this observation is what determines how long a stimulation should be applied. I would not pay extra money for a collar unit because it has a "momentary" stimulation function. I have found that when using collars with a "momentary" feature, I never have the occasion to use it.

The first two modes mentioned above apply an electrical stimulation the dog feels as a physical sensation at the point of contact (where the collar's receiver unit electrodes touch the dog's body). This is most frequently at the neck. As an aside, the collar can also be positioned around the dog's withers on the belly, or at the top of the dog's hips.

The third type of stimulation often featured in collar designs is auditory. A button is pressed at the transmitter and the dog hears a slight auditory tone emanating from the receiver unit strapped around his neck. Some unit designs incorporate an additional tone feature that sounds before, or at, the application of electrical stimulation, depending on how the transmitter was programmed. My personal preference is to control the auditory function manually.

I use an auditory association frequently in training and handling dogs in the field. I think it is an important and necessary feature of any collar design. I wouldn't want to use a collar that didn't offer this feature. The tone allows a handler to communicate with a dog without using anything that the dog might consider negative or suspect. The tone functions as a marvelous communication association to: 1) let the dog know there is an expectation pending and; 2) remind the dog that he is, in fact, wearing a collar. It reinforces the fact that if he chooses not to comply with the expectation, there is a means for the handler to enforce compliance.

The fourth type of stimulation function built into some collar designs is called the "page" function. This technology is similar to putting your cell phone on vibrate mode. The page feature causes the e-collar receiver unit to vibrate at the dog's neck. It is a physical association that literally touches the dog. This is a new development in e-collar design and, as of this writing, I have not used any of these units in training. I have played with some samples, however, and I can envision some real benefits in a training program, particularly with sensitive dogs. In addition, it is not uncommon for old gun dogs to lose their hearing and this would be a gentle way to communicate with the older canine contingent.

While modern collar designs allow the choice of stimulation type, they also allow the handler the ability to choose the level of stimulation that the dog feels. Earlier collar designs required that the handler preselect the level of stimulation the collar would deliver and program that option at the receiver unit worn around the dog's neck before the dog was cut loose to run. This meant that if a handler guessed too low and the dog decided to push the limits, the handler had a problem because there wasn't enough stimulation to force compliance from the dog. Modern collar units control stimulation levels at the transmitter and allow a handler to raise or lower the level the dog feels while the dog is running in the field.

Under the bells and whistles category, one unit may feature 4 levels of stimulation and another may have 30. This is a little confusing to the novice collar user. The additional levels are merely additional rungs on the

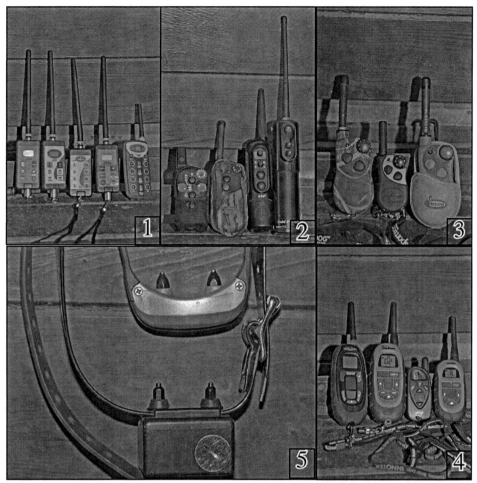

1) Previous generation Innotek transmitter designs; 2) Tri-tronics transmitters; 3) Sport-Dog transmitter designs; 4) Current generation Innotek transmitter designs featuring LED readout panels; 5) Old style bulky collar unit and modern ergonomic collar unit.

ladder. With a 4 level unit, 1 is A and 4 is Z. With the 30 level, 1 is A and 30 is Z. Having more levels does not indicate that the collar is stronger or delivers a higher level of correction.

Having said that, the number of levels is an important consideration. The proper way to introduce a dog to a collar is to find the level at which the dog barely feels the stimulation. The more levels the collar unit has available, the easier the fine tuning to find just the right level for a particular dog. Typically, a person can turn on the new collar, place it on the dog, and walk away. A half hour later, while the dog is otherwise occupied patrolling the backyard and the handler is watching undetected from the window, the handler applies a correction at the absolute lowest level the system allows. The handler then looks for a response.

Dogs and people are similar in that we all have varying responses to stimulation levels. I don't tend to feel electricity and a collar will need to be halfway up the ladder for me to feel it. It is different for others. While doing public presentations I will often ask the group if they would like to feel e-collar stimulation. Typically, a few folks will raise their hands. Included will be a big, burly guy and a small-framed woman. I set the collar to apply a correction at the unit's lowest level and pass it out to the interested participants. The man will take the collar, apply it to the palm of his hand, hit the button and react immediately: "EEEEEEEEEE!" The woman, with 100 pounds less body mass, will apply stimulation at the lowest level and say, "No, I don't feel anything." I'll have her go up incrementally through the levels until she says, "Oh, there it is. It tickles a bit."

For our dogs in the backyard we go through the same process. This is why it is beneficial to have multiple, incremental levels of stimulation. We need to see at which level the dog feels the stimulation being produced by the collar. What a handler is looking to see is a mild reaction from the dog. Often the dog will tilt his head and cock an ear. Sometimes he will lower his head and roll his eyes like a gnat is buzzing him. If the dog experiences discomfort or becomes agitated, it is too much stimulation. Once this level is identified for a particular dog, this will be the level used by the trainer to make associations during the training process.

Regarding the introduction of a collar to a dog, in the old days collar units used to ship with a dummy collar unit included in the case. I still see dummy collars offered for sale. The purpose of this counterfeit was to have the dog always wear the dummy unit when not training with the real collar, so that the dog would never realize that the collar and by extension the trainer was the responsible party delivering the electrical stimulation. It sounded like a good plan to me, but at ten bucks a collar, times twenty-five dogs, it was cost prohibitive. Instead, I ordered a couple dozen split-ring collars mail order, and then went to the local hardware store to pick up a couple dozen plumbing elbows. I attached the elbows to the collars with nylon cable harnesses and outfitted the usual suspects with some new accessories. What I learned is that dogs know everything all the time. I think they enjoyed the extra time it took for me to mess with them while messing with the dummy collars, but I sure didn't fool anyone. I still have a bunch of those collars, the ones that weren't buzz sawed by Brittanies, hanging on a hook with the dog stuff. Anyone out there want to buy some dummy collars cheap?

Another feature mentioned on the box is range. The absolute low end collars will function out to about one hundred yards. High end units will reach out to over a mile. Some manufacturers offer antenna upgrades to boost the effective working distance of their units. Most solid, serviceable collar units today fall in between 300 and 1000 yards.

Regarding range of collar use, there is a thing to be considered here. One of the rules of gun dog training goes: "a trainer should never apply an electrical correction to a dog unless the trainer can see the dog." Why? Well, it may be that the reason the dog isn't coming when called is he's just pointed his first covey of wild birds. This young dog is doing everything right, but the handler doesn't see the dog to know this and then the handler hits a button. Ouch!!! The handler has just added a month or two to the training process to undo what was just done.

The one exception to this rule would be with a hound running trash game and, in truth, most houndsmen know as much about what a dog is up to by listening as by seeing. Cover is going to determine how far a handler can see a dog. In trees, that could be thirty yards. Even in open grass a dog will find a cut to drop into or horizon out in a few hundred yards. I just don't know what a mile range is going to do for a handler.

Often, novice trainers are enamored at the thought of zinging a dog from an extreme distance. This just doesn't play out with practical use. In truth, once a dog has made the first couple hundred yards off the reservation, he is effectively out of control and anything a handler does with a collar at that point is damage control. The concern when a collar is used is that it may be more damage than control. The time to stop a behavior is before it gets that far. Problems should be dealt with no further than one hundred yards away. Actually, sixty is a better distance. If a dog is inclined to self-hunt or chase off game, than whoa him at 80 yards and keep him whoaed until you reach him. Release him to hunt again, and let him know that he is to mind his manners and work as a team player.

When using a collar, a handler needs to read the subtle cues a dog will exhibit. A handler is anticipating and interdicting behaviors before the dog acts on them. A dog needs to be well within a hundred yards for a handler to effectively watch the dog and accomplish this.

In most cases, a 300 yard range collar unit is ample.

The one reason to buy an additional range unit is to get one with a beeper collar unit. It's nice to know that the beeper can be activated at half a mile when there is more than one person searching for the dog. While searching alone, the limiting factor is the handler's ears. During a good day, in grass, on flat ground, with the wind just right, I might be able to hear a beeper out to two hundred yards. In trees, for me, the distance can shorten to sixty yards.

On the issue of rechargeable versus batteries, a collar shopper will need to determine what will work best for him or her. There are pros and cons for either option. Rechargeable units don't require the expense of buying batteries, but they do require frequent visits to an electrical plug. If one is working out of home or a motel, electrical plugs are easy to find. If, on the other hand, the handler is spending a few days out on a piece of big grass, the plug isn't available and it is nice to be able to pop in a throwaway battery. I have a number of collar units and it seems like I am constantly plugging stuff in to charge. When I mess up and forget or don't have an outlet available, the battery units sure come in handy. I just pop in a spare battery and we are back in business.

The final consideration on which collar design to buy would be a realistic evaluation of just how much collar the handler will be using during the training process. The options and features a collar unit ships with determines how high the price will be at the cash register. Does the trainer want a beeper function built into the transmitter? Will the trainer be working with multiple dogs? Two and three dog units are available. These multiple dog units ship with one transmitter keyed to operate multiple collars. In addition, some of the higher end units also allow the use of accessories such as bird launchers and backing silhouettes. These are expensive toys, but they really can provide just the right trick at the right time to polish out a dog in training. The trainer can buy the base high end training system with just a collar unit initially and leave the door open to pick up other accessories later when need and finances allow.

E-collar technology is evolving quickly, and like the computer industry, units become obsolete in a short period of time. Designs are becoming increasingly smaller, with more features, shorter battery recharge times, longer battery life, and a lower price tag due to marketplace competition and technological innovation. At this point, Global Positioning Satellite functions have been added to the newest models of electric dog collars so that a handler won't need to listen to a beeper or worry about losing a dog in the field. A handler in the field can just look at his handheld GPS unit and walk to the dog, whether the distance is one hundred yards away or six miles.

Author in the field toning a dog. Here he is maximizing the unit's range by elevating the transmitter above his head, thereby improving the transmitter's line of sight reception to the receiver unit worn around the dog's neck. (photo by Nicole Poissant)

Using an E-Collar

With the dog's proper collar features and stimulation level identified, a trainer can start using the collar to layer in associations during the training process.

There are two ways to use a collar: proactively or reactively. The common misconception regarding e-collars is that they are solely reactive training devices. The dog does something "bad." The trainer applies a correction and "punishes" the dog. The dog doesn't do it again. Specifically, the dog doesn't do it again, around the owner, while wearing a collar.

Certainly many collars have been used in this manner, and they are effective as such, but this approach is limited and not the most constructive way to utilize a collar in dog training.

Let me be clear. There are limited types of training where reactive collar use is beneficial and appropriate. An example would be avoidance training, where dogs are taught to avoid rattlesnakes, porcupines, poisons, automobile traffic, etc. This is covered in the reactive e-collar use training section of this book. Another would be with a willful dog who understands what he isn't supposed to do, but does it anyway.

In this section I will address pro-active collar use and training. An e-collar is essentially a communication device. It allows a handler to physically touch a dog up to 200, 300, or 500 yards away. That touch may literally be the sensation of an electrical tickle on the skin/contact points, a slight auditory vibration on the ear drum, or a vibrating page feature at the collar unit. This contact is perceived by the dog as an association, not a punishment.

When working with dogs, the zone of compliance is essential to keep in mind. This zone is typically from 10 to 30 yards away, depending on the dog's history with the handler. The dog's knowledge of the handler's training style translates into what the dog knows he can get away with. The compliance zone is the distance from which a handler can maintain eye contact with the dog. In dog culture, dominance is communicated through staring and body language. In addition, within the limited zone of compliance, the dog believes the handler can catch him and enforce compliance.

This zone of compliance is important. It determines the success of the training being conducted. As the training process evolves, different tools and methods are used to extend the distance of the compliance zone. In the old days, it was a horse. If a dog took a flyer, the trainer would simply ride the dog down and bring him back under control. This method does

Drag chains used to control a dog's range in the field.

work well, but you've got to have open country and a horse.

It is possible, however, to come at this problem from the other side. Instead of a trainer getting faster, a dog can be made to go slower. Methods like putting rubber balls on short pieces of cord dangling from a dog's neck will cause the dog to stumble if he moves too quickly, or so I've been told. My experience is that dogs run right through it. As a kid, I remember one of the old trainers using a two foot piece of 6"x 6" post attached to a dog with a short piece of chain. I have a short length of extremely heavy boat anchor chain that I hang off a dog to slow him down. Even if the dog manages to make some distance, the drag leaves a walking trail to follow

205

him up with.

Modern day trainers mostly use check cords to extend the range of the compliance zone. We hang a rope on a dog and the dog learns that with the extra weight dragging behind him, the handler has a tool to extend the compliance zone from ten yards to around thirty. The trainer can step on that rope and reel the unruly canine in for an accounting if he decides not to comply.

Ropes longer than thirty feet get hard to manage in the field. I have tried using check cords as long as fifty feet; but as a practical matter, I usually find myself grabbing a twenty foot check cord and then running like hell to catch up with the rapidly disappearing end of the dog-dragged rope. Getting first your boot, and then your entire body weight somewhere on that moving line of dragged check cord is an acquired art.

All life resists control and if a dog doesn't have to comply, eventually he won't. With a quick dash a handler can usually catch an unencumbered dog out to ten yards. Past that, something non-human has to be employed, and the ideal tool for this is an electric collar.

The e-collar doesn't have a tether, weight, or any other kind of coupling to fail, tangle, get caked with cow feces, loaded up with cactus spines, or otherwise complicate the trainer's life. It is a small, self-contained little unit hanging around a portion of the dog's anatomy, always there to "touch" the dog at the trainer's discretion. It works farther than the trainer's glare can be seen and his soft training voice can be heard.

Pro-active collar use means that when the dog feels a light tactile stimulation from the collar, the dog references it to an association he learned in previous training and the dog has the opportunity to comply. The stimulation the dog feels is not perceived as punishment or a negative. It is simply a request or command being given by the handler.

You will notice that I wrote: the dog has the opportunity to comply. Here is where the real strength of the collar as a training tool comes in. The collar is ideal for convincing a willful, overly enthusiastic, or otherwise non-responsive student that it is in his best interest to comply immediately to the first gentle request (be it mild electrical stimulation, an auditory beep/tone, or a vibratory stimulation). The collar, as a device, has built-in options should a dog refuse "the opportunity to comply." The trainer can go incrementally up the stimulation level ladder and convince a dog to be pro-active and comply with the first light tactile request and avoid experiencing a more stern directive.

This pro-active association should be kept as simple as possible so that its influence is not diluted through arbitrary use. I reserve that

The benefits of electronic collar training: three well-mannered team players pin a Nebraska ringneck pheasant.

association for the whoa command. For a pointing breed this would be to freeze standing on his feet. For a flushing or retriever breed it means "Hup" or "Sit" and freeze in a seated position. With this association, the collar becomes a freeze frame device. When a situation in the field starts to train wreck, I can blow a whistle, stop everything in place and unravel it before it goes any further. I cover this training in depth in the section on Whoa/Hup breaking.

Little Lucy Belle Celmer, of Tucson, Arizona, a female Jack Russell terrier, charges a defanged rattlesnake to grab and throttle it. She intends to bring it home and play with it on the sofa. Note the transmitter unit in the author's hand and the collar unit around Lucy Belle's neck. Lucy Belle quickly learns that this is a mistake. The timing of the stimulation to coincide with the strike of the snake teaches Lucy Belle that this is a critter she never, ever wants to meet again. From this instant on, when she hears, sees, or smells a rattlesnake she will run the other way. (photo by Nicole Poissant)

Reactive E-Collar Use

Avoidance Training Overview

Left to his own devices, an unsupervised canine can get himself into some real problems. The maladies of both the natural and man-made world seem to be ever present, and always at the worst possible time. Things like roads or rattlesnakes can prove fatal for a dog. The long list of things to be avoided would include: skunks, roadways, porcupines, trash bins, javelinas, mom's garden, a neighbor's livestock, etc.

It is possible to teach a dog to avoid a thing before he encounters it accidentally. This saves all parties concerned a beating and eliminates the need to write large checks to veterinary practitioners.

This book has covered proactive e-collar use, but now let's explore the flip side: reactive e-collar training. This happens when the dog does something he shouldn't, and this is followed by a sure, swift and negative electrical reaction. This causes the dog to associate the negative event with the thing that immediately preceded it. The dog makes the association that to court this thing is to court "disaster." The more negative the initial electrical reaction, the bigger the "disaster" that follows it in the dog's mind.

Dog training is about creating associations for the dog. The first step in avoidance training is to identify all the possible associations a dog can make with the thing that is to be avoided. In order to identify those associations, it is important to realize that a dog's world is broken down into three external sensory forms: sight, sound, scent. For a canine, the most trusted of these three is scent. If a dog sees or hears something he has to smell it to verify and understand it.

This concept is foreign for humans because it is different for us. If we hear or smell something, we need to see it to verify and understand it. Humans often seem to think that if they show a dog something they are making the most profound impact possible. For the dog, the most profound impact is made when he is directed to smell something. What a dog can smell, he remembers most completely.

When studying the thing to be avoided, find what scent associations are possible for the thing or situation. This is ultimately where the training will need to lead, and generally this scent association is the point at which an electrical stimulation is applied to teach a dog to avoid the thing or situation in the future. An example would be the scent emanating from an animal like a snake, skunk, javelina, or porcupine. If an easy scent source is available, the avoidance training can be easily structured to teach the dog never to go near such a smell, and by association, creature again.

Some avoidance training items or situations are more complicated than others. In some instances, there really aren't any usable scent associations for the trainer to structure avoidance training around. An example would be roadway or car avoidance. Here the only scent available would be the smell of asphalt and the exhaust generated by automobiles. Both of these scent cues are secondary to the sight and sound generated by the same roadway and autos. These are not controllable scents to be used as associations in an avoidance training session.

Teaching a dog not to chew garden hoses would be another example of a scentless training situation. There really isn't any scent associated with garden hose chewing that could be used in a structured avoidance training session. Without a scent association to train to, avoidance training possibilities are limited. That is not to say that it isn't possible to create a negative association for the item or situation in the canine's mind, but it is more complicated and ultimately less profound for the dog.

I have used structured avoidance training heavily over the years in conjunction with gun dog training to convince dogs that there are some things in the world that are bigger and badder than they are. Dogs learn this lesson easily when it is taught properly. Here are some examples of structured avoidance training.

Rattlesnake Avoidance Training

This is an example of the easy, scent specific avoidance training outlined in the previous section. I do a lot of this work here in the West because snakes are an ever present danger to dogs.

As with any avoidance training, it begins with the thing to be avoided. I use a live rattlesnake. The animal is de-fanged as a safety necessity. In the case of a snake, all three association sources, sight, sound, and scent are readily available for the dog. Snakes move so they are easy to see. They rattle and make a distinctive sound. They emit a distinctive scent that dogs discern easily.

First, I define the training area. I set aside a safe staging area the dog identifies as snake free, safe ground. This is the area where his owners are waiting for him after each successive phase of the training. Secondly, I set aside the snake area where the dog will meet the snake. Then thirdly,

A de-fanged Western diamondback rattlesnake used in Snake Safe training.

directly downwind from the snake area, I set aside a small, fallback, safe area to get the dog away from the snake during the initial introduction. Wind permitting, this small safe area is on the far side of the snake. The purpose of placing the snake between the dog and the safety of his owners is that he will have to go by the snake again to get back to mom and dad.

    I begin by placing an e-collar on the dog and hooking on a twenty-foot check cord. I make it a point to get the dog comfortable with me during this process. I greet the dog on his level by kneeling down or sitting with my back facing him as he approaches. I drape my arms down the sides of my body and make my wrist available for the dog to press his nose against. I let the dog approach me from behind and I do not make eye contact until after the dog feels comfortable and initiates eye contact. Finally, I give the dog my breath by breathing into his nose. I do this to fast track the introduction process and to allow me a chance to get a sense of the dog. I am looking for temperament and personality traits. I want to see if the dog is bold or standoffish. I am evaluating what level of stimulation will be necessary to get the desired effect with this particular dog.

    I have a helper place the snake on the ground at the predetermined snake area and then move off to the side so that he is out of the dog's view. This snake wrangler stays close enough to monitor the snake's position and keep the snake in place. The snake wrangler is there to make sure that the snake avoidance training session doesn't turn into an impromptu snake hunt.

Leading the dog on the check cord, I approach downwind of the snake and stop short at the predetermined small safe area, approximately ten to fifteen yards downwind from the snake. At that point, I stop and get down on the dog's level. I talk and pet the dog. I give him my breath. I wait to see the dog relax. Remember, dogs are very place specific. I establish this spot as safe so that once the dog has been exposed to the snake and is in some degree of panic I can immediately get him to a safe position, calm him down and reassure him. Once the dog's body language goes soft, he is ready for the introduction.

I lead the dog upwind through the snake's scent stream to the snake and wait for the dog to realize it is there. Of the three possible cues (sight, sound, scent) available to the dog, the first to get the dog's attention is almost always sound. Dogs almost never see a snake and will step right over it unless the snake moves or rattles, and they don't generally react to the scent until they know there is something there. I push the dog forward until he is at the snake and the snake responds to the dog's close proximity with a warning buzz.

At this point, the dog seeks to locate the source of the sound and sees the snake. Generally, one of three things happens. About 10% of the dogs tuck their tail and run the other way. Another 10% don't blink or hesitate. They drop their heads and charge the snake to grab it, and never take the time to smell it while charging. The final 80% upon hearing and seeing a rattlesnake, stop any forward movement and look to use their noses, circling downwind of the snake to smell it.

If the dog cuts and runs, I do not apply an e-collar correction. I wait until the second test. I just lead the dog back to its owners.

If the dog is a member of the second group and charges the snake without taking any time to smell it, I do apply a correction. That dog then joins the 80% group which, upon hearing and seeing a snake, circle downwind to smell it. When all three associations are present (the dog sees, hears, and smells the snake), I apply a severe correction. I am looking to make a profound impression upon the dog. I often tell dog owners during the pre-training orientation that we are here to traumatize the dog for life. This is the intent of the training. We want it vividly etched in the dog's mind that whatever this funny looking, funny sounding, funny smelling critter is, they don't ever want to go near it again.

I make this association with a stiff, short "bite" delivered by the collar. The e-collar is the ideal tool because stimulation literally feels like a bite. When muscle is stimulated by electricity, the muscle constricts and at the end of the stimulation the muscle slacks to its pre-stimulation tension. The neck muscles of the dog during stimulation feel like they are experiencing a bite.

The level of the stimulation needs to be very stiff. Each dog is different, and one of the most difficult parts of avoidance training is guesstimating just how much will be necessary to attain the required impact. A professional trainer could do hundreds of dogs over the course of a year. As he or she meets each new dog, he or she has a very short window of lead time to make the determination of what level will be required for each dog. I always make it a point to err on the side of caution and start low. If I need to, I can reset the stimulation level at the transmitter and apply a stronger correction. The dog's temperament, personality, and age all factor into the stimulation level choice.

I time the delivery of the stimulation to reach the dog when the dog is closest to the snake. With experience, a trainer learns to gauge just how close the dog is willing to go and holds off applying the correction until that instant. I wait to give the dog all the time he needs to get as much of the three associations, sight, sound, scent, as he wants. This memory will need to last the dog's lifetime, so an extra second or two of the initial contact is time well spent. After the correction is applied, the dog will never willingly go near another snake again.

Training Problems

"Good judgment comes from experience. Experience comes from bad judgment."
                                                        Mark Twain

---

So, it's the full catastrophe. The train has derailed.

There is a trajectory to life, just like a rocket launched into the sky. It starts with some rumbling and hissing. Then there's a lot of spark and fire, commotion and confusion. A controlled explosion. The projectile leaves the ground slowly and gets a little squirrelly, fishtails for a while until it builds up enough momentum to develop the speed needed to straighten up and fly right.

This is what we face when we bring on a young dog. I don't want to diminish the problems that a trainer can face with the first couple of years of a bird dog's life. Trust me, I know. But there is stuff we can factor in to help the two of you get through it.

First, let's acknowledge the best case scenario. Sometimes, everything goes right. A young pup grows into a model citizen and progresses in a perfect arc across the sky. If the heavens have been that kind to you, then just keep your mouth shut. We don't want to hear about it.

If, on the other hand, you are like the majority of bird dog trainers, there are going to be "things" that come up as your dog progresses into adulthood. I trained professionally for a number of years and I have seen some strange behaviors show up in young field dogs.

Dogs that run out for the retrieve, scoop up the bird, and just keep going...until they get to the end of the check cord where they dig a hole and bury the bird.

Or the scary smart, generally German, dogs that unweave the chain link wire on kennel gates. With their teeth.

And the male pudelpointer who used his front feet like hands and would empty out his neighbor's food bowl, then pull the individual kibbles over into his run one by one for inhalation.

That same male pudelpointer, once he progressed to planted pigeons, would establish a point, look at me, then look at the bird. He would then jump in to grab it. He wanted what he wanted.

None of these were bad dogs. They were just creative progenies in the making. So, what do you do when challenges crop up?

First, let's look at the ground rules. Canine culture is predicated on dominance. If there isn't a dominant entity above them in the pecking order, their culture dictates that they fill the slot. Often, the train wreck sort of problems that pop up during training happen because a young dog is looking for advancement. If a dog doesn't believe that you're the boss, then there are going to be problems. I'm not saying here that if you're the top dog, stuff won't happen. What I am saying is that when it does, you'll be in the position to get it sorted out and get past it. Would you want a dog who wasn't willing to give it a shot to get to the top of the ladder?

There are 3 foundation posts needed in building a training program: dominance, proximity, and patience. Ideally, these phase in gradually as you raise a puppy. It may be that the dog comes into your possession at a year old, and so you start there. Whatever your situation, tend to and be conscious of these foundations.

What about when something unpredictable happens with your young bird dog? The particulars aren't necessarily important. There are a multitude of things a dog can do to leave you talking to yourself. What I want to give you is a general plan on how to proceed under most circumstances.

What do you do and how do you react?

First, is this a problem you need to deal with at all? The axiom in dog training is you don't correct a fault without creating another fault. By extension, be careful what you classify as a fault for fear that you will have to correct it and in the process really screw up the dog.

Can you live with it?

The dog rolls birds in his mouth and runs a victory lap before giving it to you. Yes, I probably could live with this. Something like this will go away naturally with repeated exposure to dead birds.

How about if the dog has decided that he is not going to hunt for the gun and wants to chase birds out of the county? No, this is something I would view as a fault and get sorted out. In the fixing, the dog falls in line and straightens up. Great!

If, on the other hand, you address the fault and your dog rebels and refuses to comply, you have a problem.

When your dog does something you take exception to, there will be a train wreck. It will happen in one of two ways: 1) your dog will boldly try to go over the top of you and get his way, or, 2) your dog will fold, shut down and refuse to comply and, once again, get his way. The "way" that we are referring to here translates to some sort of interaction with birds. The list of possibles is long and varied as in bury, chew, chase, eat, lick, pluck, ad nauseum.

If your dog takes the direct route and tries to go over you, then you have a fair fight. Don't let him have what he wants, and don't lose your temper. Restrain and remove him. The hunting or training session is over. Save it for another day.

Go back to the structure you used in yard training and physically control him. Let him know that if he wants the bird, he has to go through you to get it. If he wants the controls removed, he will have to mind his manners. He'll make a deal and modify his behavior because he wants to get the bird. After going back to yard basics and then returning to the point where you had the problem, physically control the dog until you get compliance and the dog proves himself. Depending on what you used in your early training, run him with a check cord, hobbles, pinch collar, e-collar, etc. Use the tools he is familiar with and that have shaped compliance in the past. Expect compliance. Leave no option but compliance and your dog will have no other choice.

If your dog goes the other way and shuts down, it gets trickier. It can be very frustrating to deal with a folding dog. This is passive-aggressive behavior in the truest sense of the word. What the dog is doing is throwing a bargaining chit on the table. He wants you to deal with his affect and not the original behavior. You are being lured. Don't go there.

If you try to force the dog into doing what you want, you won't like what happens. He will escalate his behavior and it will go downhill from there. If you get angry and frustrated, the dog wins.

You have just entered the realm of psychology. Force will not help you here, but envy, jealousy, boredom and time will.

The most effective tool for boldening up a folding dog is other dogs. Leave the problem dog out of the mix, but close enough that he has to watch everybody else having fun. Abandon him in the center of the chain gang so that he gets no rest and has to be pulled by every other dog in the mix. Run him with a check cord so that when the other dogs get into birds, he is held back, at a distance, and can only watch. Let his buddies make retrieves on birds lying five yards off the end of his taut check cord. When you see him chomping at the bit, then slowly stir him back into the mix.

It's harder when you have only one dog to work with. In this case, use birds to your advantage. Fly pigeons for the dog that he'll want to chase. You may need to give him a little slack and let him chase. You can reel him back in later, as needed.

Often, with a passive-aggressive dog, problems evaporate of their own volition once the dog believes that he isn't going to get his way. Wait. Watch. Let time pass, back off and try again later. Go back after a refresher course in yard work where the dog experiences some positives. Is the dog a little immature? Does he need some time to grow up?

If a dog likes birds, you can fix anything. Think it through and reason it out. Go slowly. Always ensure you are in position to physically control the dog and enforce commands. Stuff has a way of sorting itself out.

I used to tell clients that it takes three months to train a dog. One month for yard work, one month for bird work, and then a final month for fixing anything that's broke. We are at the end of two months on this calendar. We need to take an inventory and see what needs attention on the dog. Each dog is an individual with a unique personality and temperament. I was always amazed at the strange takes and reactions individual dogs had to different portions of the training process. It is mostly unpredictable. Sometimes faults would come to the surface like gun shy, bird shy, man shy. Self-hunting. Generally, there was clean up work on retrieving needed. In this next section I will address more specific issues.

Buster and Boo

Buster was a looker. He was a fifty-pound, perfectly marked male tri-colored English setter from our foundation stock blood. I had gotten him young, at less than a year old. A young man who had bred a few litters of setters had whelped the dog from one of his breedings and kept him to raise. He shared his house with a roommate who had been leaning on the dog about barking or some other thing. I don't remember the particulars other than the dog had been worked over pretty good, and he had become fearful and unresponsive. The owner didn't know how to fix it and, at the dog's young age, the owner couldn't handle him. I don't remember if the roommate was still in the picture, but in truth the question was academic because the damage was done.

The dog was man shy and ultimately proved to also be gun shy. This was all fixable, but unfortunately there turned out to be a deeper problem. The dog was oppositional in nature...if he were human, he would have been called a jerk. I would bring Buster into the house thinking we were finally turning a corner, and about the time I would think I was seeing progress, he would urinate on the furniture. All we had to do was trust him to have him turn on us. He did this because he could, and he did this to maintain status quo. He didn't want to be better. He liked staying the way he was, and if peeing on the book case got him there, so much the better.

I put him through yard work and made bird introductions, expecting the switch to flip on as we went through the process. We got through a piece of the gun shy only to have him start self-hunting. Again, he did this because he could. He did respond to kindness, but his response was ultimately manipulative and self-serving. He lived with us for a year or so. I could have trained three dogs with the time I put into him. It finally broke for me when I looked over one day and saw something on the roof of our neighbor's house, chasing their cat. I walked over to discover Buster was the culprit.

A bird hunting friend needed a backyard dog for his parents back East. I offered Buster. I drove Buster over and when my friend saw the dog, he said that he would like to give him a try in his own string before bringing him to his parents. I wished him well. He messed with Buster for a couple of seasons with the same host of oppositional behaviors I had seen: gun sensitive, man shy, self-hunting, and urinating in the house the minute you turned your back on him.

One day while trying to hunt him out on the flats, Buster took yet another self-hunting flyer. My friend did the obligatory looking and waiting, and then he wished Buster well. He had come to the same conclusion I had, that he was best shed of him. Buster would no doubt find another house in which to pee on the furniture. He did have his good looks, after all, to fall back on.

Boo was a female GSP around a year old. Someone dumped her at the edge of town and she turned up at one of the old guest ranch communities needing water. The owner took her in and tended to her. Then she called me and asked if I knew of anyone missing a bird dog. I hadn't gotten any calls. She asked if I wanted the dog as she couldn't keep her there.

I drove over to see the dog. She was a well bred, old blood GSP. She was also gun shy and bird shy. She was a little touchy around people as well. She looked like she had been wandering the desert for a time. She was thin and worn, but she responded to kindness. It was Halloween, so I called her Boo.

I brought her home and offered her food. She responded with panic eating. It was clear she had been short on food for a while. We brought her in the house and tried to reassure her. It took a few days, but she came around. Unlike Buster, she was very honest when she was afraid. She would look in my eyes and say this concerns me, and then she would trust me to walk her through it.

We got the gun shy fixed and then put her on birds. She never looked back. We crossed her over to wild birds and she just did everything right. She always had a kind response when I asked her to trust me one more time with the next thing I needed her to do. When she was ready, I sold her to a single dog hunting home where she would be valued and hunted.

The difference between Buster and Boo was resiliency. Bad stuff had happened to both dogs, but they had responded in very opposite ways.

Shy: Gun, Bird, Man

The full calamity. The things that end in shy, like gun shy, bird shy, man shy. These will show up somewhere in the process and may derail training before you get to the end of the second month. It is hard to shoot birds for a dog if the dog is cowering under the trailer. It's hard to complete whoa introductions with a dog if he rolls over and urinates on himself when the trainer gets within ten feet of him. Shy has to been addressed when it appears. A handler can't move forward because the "shy" acts like a brick wall. All forward movement stops. That's the tradeoff for the dog, because the behavior is designed to control the situation and insulate the dog from something that frightens him.

Notice that I address gun shy, bird shy, and man shy as one term, "shy." It is the same condition and most dogs that are so afflicted, are some percentage of the three. The genesis of "shy" is either genetic or man-made. With either of the above causes, the cure is birds. If the dog likes birds, he can be fixed.

If it is genetic, it can be tough to address. It's doable in many instances, but you often won't get a 100% fix. All you can do is to do the right things and wait until the dog comes around. The dog may come quickly. Or, it may take time, with multiple wild bird contacts and two to three seasons under the dog's collar.

The other cause is man-made. Something bad happened somewhere involving some portion of the trilogy of gun/bird/man. A dog was completely unprepared: the bird blew up in front of a young dog's face.

Image of a "shy dog." The fear in this dog comes through the photograph. This dog learned to trust again and completed training, able to hunt and work birds.

Following the explosion of scent, commotion, cackling and feathers, explosions of sound pounded down on the dog from the funny looking stick right above him. The human that he was with got frustrated and preoccupied. The human may have gotten angry when the dog was afraid to approach the feathered thing now lying on the ground in front of him. There was another smell on the feathered thing now. Red and warm. Coppery. Then the angry human picked up the feathered thing and tried to push it into the dog's mouth. The human kept yelling something. It sounded something like "fetch," whatever that means. When the dog balked, the human got really angry and…See how it looks from the dog's side of the exchange?

The dog's age is the mitigating factor in this. If the dog referred to above is eight months old, he has some level of maturity and context to deal with the insult. If, on the other hand, the dog is three or four months old, the insult can become mythic and buried, and really difficult for a trainer to uncover.

Whether in "throwaway" dogs I got from the pound, or dogs brought in for training, eventually pieces of "shy" would show up in some as we started the training process. Often, the first appearance would be a reaction to the blank gun when the shot was first introduced in yard work on the whoa post. I was good at fixing shy dogs, and over the years

I've done lots of them. When a person trains professionally, dogs aren't brought to you because everything is going right. Most of the time, something has derailed along the way.

When I first started training, I would query the owner to get a take on what had caused the problem. Some of the dog owners were sincere when they said they didn't know. Others described an event that may have been the genesis of the problem. Some were uncomfortable and less than candid because they knew they had done something dumb. Ultimately, I stopped asking. I was making some folks uncomfortable and knowing didn't change anything. If a person ends up with a hole shot through his foot, it is kinda irrelevant how it got there. The thing to be concerned with is fixing the hole.

The way to fix shy is to evaporate out the fear. It generally takes about a month. First, you build trust with the dog and show him something he likes. In this case, that would be birds and other dogs who like birds, if such dogs are available. Next, you wade through the fear with him until he comes out on the other side of it. The two requirements are that the dog trusts the handler and likes birds. If you don't have that, then there is nothing available to use to pull the dog through the fear.

Some trainers make the distinction between gun shy and gun sensitive, and the distinction is valid. Shy happens in degrees. The dog may get a little stoic at the shot or he may run and cower under the truck. He may back up and stand behind the handler when a bird flushes, or he may see a bird being loaded into the pouch before a training session and jump back into his box on the trailer and refuse to come out. Obviously, one is less of an impact on the training process than the other, but the cure is the same for both.

Something bad happened during training around guns and/or birds and a human was present in the exchange. A trainer must reintroduce the three elements of gun/man/bird in a structured, safe manner. The reintroduction needs to be cut up into small increments. The initial increments should include only the good parts and none of the fearful stuff, until the dog gets to liking it. Once a handler has the dog on board, then he starts mixing in a little of the bad, letting the bad neutralize out, and then stirring in a little more. The two of you will reach a balance point where the dog figures, "What the heck, I'm willing to tolerate this to get that."

Some of the cures I see touted for gun shy are really counterproductive, if not downright destructive. They focus solely on the sound of gunfire and attempt to fix the problem by desensitizing the dog to the sound. It's not about sound. It's about what the sound associates with for

Do not discharge firearms around an unsure dog to see if they are gunshy, and thereby make them so.

the dog. Stuff like banging pots at dinner time or audio tapes with gun fire woven into them don't make a lot of sense to me. Then there's the proverbial fix: drive your dog to the shooting range and park off a ways from the sound of the discharging weapons. I can only image how confusing that trip would be to a dog.

Birds are left completely out of the equation, which is a serious omission. The purpose of the exercise is to get birds. A shy dog may get to the point where he trusts gunfire and people together at the same time. However, once the dog is put on a planted bird, and the fear of birds is part of the association for the dog, the dog's elevator goes right back up to the top floor and the trust that was built up goes out the first available window.

Start by bonding the dog to other dogs that like birds. I always gave new arrivals some decompression time to romp in the dog yard and make friends. Two of the best tools to recover a shy dog are envy and jealousy. They may be afraid to proceed, but the fear doesn't have near the motivating power of having to watch your buddies have fun while you

223

are excluded. If a handler has other bird dogs, or can train with other dog owners, this will expedite the entire process.

I begin by assessing the dog around people. How much of a connection does the dog have with me? Does he respond to kindness and affection? Some of the dogs I got out of dog pounds were in shock and completely shut down. It took awhile for them to come out of it. Some of the customer dogs were collapsed with fear, "There has been a terrible mistake. I don't belong here. Who are you? What am I doing here?"

I never pushed those dogs. I just watched them, waiting until the time that I saw them come out of it and start playing with the other dogs. That could take a few days, but when I saw them playing and rough housing I knew we were ready to start. It was important to make them a part of the group and when the time was right, I did that by making them part of the training string.

Depending on how much is rolled into the "shy," the first road block may appear on the chain gang at the beginning of yard work. This would be "man shy." Will the dog come to the gate to be taken out and snapped onto the chain gang? Is he the last dog hanging back at the end of the yard while everyone else is jumping at the gate to get out into the training yard? All you can do is wait. Wait to see when he comes out to the front of the fence and watches his buddies having fun training. When he spends the training session watching from the other side of the wire, you know you got him.

Clip him on the end of the chain gang and let him coast for a couple-three days while the other dogs are worked. My training chain gangs had 8 to 10 dogs on them, but yours can hold two or three. Use the number of dogs you have available. This is the time to start with a man shy dog. If he folds or cowers when you get near him, ignore his affect. Treat him like every other dog. When you get to his slot on the chain as you work each dog, sit down with your back to him. You will have to determine the distance by gauging his comfort level. At the distance where he gets apprehensive, sit down. I had a book and a mirror. The book was to kill time, and the mirror was to check on the dog without alerting him to the fact that I had any interest in him. It may take ten minutes, it may take forty. When the dog stopped monitoring me and laid down, or better yet broke eye contact and dozed off, he was done for the day. For the next session, we closed the distance a bit.

This sounds like it could take some time, and it will in the beginning. There is a cascading effect and the dog will come along more quickly the longer he is in training until you reach a point where it crumbles and you break through the wall and can leave it behind.

At some point you will be sitting close enough, with your back to the dog, that he can smell you and press his nose against you. Let your hand extend on the ground behind your back so that the dog can get access to your wrist. When the dog is comfortable with you petting him and making eye contact, use your breath. Speak into the dog's face so he can get a read on you. Give the dog some house access and use intimacy to build trust. When it's time, clip him on the whoa post and go through some laps.

The dog will come around.

The next place to expect a problem is on the whoa post when the introduction of pigeons and gunfire comes into the training process. If the dog has a problem here, it will be evident. You can continue and complete the whoa training, just omit what you need to from the process, whether it be birds or gunfire or both. Hold those introductions until you get to the field. Once the dog is in the field, the problem can be addressed effectively.

When you get to the field, start with birds. Keep field whoa work to a minimum. Let the dog chase and have fun. Don't do anything that is going to put pressure on the shy dog or make him feel there is an expectation. You are looking for the thing that makes the dog excited. Typically with the bird dog breeds, it's chasing flyers. With the versatile dogs it could be flyers or wing-pulled pigeons thrown for the dog to carry and retrieve. With the retriever breeds, it's wing-pulled birds thrown as retrieves.

Keep the number of drills per training session low. The dog needs to be left chomping at the bit and wanting more when you put him up at the end of his session. If you have trouble getting enthusiasm from the shy dog, pick out his best buddy and give him the treatment and let the shy dog sit it out and watch. After two or three sessions, try him again and see if he hasn't come around. If he's still a little lackluster, have an assistant help you and work both dogs at the same time so it's a contest to see who can get there first- only rig the game so that his buddy wins the race and gets to the bird. That should do it.

When the shy dog is pumped up and zooms out to chase or pick up the bird, start adding in a little of the negative stuff.

Throw a bird and wait until the dog is in the thick of the chase or is just about to get to a bird on the ground. Have an assistant at an extreme range from the dog fire a muffled blank pistol. The blank gun can be surrounded by a pillow or buried inside a game pouch. Experiment beforehand so that the sound of the discharge is appropriate. Err on the side of caution. Don't make a mistake on this.

You will no doubt see a response from the dog. However, the bird is right there in front of him and it was a very minor noise. He may stop or hesitate for a moment. Praise him lavishly when he comes in and continue the drill without the sound of the shot. No more shot for the first session.

Do it again the following day, but with a second shot on the follow up drill. Go for three on the third day. Roll the sound of the blank gun into the drill incrementally raising the volume of sound as the tolerance of the dog increases. Just as we did in earlier training, play with the sequencing of the cues the dog is getting.

Initially it was whoa/bird/chase/get to bird/shot. Move shot up the line until the drill runs whoa/shot/bird/chase/get to bird. Done properly, for the dog, the gun report will be an announcement of a coming bird. When this shift occurs, then start moving the blank gun closer to the dog. Take the muffle off the blank pistol. Point the gun in the direction of the dog so that the sound waves carry directly to him. Switch to a 410 shotgun, again at a distance, pointed in the opposite direction and then gradually work in closer and closer to the dog. Switch to a twelve gauge.

Do this incrementally, until your assistant is flying birds in front of the dog and shooting them for him. Then switch to the handler taking over the shooting chores where the dog has everything happening right out in front.

At this point the shy is behind the dog. You may see pieces come floating out later in further field work. Don't make an issue of it. Once you cross the dog over to wild birds he will be fine and can be considered cured.

Blinking

When a person trains for the public it is fair to say that, generally, one doesn't get the dogs where everything went right. In worst case scenarios, the dog shows up as parts in three or four separate boxes. The owner hauls them in one at a time, puts them down on the counter and says, "Can you fix this?" On one of the boxes is an old, dirty masking tape label. Scrawled in big black permanent marker across the tape is the word: Blinking.

Blinking is a major fault and refers to a dog that deliberately pretends he sees no bird there. The dog figuratively closes his eyes and refuses to see. Around humans, these consummate actors have no interest in birds.

"See no Evil." A blinking dog pretends that birds are not there, rather than be around birds and people at the same time. Something bad happened somewhere.

      This is a very tough fault to fix and the problem is amplified because this is the affect of a very smart dog. It takes intelligence to pull off this ruse and make it believable. Remember that the primary motivator we have when working with gun dogs is their interest in birds. Without that, the tool box is empty. The dog with no interest in birds is a dog you cannot fix. Therefore, the only redress with a blinking dog is to make him feel safe enough to be around a human and a bird at the same time- again.

      Now, here is the deal breaker with a blinking dog. It is rare, and I can count the dogs on one hand, but it is possible to get a bird dog that really doesn't have an interest in birds. If you can read dogs fairly well you will see it quickly and thereby save both you and the dog a beating. Find him a nice backyard somewhere, preferably with children. He will probably make an exceptional family dog for some lucky folks.

With the exception of those few dogs that just didn't get it at birth, blinking is a man-made malady. Something real bad happened somewhere. Often, it involved youth and electricity, or some combination thereof. The dog figures that he just isn't going to be put in the position of being in the same square mile as a bird and a human being ever again. In truth, this is a shy dog, meaning man shy/gun shy/bird shy carried to another level. Once the trainer is able to break through the blinking, "shy" is waiting on the other side and it will also have to be addressed in training accordingly.

With this sort of fault each dog is unique. The best way to illustrate this, for the purposes of this book, is to tell you some stories.

Let's start with two dogs who are examples of dogs who found nice backyards because they really didn't have an interest in birds.

The first was a beautiful male tri-colored English setter out of a well known Mid-Western kennel. A gentleman I know had purchased three puppies at the same time to raise up and train himself. One of these puppies, the tri in question, had never shown any interest in birds. The other two came on and made bird dogs, and this gentleman kept waiting for the tri's switch to turn on. At a year and a half he gave up and asked me if I wanted the dog.

I generally kept a list of folks who were looking for dogs. This tri sounded like a good candidate to train out and sell, so I told him to drop him by.

When he arrived, he was a sweet dog and a real looker. He wasn't afraid of people. The only thing that was out of sorts was that, as is the philosophy of the breeder, the male had been castrated.

I have never met the breeder personally, but I have read his literature regarding his preference for castration. My sense of him from his writing is that he is very opinionated and I think this had been the influence that caused the dog's owner to alter the dog.

For the record, let me state that I think this is a really dumb thing to do. It changes a dog, and if done too young I think it may ruin him for hunting. I do know that in the dog yard these dogs are not perceived as male by the other males and are excluded from the male culture of the yard. When castrated dogs came in for training, it generally took some time for them to be included in the yard and mostly, they never came around completely. I would wait and watch to see them start lifting their legs to urinate. I know that it is common for humane societies and Veterinarians to recommend this procedure, but I would caution gun dog owners to just say no, thank you. My best guess is that the castration was an influence in this dog's lack of interest on birds.

The tri, as I stated, was a sweet dog and easy to work. I included him on the chain gang. I ran him and flew pigeons during training sessions. He kinda ran. When he showed no interest in birds I tried using jealousy by pitting him against other young dogs on the string, to no avail. I watched him in the yard with the other dogs. While every other dog was tracking the pigeon trying to land in the yard to steal dog kibble from the feeders, he laid off to the side and slept. When I had loaded the other yard dogs on the trailer, I put wing-tied pigeons in the yard for him to get. The birds walked around him as he yawned. I used other youngsters in with him to see if their getting the pigeon would pique his interest. He watched the fun from the sidelines with no interest in participating. If my memory serves, I spent about two months on him with zero progress.

Then a young single mother called me to say that her child's dog, a male tri-colored setter, had gotten out of the yard the day before and was killed on the road. She was desperately trying to find a replacement setter and they are hard to find in this part of the world. Cost was a concern. I told her that she was in luck. I had just the dog and today the dog was free. She picked him up that day. I heard from her a time or two over the next couple of years. The dog was a perfect fit, and I was glad to hear that he had found the right place to be.

Next, is the story of Smokie. I received a call from a woman in the Phoenix area who did dog rescue work. She told me a man had left the remnants of a litter of German shorthair puppies with her to be placed. The puppies were six-months-old when she first received them. They were three male dogs who were pushing a year old, and they needed homes. As a gun dog trainer did I know anyone that was interested?

I mentioned the call to an acquaintance who had asked me to keep an eye out for a free dog. This person picked up one of the dogs and brought him by, and he looked good. Additionally, I also told a friend who was interested in a shorthair. He picked up the second dog and left him here for training, and he trained out pretty well. It weighed on me that one was left there alone, and so after a couple of months I arranged for my wife, Nicole, to pick up the remaining dog. I figured we would train him out and get him placed somewhere.

The story Nicole told of the facility was entertaining. Bless the woman's heart that had taken the puppies in, but her rescue work was with little dogs. Toy poodles, if my memory serves me. She lived on a very small lot in a double wide trailer. Nicole said there were about thirty of the little poodles and they moved en masse like a school of tropical fish and towering over the moving mass was this large male shorthair.

He, unlike the other two, was overweight. He had also been castrated. We brought him into the dog yard and he was sweet enough, but you could tell he felt out of place. A herd of poodles, this was not. I rolled him into yard work on the chain gang and whoa broke him. My intention was to try to bold him up. He did the repetitious training well, but never really clicked as a member of the pack. He didn't roughhouse and engage with the other young dogs in the yard. This wasn't unusual with castrated dogs, so I waited to see when he would turn on.

He never did.

I pushed him with birds. I timed him out and had him watch other dogs with birds. We brought him in the house. I tried all the usual tricks. It just never happened. It came to a head about four months into his time here. I had been trying him on and off to get a response. He had ridden out on the trailer with me to train on the flats. I set up a training course and he refused to walk with me. He ran back towards the trailer and hung about a hundred yards out in the tree line. I called him over and he refused to come. I finished working dogs and loaded gear and he refused to come. I got in the truck and drove on down the road. I wanted to see him follow me. I got to the end of the two track and gave him a few minutes to show and he didn't, so I turned around and found him frozen in the same spot in the mesquite. I walked out to put a lead on him and bring him in. I could see in his eyes that it wasn't anything personal, this was just a thing that wasn't in him to do.

We ran a newspaper ad. The mother of a young boy made an appointment to come and meet Smokie and he went home with his new family. I got a follow up thank you note from Smokie a year later, transcribed by his new owner's hand. It was complete with pictures of Smokie reclining in his bed besides his new young master's bed, and an image of Smokie running on the golf course where his new charge walks him daily. Years later, I got another letter from Smokie's family saying that Smokie was getting older and slowing down, and that if I came across another Smokie they had a place for a new family member.

All I can take from it is that Smokie knew where he needed to be more than I did.

Third, I have a sad story. I was offered a very well bred, Crockett blood tri-colored male setter. The owner sent me pictures through the mail. The dog was a real looker. He was probably four or five years old at the time. He had been trained by a pro as a youngster, and then transferred to another pro training on the prairie for campaigning during his derby year. He had a derby win. The owner said that he wasn't using him and he was going to seed. Could I use him for a good price?

"Well, yeah, I could. Particularly for breeding," but beware the gift dog. Then we negotiated down the price to puppies if a litter was produced- never a good sign.

I arranged a time to drive out and pick up the dog. It took two hours to get there and the last few miles were on dirt, out and beyond. I found the obligatory rural mailbox and gate, and turned onto the acreage. As I traveled up the entrance road I passed a large horse corral with a large covey of Gambel's quail scurrying through to get out from in front of me. I made a mental note.

I parked and walked around to the back of the house as instructed, and there sleeping on the back patio was one looker of a setter. He got up to greet me. I talked briefly with the owner and asked if we could take the dog for a loop around the property. I steered us back around the front of the house and lined the dog up to go through the corral. I watched the dog cross the quail scent, drift sideways and avoid the birds completely. He did it so effortlessly I was impressed. He was one hell of a dog, or would be when that was fixed.

I asked the owner about the blinking and he said there had been some issues. He said it had happened during his training and each trainer had blamed the other. The sum total was that the dog was sent home broken, and I don't mean steady. My take was that the owner had tried and didn't know how to fix it.

I brought the dog home and started trying to work through the problem. He was really good. If he knew a human could see him, any birds present did not exist. He would not acknowledge the bird in any way. Yet, I could watch him through the curtains while he was in the dog yard and he was at the head of the pack trying to snag pigeons out of the air as they came to raid the dog kibble bins and splash in the dog water troughs. I took him back to basics on the chain gang and whoa post. I figured to let some time go by and see if we couldn't evaporate some of the problem out. He settled in, but whatever had happened to him had left a reinforced brick wall in its wake. I took it for progress that he was more open in the dog yard on acknowledging the pigeons flying overhead when I was in the yard with him.

This was at the beginning of Arizona's late summer monsoon cycle. When the first afternoon monsoon lightning storm hit, thunder sent the dog straight over a six-foot chain link fence. The dog disappeared and

I found him several miles away down by the main highway. The scenario repeated again. At the slightest rumble in the distance, the dog departed. I found that the setter could scale the dog yard chain link at will. When I couldn't be there to monitor the sky, I was forced to contain him in a covered dog run within the dog yard we reserved for females in season, a run which we affectionately refer to as Alcatraz for its impenetrability.

The dog didn't handle lockdown well, and it seemed that any movement forward on his training was negated by his reaction to the rumble of lightning. One step forward. Two steps back. In addition, I was acutely aware that when we got through the blinking, gun shy was on the other side. Judging from this dog's reaction to distant lightning and thunder, the gun shy was going to be a doozy.

One afternoon, during a monsoon, the setter found a way to breach Fortress Alcatraz and disappeared into the storm. I lost the better part of the day recovering him. I knew that it was only a matter of time before a car hit him on one of his forays. I made a call to the original owner and drove him back to the safety of his porch. He would have the freedom to hunt his horse corral Gambel's covey free of human involvement.

Lastly, I have a story about one of these difficult blinking dogs that actually worked out. A gentleman called me with a two-year-old male shorthair that was not working out. He stated that he had been working with the dog and the dog just wasn't reponding. That can mean a lot of things. I asked him for some history. What was his training background? He stated that he had an older male GSP he had trained that was doing well on desert quail. He had done the same training with the new kid, but he wasn't coming around. I told him to bring the dog on by.

When the dog arrived, I looked him over. I could see from his lines that he was old school shorthair. No foofoo show breeding or screw loose AKC field trial blood. He was the real deal. He wasn't afraid of people. He seemed to genuinely like his owner. He was burley and gruff, but so was his owner so it seemed to fit. I put him in the dog yard and right away he got surly with another male, as I would have expected, so we arranged private quarters in the corner suite for him.

The owner told me that the dog wasn't interested in birds, so that is where I started. I found that he really wasn't interested in birds. A wing-tied pigeon could walk between his feet and he wouldn't look down, which tells you something in and of itself. I could tell by looking at him that whoa and manners weren't going to be an issue. With his blood that would come fine, but all would be for naught if we couldn't get him started on birds.

I asked the owner for more information. Was he housed with this older male GSP? I wanted to know if the older male had somehow cowed him off of birds...not an unusual thing, particularly with male German dogs. The owner said no. The two dogs had separate runs removed from each other.

I asked, "What contact has he had with birds? How were birds introduced?" The owner said that there really hadn't been much because he showed no interest in them.

I asked, "What about tweety birds or doves landing in his run... or flying overhead? Does he look up? Does he try to grab those that land in his run? Do you have quail coming through your property that he can see?" I was looking for anything here.

The owner responded, " Well...no! There's just the chickens."

"What chickens?"

The owner then explained that they raised and fought fighting roosters, and that they had several hundred spread out and staked on half barrels on the property and surrounding the dog runs. I was beginning to get a picture.

"Have you ever disciplined him for killing a chicken?"

The owner stated, "No." I made a mental note to reserve judgment on whether I believed that.

"How does he respond to the chickens?"

The owner stated, "He ignores them."

"OK," That gave me a place to begin.

Over the next few weeks I was able to spend time with this gentleman when he came out to train with us, and I grew to like and respect him. I learned that fighting roosters were one of his passions and he was very involved in breeding and fighting birds. I had the opportunity to attend a fight and was impressed with his level of knowledge and commitment to his birds. And...I believed him when he said he had never disciplined the dog for killing a chicken that got in his run. But I knew he didn't have to because he had raised that puppy. The little guy learned early on, at a very deep level, how much his owner valued those birds. It would have been easier to fix the dog if he had gotten in trouble for chomping a chicken or two. It would have given us a baseline to start with.

The dog had private quarters so I tried giving him wing-tied pigeons and leaving them in his run. I switched to quail and chuckars. I left a gate open so the adjoining run was full of dogs salivating to get at the birds wandering around his feet, which he refused to acknowledge. Nothing worked. I would have to go to Plan B. I called the owner to get his approval and I explained that you don't correct a fault without creating another fault. He told me to get it done.

I went back to the old books that were written before humans got so clever. Back then you used the basics: dominance, hunger, sex, jealousy, a whistle, and a rope.

We began with hunger. The one way we could get him to condescend to look at a bird and jump start his prey drive was to make it his only source of food. I removed the dog's food bin in his run. Every morning I came into his run and laid out a fresh killed pigeon on the gravel. It took me about half an hour to do my kennel chores, and then I returned and removed the uneaten pigeon. If my memory serves me, it took about five days. I had opened a couple of the earlier birds up a bit to make them look more like food, and I was contemplating doing the same with that day's bird when the boy came up, grabbed the bird and inhaled it.

He repeated the maneuver for the next couple of mornings, and then I noted that he was anticipating my arrival, or more importantly, the arrival of his feathered breakfast. When I saw this I upped the ante. All the previous birds had been fresh killed. Now I delivered him wing-tied birds he had to kill himself. When he got the hang of this, then I started bringing in several healthy homers and I would fly two or three birds for him to chase and not catch before I dropped a wing pulled bird that he could catch.

So far, so good. We now had a dog that would eat the first bird of the hunt, provided he was hungry. I now needed to jazz him up and get him chasing birds just for the joy of chasing them. I brought him into the training schedule and let him ride the chain gang while I flew homers over the top of the dog string. He didn't give me much, but I did notice that he didn't like our dominant setter named Jasper. Not a lot, but a little. Thus, when I began his whoa breaking we went to the next step: Operation Hate Jasper.

Every morning when I fed our boy, I would put Jasper in the run next door so only a line of chain link separated one from the other. Every other morning I would put down his food pan, let him get a few mouth fulls of kibble, and then remove the pan and give it to Jasper on the other side of the wire to finish. The sounds coming out of the shorthair would have run off a badger, but Jasper was the dominant male in the yard and he wasn't letting it bother his meal as he cleaned the pan.

When he was bristling good at the sight of the white dog, I then started short tying him in the training course I had laid out for the morning. I positioned the shorthair to the side of a planted pigeon and I brought the setter in to work the bird. I would let the setter point and hold the bird. I would fly it out of a remote launcher, and as the bird flew away, I would throw a drop pigeon just short of the end of the tether holding the shorthair. First, the pigeon was fresh killed and then later, to up the adrenaline, I used wing-tied birds.

The shorthair would watch the setter come in to work the bird. Initially he just sat at his stake, but after a couple of training sessions he started rising up and tugging at the end of his tether to get closer to the flush. I upped the ante a few more notches by dropping two or three pickup birds at the flush, and I let the white dog have all of them until it looked like the shorthair was going to pop the chain holding him to the tie-out stake. Finally, I threw a drop bird within the shorthair's confinement circle. He grabbed it before the setter could and carried it back to the middle of the stake. I went in and praised him, accepted the bird, praised him some more, and then gave the bird back to him and walked away. We were ready for the next step.

I placed the shorthair on a check cord and had a helper hang onto the end of the rope to keep the shorthair clear of killing the setter. We sort of worked the two dogs together. First, the setter went in on the bird, but quickly we reversed it and gave the shorthair the opportunity to get the bird before the setter. Over a period of a couple of weeks, the shorthair turned on and started seeking birds. Of course, the setter was tied up on the chain gang behind him in case he thought about balking the find.

He did start pointing. It was partly instinct and partly whoa breaking, but once the switch flipped he came around. I ran him with females he wasn't inclined to kill and worked on backing and minding his manners. As expected, we had to go to the force table to address the fault we had created by allowing the dog to eat birds. It took four months and he did make a dog. I wouldn't want to be a white male setter around him, but he did make a dog.

These are some illustrations of blinking and how individualized each case can be. Blinking is not an easy fix, and it may be beyond the capability of an amateur trainer to address. Tarrant once told me that it's the hard cases that make a trainer, and once you have fixed a few blinkers you can honestly call yourself a trainer.

Self-hunting setter outfitted with drag chains to control his range.

Self-Hunting

Self-hunting is another common problem that shows up, particularly in the field trial bloodlines. With the structure used to control a dog during yard training and during the early stages of field work, the self-hunting dog is effectively thwarted. At some point, though, a handler has to let go of the reins and that's when the dog has the opportunity to take a flyer, if it is so inclined. It will typically begin when the dog disappears upon entering the tree or brush line, or when dropping over a rise. His affect may be that of non-concern until he is out of view, and then he switches over into warp drive in a straight line to leave the handler behind.

A dog can be controlled by whoaing when he reaches the edge

of expectable range, but all this does is postpone the inevitable. This is something that has to be dealt with, and two months into training is a good time. The training and means of control are in place. There won't be any confusion on the dog's part. He knows what you expect and he knows what he wants to do.

Let me be clear about the issue of range here. Flushing dogs have to work within gun range. That means thirty to forty yards.

Pointing dogs have a different function. It is common for folks to say that a pointing dog should also work within gun range. This point is often espoused by people with untrained or ill-mannered dogs. I don't care how far a pointing dog ranges. If he is properly trained, he will point and attempt to hold any birds he finds no matter the distance from the gun. In reality, the mark of a good dog is one that moderates its range according to availability of birds and type of cover. A good dog will push until he finds birds, expanding his search until the birds are located. Once into birds, that same dog will tighten up and start working singles within gun range. It is the same with cover. On flat, open grass the dog will run at two hundred to four hundred yards out, or more. In heavy, visually obscured brush and trees, the same dog will work in close from thirty to eighty yards, depending on the thickness of the vegetation. A dog who loses his handler will circle back, cut the handler's back trail, come running up from behind and then back out to front to resume hunting.

A pointing dog is said to cover ten miles to the hunter's one. I don't want to have to walk those extra nine miles. That's why I have a dog.

With self-hunting, the problem is not a matter of range or distance from the gun. It is a failure to work to and for the gun. This is an important distinction. We have the means to control distance. What we need to impact is the dog's intent.

Set the dog up to fail. Let him do what he wants to do, but be prepared before the fact. When I had a self-hunter, I would keep him under wraps with structure until a warm day came along. I held him off until the very last training slot of the day, when the sun was nice and bright. I got everybody else stowed on the trailer so I didn't need to come back and tend to dogs. I loaded myself up with water and we went for a walk.

I would take him into the tree line where I knew he would make a break and I let him do what he wanted to do. When I saw him disappear on me, I gave one single whistle cue, "come." I never made another sound. Then I started walking straight out on his line of departure. It might be that I had to walk a while before I saw the dog. At some point, I would have a line on the dog and he would notice me. What the dog wanted was for me to be vocalizing, and whistling, so that he could track my location and thereby avoid me.

What happens by default in those situations is that the hunter keeps track of the dog. That's not the proper order. The dog needs to be keeping track of the hunter. I don't have time for those kinds of games and this is one of the few things in handling that I will not tolerate. If a dog tries this nonsense on me, there will be consequences. We have all seen a handler in the field hacking a dog with voice and whistle, afraid that he or she is going to lose sight and thereby lose contact with the dog.

No, thank you.

When that dog sees me coming, he figures he's in trouble. I don't give him any cues. I don't make eye contact. I just keep bearing straight down on him. The dog will pick a range that he is comfortable with and keep bumping off of my approach to maintain that range. It generally falls within 50 to 150 yards. The dog is postponing accepting responsibility for his transgressions.

The dog is wearing an electric collar and I could use it to stop and whoa him. But, to do so would make me the responsible party, and what he needs to learn is that he is the responsible party. If I used the collar, the dog would learn that when he is feeling the weight of the collar around his neck he has to comply, but turn him out without a collar and he is as good as gone.

Some of these walks lasted two to three hours and when the dog eventually folded we were several miles away from the truck. Ultimately, what did the dog in was heat and lack of water. His bump range would shorten and he would begin to run from one shady spot to the next, trying to cool down. When he let me close to twenty yards, he was done. That was the length of the check cord he was dragging. I would step on the check cord and walk up to the dog.

And then we got it fixed. I left the dog with the absolute certainty that he never wanted to have that conversation with me again. I draw a very hard line here. This kind of behavior will get a dog killed while hunting in the field. The dog believed that I was crazy enough to follow him until he played out and there was no escaping me. I was the means of control, not an electric collar. Whether he had one on or not, I would find him and walk him down.

After a breather, I would water the dog, give him some time to cool off and rehydrate and then we would begin our walk back. Only at this point would I resume interacting with the dog. From that point on, with very few exceptions, he minded his manners.

It can happen. There is a genetic component involved here, and there is the rare dog that, given the chance, will always be looking for an opening to take a flyer. I bought a little German girl that was a registered AKC GSP. She had been bred by a field trialer and sold as a puppy to a man looking for a foot hunting dog. He didn't get what he was looking for; she, in fact, looked to be pure pointer minus the tail. The man couldn't control her self-hunting, so I bought her to train out and sell.

There was a standard joke regarding the breeder of the dog, that the way he culled his pups was to let a litter reach six months of age. At that point, he took the lot of them out into the desert and turned them out for a run. Whatever came back, he kept.

Some of these dogs will loosen up when they mature at about three to three and a half years old, but it is a long three to three and a half years. In fact, you can never really trust that the dog won't take off on you, generally at the worst possible time.

This brings us to the topic of lost dogs.

Lost Dog

Dealing with a lost dog is an important subject. If a person is going to consort with bird dogs for any length of time, he's going to lose, or should I say misplace, a few.

When I was training professionally, each morning would start in the gray light of predawn with my head leaning over the steering wheel, the training birds and gear stowed on board, and a full dog trailer. The prayer would go something like this: "Please, God! Don't let me get a customer's dog lost or snake bit today." With that I would pop the emergency brake and roll down the hill to start the day.

Half the prayer was answered. I never got a customer's dog snake bit, but over the years I have lost a few, both customer dogs and my own. Thinking back my memory is a bit fuzzy, but I know it's been a couple dozen or so.

If I go back to my beginnings, as a teenager, I lost my first setter working a marsh along the interstate in California's Central Valley. I looked for three weeks and never found her. Even today, I still get a tinge of that empty feeling any time a dog goes over the hill and is a little long on the check-in.

Lost dog sign on Willow Springs road, Pinal county, Arizona.

When one has experienced losing a dog, he will forever remember the frantic helpless feeling that comes when the country gets huge and that small speck of a dog is nowhere to be seen. What was once compact and familiar becomes vast and inhospitable. When a dog takes a flyer, the coyote's fading light serenade shifts from romantic to ominous.

There are things that are helpful to know when a dog goes missing, comforting stuff like "they almost always show up." While it may seem wishful when a person is in the middle of it, the truth is, they almost always do. Sometimes they show up a little worse for wear, particularly in the desert country I live in. Yet, even if they've been gone a few days, they mostly show up, mostly intact, save for the accusatory glare in the eye that says, "I turned around and you weren't where you were supposed to be! How could you abandon me out there?" In the dog's mind, it works out to be our fault.

There are some things to do when a dog takes a flyer. First and foremost, before the fact, never ever put a dog on the ground without a sturdy D-ring collar around his neck, carrying complete and accurate contact information. Like the head waters of a river, everything that happens once the dog goes missing flows from this. Once the dog is gone, there is no way to undo this critical error.

I know stuff happens, I've been guilty of it myself. I cut a dog some slack because he doesn't like a tight collar; then, when I'm in the field working with another dog, he pulls at the chain gang and then pulls right out of his collar.

Or, in my part of the world it's getting to the point where phone number area codes are changed about as often as underwear. It's a minor annoyance unless you have thirty dog collars with a now incorrect set of phone numbers. So, I order the new collars and then take the old ones and hang them on a hook with the dog stuff, fully intending to (one day soon) drill off the incorrect brass info plates and put on correct ones. Then a new dog comes in, and in his first afternoon of freedom in the dog yard, the new addition chews the collars off of half a dozen of his fellow canine cohorts. I need to train in the morning, so I grab some collars off a hook and don't bother to blow the dust off to proofread the contact info.

Life intervenes and this sort of stuff happens, but I can speak from first hand experience: it is hard enough worrying about when and how a dog will turn up without knowing that, through a really dumb move, you omitted the one best chance of recovering the runaway.

Never, ever put a dog on the ground without a sturdy D-ring collar carrying complete and accurate contact information. Enough said.

Moving on, with a gone dog, one of two things may happen. Either you will find the dog or someone else will. Give the missing dog a couple of hours to turn up. During that time, get to a phone and call to make sure someone is sitting at the contact number waiting, should a call come in. Check back frequently: if someone has managed to corral him, you want to go pick him up as quickly as possible.

When I leave to make that call or to check adjacent roads, I always leave a bucket of water and a pad or coat that the dog will recognize by scent. It has been my experience that most dogs will turn back up where the truck was parked, eventually working their way back to the place where they started. Usually, they will show up around dark or a little while after.

My main concern during the interim time is roads. A bird dog will do fine out for a lark in the wild, but they don't fare well around automobiles. I don't train around roads and I don't run inexperienced dogs off the side of pavement. We have those luxuries here in the Southwest. I know many folks reading this don't have that kind of open country, so be careful.

After checking roadways I go back into the area and walk out from my parking spot, being sure to put the truck back where it had originally been parked. I don't spend a lot of energy or travel too far across country before getting back to the truck. My job is to wait.

There are, however, mitigating circumstances to take into consideration. Was the dog pulling a check cord or drag chain? Those could hang him up and prevent him from making his way back.

If it was 105 degrees that day or if the dog was dragging gear, I didn't have a choice. I had to presume the worst and assume that the dog was at risk or hopelessly tangled up somewhere, unable to get back. In those cases, I would call my friend, Don Prentice, and say, "Don, I got a flyer." He would meet me and we would take a line out across the desert carrying binoculars, 2-way radios and water. Sometimes we got lucky and would find a lost dog by walking him up, but mostly we didn't. Often, the dog would turn up back at the truck of his own volition, while we would get back late afternoon, thirsty and shredded, only to find our MIA snoozing and well-hydrated, thumping his tail in the shade under the dog trailer.

Of course, there are the obvious things to do while searching: blow a loud whistle and call the dog's name. Over the last few years, if I had any uncertainties regarding a training dog or while guiding with our own field dogs, I ran them with a beeper collar that I could turn on at a distance. Before that technology was available, I used dog bells. I would use anything to give me some help locating the dog by sound. Many times, a dog will howl if he's hung up or if he hears you in the distance. Particularly after dark, the sound carries a long ways and it is one of the most welcome sounds a searcher can hear.

If the dog doesn't turn up by nightfall, I plan on spending the night and roll out a sleeping bag on top of the trailer. When I was training, this was the point at which I called the owner. Mind you, this is not a call a dog trainer enjoys making, "Yeah, remember that valuable dog you had? The one you trusted me with and gave me a lot of money to train? Well, last I saw him was about 7:00 am and he was headed out onto the flats. Yeah, it was hot today. Yes, I kind of know where he is, give or take twenty square miles. That noise in the background, actually that's not him. Those are coyotes howling."

Recovery pens for lost dogs at a public hunting area, Waimea canyon, Kauai, Hawaii.

      I can go my whole life without making another one of those phone calls.

      If the dog isn't back by morning, you start over again. Some dogs have taken two or three days to return. Obviously, the longer the dog is gone, the greater the chance for a non-recovery. I would like to see a dog back within a few hours, but it's not the end of the world if that doesn't happen. After three days, I get concerned. If my memory serves me, I don't think I've ever had a customer's dog gone for more than three days. I have, thankfully, been able to recover all customer's dogs who ever took a flyer. All of them returned patchable, if not healthy, and no worse for the experience.

      If the disappearance stretches into the second day, get some flyers printed up with a physical description of the dog. Even if you get a call just reporting a sighting of the dog, it will help focus the search. Contact whatever civilization is in the area and let them know you're missing a dog. The folks at our local Circle K convenience store have helped me recover several dogs. One of the few pay phones in our area is located there, and this is the first place where people will stop to call. I also call the local Game & Fish Ranger, as well as other hunters that I know will be out on the flats. Like a bad penny, sooner or later the dog is going to turn up.

      How long can a dog be gone and still show up? My friend, Larry

Hull, from Somerton, Arizona, located in the state's southwestern corner, lost an Elhew pointer on Allen Flats in the southeastern portion of the state near Willcox. That was on Halloween, 1998. The dog had a penchant for self-hunting and he hunted himself right out of sight about 9:30 in the morning. The area is surrounded by some remote country. Larry searched for two days to no avail. Finally, he had to pack up and get back to work. He drove the 330 miles home to wait for a phone call that didn't come.

Larry had long ago figured the dog for gone when the phone rang on May 27, 2000. A man calling from Sunsites, Arizona (a wide spot in the road, 80 miles south of where he had lost the dog) told him his dog was hanging out in front of the local bar. He had taken Larry's phone number off the dog's collar. The man said he saw the dog there every morning between 6:30 and 7:30 am. The man gave Larry his name and phone number. Larry asked the man to gather up and hold the dog for him. The man replied that he didn't think he could do that and ended the conversation. Larry tried to call him back but the number wasn't any good. He tried the name in the local directory to find that no such name was listed. Larry was left with a dilemma. Was this his long lost pointer?

He rearranged his schedule and got the next day's work covered, drove halfway across the state, got a couple of hours sleep in a motel in Phoenix, then continued driving at 3:00 am to arrive at the bar at 6:30 am.

Larry, feeling a little foolish about the chances that the tip would actually pan out, was not surprised when he arrived at the bar at 6:30 sharp and found no dog in attendance. He waited and no dog showed. Since he figured he had already paid the price of admittance, he toured some of the surrounding roads while whistling and calling the dog's name, all to no avail.

On the way out of town, Larry hit the main road and pointed his truck towards home. As he passed the bar, which sat in the distance across the highway, he looked over and saw what appeared to be his dog sitting by the front of the building. He immediately cut his steering wheel hard towards the bar and drove through the center median up to the dog. Sure enough, it appeared to be his.

He got out and called to the dog, who studied him for a moment and then recognized his former owner. The dog came to him. Larry petted the dog, dropped the tailgate, and swung open the door on the pet porter. Larry told the pointer to load and the dog jumped in and made himself comfortable. Larry told me that when they arrived home that afternoon, he let the dog out of the box and the dog immediately went to his old kennel run, loaded in and laid down in the preferred spot that he had left almost two years earlier.

It just goes to show that you never know. Larry was sure that the dog was long gone. The chances of the dog showing up after almost two years were nonexistent. Go figure.

A friend called last week to tell me that his little female pointer named Dixie, which I had raised and sold to him, had been lost out on the flats for the last two days. She took a flyer after a departing pronghorn antelope. We talked strategy, and I tried to allay his fear and uncertainty. It was in his voice. He had spent the last two nights lying out on the dog trailer listening to the coyotes howling, and waiting for her to return. I told him that they almost always turn up. We made a plan for him to follow.

There were some other things, however, like an undertow in the bend of a deep river, that we didn't approach: sometimes, they don't return; sometimes, the drive home is too quiet when the dog curled up in the blanket, on the seat besides you, is dead.

She turned up after a few days. A phone call came in: "Hey, you missing a little white dog?"

She'd lost some body weight, but nothing that steady grub and some sofa time wouldn't cure. I guess she'd planned on a pronghorn meal that didn't materialize. She'd given her owner a few bad days, but she didn't seem too concerned about it. Lying on the sofa, twitching in animated dreams, she no doubt was catching pronghorns. She's resting up for her next grudge match.

If you live with bird dogs, you live with uncertainty. Any time you cut one loose, there's the chance that they will keep on going and thus the old saying applies, "Ships are safe at harbor, but that's not what ships are for."

That is the nature of bird dogs.

Two shorthairs waiting for their next grudge match to begin.

Fighting

This can be a real problem. When males do it, it can simply be a boy thing, related to dominance. When females fight, they are often trying to kill each other.

Mostly, dogs get along. They live in a pack and jostle for dominance in that pack, but it is mostly puff and posturing. Every now and then, however, a dog comes along that is a fighter. Sometimes, you get a pair of dogs that are fine with other dogs, but just want to shred each other. We have two shorthairs living here with us now that wear soft muzzles whenever they have access to each other. They are the best of friends, it's just that on occasion they try to kill each other. If memory serves me, after the last bout it took 36 staples to close up one of the dogs.

Some breeds are more prone to problem fighting than others. The German dogs can be terrors. When setters go at each other there, is a lot of saliva and bedraggled hair. The setters sort it out, break for a doggy bone, and then congratulate each other on how good they looked in the fray. When the German dogs get involved, there is blood sprayed across the walls and large sections of skin hanging off of the winner. The loser looks worse. And God help a non-German dog if a German dog jumps him or her. The German dog immediately starts staple punching his opponent's legs and neck, and tearing holes.

Years ago, a friend asked me if I had ever really seen a dog fight. I asked him what he meant as I sensed there was a story coming. He told me about being in a small, two seater airplane. He and another gentleman were flying to another state to run dogs in a trial. Riding along with the men were three dogs. Because the plane was very cramped they could only fit in two pet porters behind the seat, so one of the dogs was loose in the limited remaining space. The loose dog was a male golden and one of the crates was confining a male Chessie. Apparently, the two dogs didn't like each other. Somewhere mid-flight the Chessie had had enough of the loose golden and came through the side of the pet porter. Because of the limited space, all the men could do was yell. It went on for a time and my friend said that he was quickly preoccupied with wiping the spraying blood from the inside of the windshield so the pilot could see to maneuver the plane.

Predictably, the Chessie won. The golden ultimately went limp and the Chessie gnawed on him for awhile like a chew toy. They got the plane on the ground, assuming the golden was dead. Upon getting the dogs out of the narrow confines of the back of the plane, they found that the golden was still breathing and got him to a vet. The golden survived, but my friend said the dog was never the same.

A dog that fights, really fights, is a real problem. There are no fixes or cures for this. For the rest of that dog's life he can never be trusted around other dogs. The current politically correct party line coming out of the humane societies and veterinarian industry is that all males should be castrated and this will take care of the problem. The claim that castrating a male dog will stop him from fighting just isn't true from my experience.

My introduction to Martin, a gentleman that I trained several dogs for over the years, came via a young male German shorthair named "Red." Martin lived in New Mexico by way of his home town, Lubbock, Texas. He had bought the dog sight unseen from a trainer in another state. Martin had the trainer ship the youngster straight to me. If memory serves me, when Red arrived he was about eight months old and still very much a puppy. He was a little shell shocked from being bounced around, so we brought him in the house for a time and then transferred him into the dog yard.

Socially, he did everything right. He deferred to the older males. Things went well for about a month and a half, until I caught Red stiff legging a male tri-colored setter, three years his senior, named Concho. I left it to Concho to work out, which he did. He rolled Red over onto his back and hovered over him. Enough said. Red was appropriately repentant and I figured that was the end of it.

Red grew a couple of inches and decided to try it again. I was letting the dogs out of the main dog yard gate for a run and I generally did it by seniority, calling out a dog's name and then letting him through the gate, one dog at a time. Concho had been a few dogs out by the time I got to Red. Just enough time for Concho to make a loop and swing back by the gate. At his turn, Red came through and spotted Concho. The shorthair accelerated and hit the setter broadside like a torpedo. Red never looked back. The two males locked up and the donnybrook began. They rolled and spun and all I could see was hair, saliva, and blood coming out of the ballet of blurred motion, like wood chips coming out of a planer. The water hose and broom had no effect. We live on a hill which is steep sided and a couple minutes into the battle the canine ball rolled down the slope to the dirt access road leading into our property. Concho outmatched Red, but every time the old setter would let go of the shorthair, the shorthair would spring off the ground and jump him again. I ran back up the hill and got a throwing rope, got a loop on the shorthair and was able to pull him off and tie him to a fence post and end the fight.

I called Martin after I finished doctoring. Martin was concerned to hear about the fight. Red was going to be kenneled with another dog and Martin didn't want to have to deal with problem fighting. I heard from Martin a few days later and he asked me about having Red castrated. I told him I didn't think it would impact the fighting issue. Martin had a real problem because he couldn't have a fighting dog in the kenneling arrangement that Red would be entering after his training time with us. I told Martin I would arrange the surgery if that was his wish. Martin opted for the procedure and Red had the surgery.

It didn't change Red's desire to fight one bit. He had separate quarters from that point on in our kennel, and he never missed the chance to challenge Concho, and other male dogs through the wire for the remaining time that he was with us.

I generally hear from Martin every year or so to talk dogs or birds. Several years after Red went home, the phone rang. I heard Martin's West Texas drawl coming through the phone receiver.

"Web!"

"Yes, Martin."

"Well...I bought me a pomeranian!"

"Really, Martin," I replied. "Have you finally come to your senses and given up running bird dogs?"

"No," Martin returned, "The wife of the guy that owns the kennel where I was boarding Red let her pomeranian out when Red was loose. He killed it deader than a rock."

If the dog is a fighter, there isn't a fix. You can never trust that dog around other dogs. It is a condition that will have to be managed for the rest of the dog's life.

The Broom Dance: What to do about a Barking Dog

It is probably safe to say that the oldest conflict between man and dog is barking. Since the very beginning, when the two of us started sharing the same cave, some sleepless fellow rolled over, picked up a bone remnant of the previous night's dinner, and flung it into the dark hoping to hear a yip. He threw it towards the sound that his canine companion was making and uttered the caveman equivalent of, "Stop that *#@$!%& noise!!!"

Things haven't changed much in 200,000 years. The string of expletives has the same intent and one of the most often asked questions is: How do I stop the barking?

Well, it's probably best to start with an acknowledgment: You can't completely, nor would you want to. Just like the cave man looking for an early warning when the cave bear came sniffing around, there are times when you want a dog to bark. However, there are probably many more times when you would prefer that he didn't. So, it's really a matter of controlling barking, not stopping it. Dogs can learn when you want them to bark and when you don't. They also learn when they can get away with barking and when they can't, because fundamentally, one of the great joys in a dog's life is to bark.

Let's start with the "sure fixes." Things that are billed as simple and easy always come with a price. The most draconian method is to have the dog's voice box surgically removed. That seems to be as sure a fix as possible, doesn't it? However, I had a dog in for training that had undergone this procedure, and the resulting effect was worse than the original barking. She no longer barked, to be sure, but the surgery didn't impact her enthusiasm for the process. Following the procedure, she sort of whistled. Not a pretty, lyrical, melodious kind of whistle, but a grating, fingernails on the chalkboard kind of sound. Her barking was executed with the same frequency and gusto as before, but minus some volume and range. This meant that far neighbors were spared, but close range listeners

The night time choir convenes.

had a whole new sound to contend with.

The whole concept of surgically altering a dog to control barking is just a bad idea and should be dismissed as a non-option.

The other "sure fix" is an electric bark collar. This option really works, but again at a price. Some of the early units were really kind of a pain to operate. They worked off of magnetic keys, which routinely made people mutter to themselves in frustration. In addition, the units required constant recharging. I don't know about you, but I don't need another thing to remember to plug into the wall at night. The latest generation of collars are well-engineered pieces of equipment that run on rechargeable or interchangeable batteries. These units are dog-proof and will keep a yard quiet. They have been billed by some as the cure for problem barking, which conditionally, on a part time basis, they can be, but they also can generate their own range of problems.

The first thing I've noticed is that early use of an electric bark collar will affect a dog's socialization and maturity. When a pup turns four or five months old and starts feeling his oats, he is prone to make some noise, as he should. This is the dog's time to enter the world with pride and confidence. With that pride comes a bit of canine bravado, in the form of barking.

If that enthusiasm is thwarted with electricity, something goes away and it will take the services of a professional trainer and a communal

An electric bark collar will control barking...but only while the dog is wearing it.

dog yard to put it back. That puppy enthusiasm is best channeled into situations where he can exercise his running gear and vocal cords to exhaustion...and where it's not going to get anyone annoyed. Find some open country and cut the kid loose.

Remember: tired puppies sleep, bored puppies bark. If the dog can't be directly supervised, then bring him in and let him nap in a pet porter. During night time hours, when barking is most problematic, bring him in again. He can't see the moon to bay at it when he's sleeping in the house in his crate.

The first six months of a bird dog's life is time intensive for the human part of the team. Plan on that, and don't try to cut corners with electricity in any form. The only appropriate application of electricity, prior to ten months of age, is for aversion training. An example would be to "snake break" a young bird dog who will be out running in the American West. However, I don't generally recommend even aversion training until at least 10 months unless absolutely necessary.

When a young dog isn't allowed opportunities to make some noise and figure out how the power train works, his normal development short circuits and disconnects. Dog training is an incremental process. Pup won't comprehend G, H, and I before he has mastered A, B, and C. A time line might go something like this:

Birth to six months old: Use structure and exhaustion (his, not yours) to control unwanted barking. Time him out in his crate and bring him in at night. Throw in a chew toy for the buzz saw. Consider raising several pups together so they can entertain each other. Give them ample opportunities to vocalize and play in safe areas during appropriate times, when the commotion isn't going to get anyone riled up.

Six to seven and a half months: This is the time when an owner basks in the glow of a canine Superpup who will do no wrong. All your hard work has been rewarded and when Junior gets rambunctious, you ask where his toy is and he goes and finds it, brings it to you and then quietly sits by your side waiting for your next request.

In the field, all the systems are coming on line. Junior is running like a big dog and the nose is starting to tune in to the smell of birds. Well, ok, meadow larks, but they do have feathers and fly. Pup chases them in big arcs across the open fields until you blow your whistle and he comes running in. Everyone sleeps quietly at night.

Seven and a half to nine and a half months: During this time period, a terrible trick of fate intervenes and somewhere in the dead of night a malevolent force enters your home and swaps your model pup for his demon seed identical twin. Junior is gone, and in his place a contrary little beast conspires to break all agreed upon rules and regulations.

This is as it should be. Your little one is growing up and maturing into a bird dog. Remember what your parents said about you as a teenager. Get ready, it's canine pay back time.

Don't pick any fights here, because there is no way you can win. Just stay out of the way when possible, and go back to the structure you used earlier, when necessary. The sole responsibility of a dog owner during canine adolescence is to find a way for the two of you to survive to Junior's ten month birthday without losing a sense of grace.

Oh, and about the barking. What were once endearing little puppy woofs are now big dog noise. I don't have any words of wisdom here. Do the best you can.

Ten month old Emancipation Day: This is now the time for pup to begin training, and you have a fair fight on your hands. The first order of the day is the command, "Stop That Noise."

Junior has lived an idyllic puppyhood. He was nurtured as a little guy. He has broadened his horizons through his "teenage months" and now he is certain of several things. He knows that he can run, that birds can fly, and he figures that if he can run fast enough, he just might catch one. He also thinks that if he plays his cards right, he can be master of the universe. Given the opportunity, Junior will try to yodel that pronouncement to the moon nightly.

Regarding the master of the universe stuff, at ten months old, it is now time to dispel Junior of such delusional thinking. Canine structure is predicated on dominance, and it is now time to introduce Junior to the top dog.

This will be Junior's first mandated lesson and it will be a completely safe one that will carry no negative associations to his future career as a bird dog. It has nothing to do with birds or guns or hunting.

You are going to tell him to do something, and he is going to ignore it because he doesn't believe you when you say it. The command is "Stop That Noise" and it is said in a firm, controlled, direct voice, not an angry shout. It is given once and when the training is complete, pup will believe it and any other command that comes on your voice.

Let me set the stage for this all important first lesson.

First, the only tool necessary is a plain wood-handled, yellow straw broom. The one I am currently using is 14 inches wide and 17 inches tall, not counting the wood handle. The handle is 40 inches long, in order to afford a good long reach. It's a plain Jane model that I bought at Costco. There's nothing hard on the straw portion of the broom that could hurt a dog in the all important whoomping portion of this lesson.

Wait until the full dark of night, with a bright full moon being preferable so the dogs can see a little better. Wait for the first song to Orion to begin. It's a safe bet that after the last two months (the teenage period) an owner can pretty well predict the start time. When you hear the first bark, calmly go to a house window nearest the barker and in a calm, direct, firm voice give the command, "Stop That Noise" once. Remember, there is to be no anger or emotion in your voice. At the next sound you hear coming from the dog yard, exit the building and grab the broom which was left in the staging position at the building exit.

As you approach the dog yard gate, remain absolutely silent. Give the dog no more verbal cues or recognition. Remember: no anger, you are simply performing a training drill. Enter the dog yard and get a good, two-handed grasp on the broom handle. Go directly at the dog. At this point, let me interject a comment on technique: I live in Arizona, where it is mostly warm. As a consequence, I don't sleep with a lot of clothes on. My experience has been that the more pale bare skin left to glow eerily in the moonlight, the more profound the effect on the student.

When you get to the dog, with a clean fluid motion, swing the broom and give the barker a firm whoomp on the derriere. If the dog flees as you approach, follow until you can make this point of association. Remember, no anger and no verbal cues. You are not trying to hurt the dog: just deliver a clean, firm swat with the broom. Then beat some of the surrounding real estate. Anything that makes a lot of noise, like rattling chain link fencing or the tops of dog barrels, especially if he's in one of them at the time. Gauge it for about 20 seconds worth of high drama, but remember, no human voice.

If you are using a communal dog yard you will have the assistance of the other dogs, because the second they hear the window slide open for the, "Stop That Noise" command, they will be running for any available bunker and the offending barker will be sitting in the yard alone when you arrive, wondering what everybody got so worked up about.

When the theater session is completed, calmly and quietly leave the yard. Leave pup wondering what the hell was trying to kill him, from deep within the recesses of the first dog barrel he could find to scramble into.

The impression that pup will come away with is that there is some creature that walks the night looking for barkers like himself and that all he has to do to summon this broom wielding manifestation is to utter a peep. Now you, for your part, tried to warn him but there are certain things that are just out of human control and this night walking creature that materializes at the sound of barking is one of them.

Over the period of a couple or three days, the lesson may need to be repeated. During daylight hours, make no changes in the procedure. Pup will quickly ascertain the true identity of the broom-wielding maniac, but he won't fault you for it. This is not about anger; rather, there is some strange control that this "bark sensing broom" has over the normally neat human that is his keeper.

For your part, you must show pup that every time he barks, without exception, the broom shows up. It generally takes three exposures to bring pup around. This is not a permanent fix, but the set up of a method to control the problem.

The true value of this training is that pup obeys you when you say something. He believes you. If you are rigid as a handler for the rest of the dog's life and only give your commands once, expecting compliance, he will believe you for the rest of his life and comply. You are laying a foundation for all future training.

If someone can not be there to monitor the barking, Junior will eventually learn that he can bark when no one is there to escort the broom out into the yard. If you are diligent about 100% follow through, but your spouse is not, the dogs will learn that the broom has control over you, but not your spouse. So when you are home, silence will prevail, when you're not, it won't. They are all such clever beasts, after all.

The broom dance is the initial lesson. There will need to be provisions for a maintenance program. Now, we can discuss Plan B strategies.

I have gone to extraordinary measures to control problem barkers. I have set up a sound activated water spray system that turns on at the sound of barking, otherwise known as the "Bark 'N Spray." The problem is that the sprinklers don't get every square foot of the dog yard, and so, of course, that is where the dogs stand when they hear the first hiss of the sprinklers turning on. They don't make a peep when they know I'm home because I'll show up with the broom, but when I return home after being out, the yard gravel is wet. I have one Lab who loves water showers from the garden hose and discovered, after I installed the sound/spray device, that the yard was now equipped with his own personal, on demand water shower.

The only sure control is an electric bark collar. Not the kinder/gentler versions that make a noise or emit a spray to let the dog know he's being naughty. No, something with a bite is in order. Use an electric bark collar.

Once you have identified the offending culprit, fit him with a collar with a sharp enough stimulation level and the noise will stop. Offender Identification can be difficult if you have a yard full of dogs, and I have often, in the wee hours of the morning, wished for a unit that would light up rather than issue a shock. This way, I would have instant target acquisition and the broom would know exactly who it should be dancing with.

The electric bark collar should be removed when you are there to supervise the dog's barking. Long term contact with the probes on the collar can cause skin irritation on the dog's neck. Even a period of a few days is too long. If there are times when you can't be present to curb barking, then the electric bark collar is a sure short term control. Ultimately, the dog must remain silent because you told him to and he knows you are there to enforce it.

Barking is an ongoing struggle between humans and dogs. Dogs are going to bark. Humans are going to get annoyed with it. If an owner gets it under control and stays proactive about it, then everyone is the better. The additional benefits of this first important lesson is that it carries through to all future training.

In Closing

Saying Goodbye

It has been said that dog training is hard: a thing best left to those who have the aptitude for it. That is not my sense. It can be challenging, and frustrating. It does require an allotment of time and tools. But it isn't something that can be fairly categorized as "hard."

It is, however, hard to lose dogs. Tarrant told me that the reason dogs live only a single decade as opposed to our seventy to eighty years is that if a dog lived near as long as a human, the pain of his loss would be too much for us to bear. The dogs that my wife and I live with are bonded deeply into our lives. They leave holes with their passing. There is an arc that we see in their lives and, I don't know if this makes it any easier when we watch a beloved dog slip away after a full and productive life, but it is softer. It's hardest to lose a young pup who hasn't yet run the full arc of his life. You fight with him to come back, and when he loses, it shreds your heart in a way I can't describe with words.

I want to talk about the hard stuff of sharing your life with a dog: helping your dog make that final passage.

There will come a time when you will have to watch your dog die. At the same time, something else will be departing from your life. What will be lost is shared experience: the collective memory that the two of you lived. History. You will watch your own mortality play out in front of you, because in truth, part of your own physical being is dying with your dog. Often, with our dogs, it is the very best part of us.

Grief is a difficult emotion. It has tremendous weight. When the time comes, your dog is going to need help. Simultaneously, you may find yourself overcome with waves of grief washing through you. Despite that, your dog needs you to be there.

Our culture has developed an antiseptic approach to death. Like much that we have lost in our lives, this detached approach denies us the involvement that ultimately helps us heal that grief, and it disregards the necessity of time that your dog needs to transition at the end of his life. The end of life is messy. It can be slow and grim. There are spills and leaks to clean up. There is care giving and waiting. The end, however, also presents a tremendous opportunity for love, compassion, and kindness.

In today's world, a dying dog is taken to the Vet, who is then asked to make a difficult call. Many dog's lives end there, with a hypodermic needle and a rubber tourniquet, cold on a stainless steel table in the foreign world of a small examination room. In truth, it may be the only and best option available in an instance of severe trauma and pain. Short of that, a dog has a place of his own, a home which he protects and where he feels safe. He has a place where he knows he is cared for and, if it were in his power, that is where he would choose to die.

You must make your own choices on this. I don't want you to feel that this is a judgment, because it isn't. I know that life intervenes and you just may not have the option, at this point and time, of caring for a dying dog. I have had to make similar choices in my life.

That said, if you are in a place where you are able to consciously and intentionally help your dog with his final transition, begin by preparing yourself for the process. There are some illnesses or conditions that progress very quickly. Most, however, wax and wane. Your dog may have a bad spell and then experience a time of relative health and well being in spite of the Veterinarian's prognosis. I've had goners come back and have months of good health.

Beware of expensive treatments. Some of today's urban emergency Veterinary clinics have adopted the negotiation techniques of car lot sales managers. In particular, watch out for the emergency places that are the only ones open on weekends. After the Vet examines the injured animal the owner is presented with a computer generated itemized "estimate" by a closer before treatment. Clarity is all well and good in matters of business, but be advised that the bill is three to four times or more what a regular Vet would charge.

I had one outfit present us with an estimate of $930.00 when one of our string setters went down after hunting. I think it was giardia she drank out of a dirt cow tank. Her system shut down and we needed to get her on a saline IV to rehydrate her. I hadn't been able to reach our normal Vet and so I went to an emergency place. There was back and forth and waiting for the estimate. A person other than the Vet presented us with a price and I told them they were out of their minds. They sent that dog out the door to die. I was able to get ahold of our Vet later that evening, got the dog tended to that night, and she was fine a few days later.

To be fair, the emergency clinics are filling a need, and consequently they charge fees to compensate for being open on nights and weekends. Unfortunately, emergencies can happen at any time, and they seem to always occur at the most inopportune moment. Despite the charges, it's a relief to have somewhere to take a hurt dog. Additionally, Vet health care has become as technologically advanced and therefore as expensive as human health care.

Meanwhile, along with bringing in a new puppy, shop carefully for your family Vet. Find someone you are comfortable talking with, someone who will partner with you in the care for your dog, someone who won't mind teaching you some basics in dog care, someone who will understand that a hunting dog is an athlete and a beloved companion and will treat you and your dog with respect.

I had a ten-year-old female setter who started losing body weight after the close of the bird season. I took her in for blood work and it came back acute lymphatic leukemia. We spent $1500 we didn't have for treatment through a canine oncologist. We bought her another three months of seizures and misery. She was very patient with us because she knew we didn't want to let her go. She finally got through to us that it was time.

We learned from that to gauge the day in tail wiggles, and cat sightings, and to be judicious with treatment. Do only what is necessary to maintain comfort.

Watch for pain. A dying dog will often feel discomfort that doesn't cross the line into pain. It may be momentary, and he will feel better in a little bit. That line is a judgment call that you will have to make, but I know that when it is too much for your dog, he will let you know. You will see it in his eyes and you will know that it's time.

He may lose mobility at the end. We have an old wicker dog bed that makes a pretty good carrier. We use it to move him to the part of the house where the action is ongoing. You will find that towards the end, your dog will be most comfortable if he can be near you and the dogs he has lived with. You can put him by your bed at night and out on the porch to smell the breeze and get some sun during the day.

Line the bed with one of those cheap tarps and have a stiff rug above it so you can lift him in and out. Then lay in some soft bedding that can be thrown away later. Go to a thrift shop and get some soft blankets. Try to keep up his strength with food as long as he has an appetite and use a squirt bottle for water. Set up an outside wash area for your dog, using a plastic reclining lounge chair and garden hose for clean ups. When he decides to stop eating, respect his wishes.

If God is kind to you, your friend will slip away peacefully, at rest. Or...your friend may need your help. I don't know how to advise you regarding this. Our dogs live with us and know they are loved by us. I feel strongly that this thing should remain within our family. I am certain that if it were in their power and they had the means to accomplish it, they would do the same for me.

It is very hard. It is also part of the deal. To accept life is to accept death. To sit with a dog at the end of his life and have him look at you with love in his eyes, feel him lick your hand as it rests on the side of his shoulder, and hear the soft tick of a tail thumping bedding when he is too weak to move anything else, is a shared life's ultimate reward. Once you have gone through that you will never look at another dog the same, and when you spend time working with an energetic youngster and things get interesting, "hard" isn't the word that will come to mind.

A Walk in the Wind

Soft white clouds held the high ground as the West Texas wind buffeted the clumps of bunch grass crowded in among the brush and short, stunted mesquite trees. The wind pushed towards a small impromptu collection of RV's and trailers bound into a little community of sorts alongside the muddied dirt road. The dwellings were festooned with electric cords and dripping water lines, and bunched together off to the side of a small ranch complex on any quail lease, West Texas.

My season had ended in Arizona the week before and I was there with a short string of dogs: six to fill the six-hole trailer. Two seasoned shorthairs loaded up with me (so they didn't kill each other at home), along with four young setters. The setters were in their third year and had mostly ridden the dog trailer for the past two seasons while more experienced string dogs performed for paying shooters.

The setters were four very different dogs. Three of the dogs were litter mates: an orange and white male and two females. The third girl, a tri-colored looker, had been born three weeks later and was raised with the group. All four were of the same blood. They had all gone through three months of training and were whoa broke.

Beryl, one of the orange and white girls, had been born doing everything right and she had been run hard, along with the shorthairs, for the previous three days. She and the shorthairs were curled up and sleeping it off on the chain gang beside my rig. The other three setters stood tall over the chain while I sat at the end of the trailer and put my boots on. They wanted to run, so I got the three of them ready.

We were looking for bird contact that didn't have to produce dead birds. The one thing I can't do for dogs when I'm with paid shooters is

A vast sweep of horizon, where only the wind holds sway and dogs can run forever.

give them the opportunity to make mistakes. I can't sacrifice bird contact to young, inexperienced dogs when someone else has paid for the day.

Carol, my camp host, and I had agreed to take a walk. West of camp was a large tract of land without a convenient road; a tract too small to make a day, and too large for a quick swing. As a result, it was pretty much left alone save for the occasional walking foray. The bobs and scaly coveys that lived there had seen the wars and knew what a shotgun was and, by mid-February, any dumb birds were long dead.

Carol came around the far side of the dog string wearing her shell belt and carrying her shotgun.

"Are you ready for a walk in the wind?" I shouted above the gusts.

"Might as well," she replied.

I hung e-beeper collars on the three inexperienced setters and cut them loose. The beeper units were electric training collars, as well. I didn't intend to use them unless I needed to locate a dog if one got separated or took a flyer.

These were three very different dogs who took off running, and this fact is what's germane for the purpose of this conclusion. It is human nature to try to distill a thing down to a simple process, be it catsup or a method of dog training. It is also our nature to assume that everyone and everything tends to begin at the same starting point. Unfortunately, life doesn't work that way. Yet, all methods of training utilize their own particular philosophy, and what isn't included in the dogma tends to be excluded, partially or completely, depending on the trainer. This one-size-fits-all approach to dog training does a disservice to both the dog and the trainer.

The boy setter, Hunter, was raised up in the shadows of three dominant males. Some young males will respond to this by boldening up. Hunter, as a youngster, hung back and didn't challenge the status quo. He liked birds, but he hadn't had the benefit of bird time focused solely on him. He was a bit soft. He would get out and run a lick and then check back in and walk with me awhile. He didn't take pushing, and would balk when I tried. He was long legged and built for covering ground and would do that for a time if I put him down with his sister, Beryl, or with Rebel, a tri-colored dominant male. When I got him into birds, he would animate and hunt with purpose. With Hunter, I was mostly just waiting for the switch to turn on and I figured that time on wild birds would jump-start him.

His litter mate, Sara Beth, had not been raised by us. She had been sold as a ten-week-old puppy and gone to live in another state. Her new owners were in the process of building a new home and didn't follow through with building a yard and kennel to contain her once she matured to the point where she had a motor. As young dogs will do, she took to running wild. Rather than having her end up under a car, they farmed her out to a pro for safe keeping. The trainer ran a "put and take" shooting preserve as part of the training operation and Sara Beth was left to run wild on it. She missed the connection, the proximity, a dog gets from being raised in a family. I got a call from the pro telling me that he had one of my dogs and that he didn't think her owner had an interest in keeping her. He wasn't a setter guy and didn't have a use for her. To the owners' credit, I spoke with them and they phoned the pro and authorized the release of the dog to me. My wife and I tag-teamed a three-day truck ride to pick the girl up.

One of the benefits for Sara Beth was that she had been running wild on birds from a young age. She definitely knew how to cover ground. The off part was that she didn't connect to the hunter, and it took some time to bring her around. Short term, she has to be reeled in to hunt for the gun. Long term, she is inconsistent. She is strong on finding birds, but then she can drift and lose focus. When she gets tired, she thinks about shutting down and I have to keep on her to stay out front.

Finally, the last little girl is Zorra, a fifty-pound tri-colored setter, who came as a trade for one of our large white male puppies. The litters were three months separated and Zorra came to our group younger and smaller. She was raised as a litter mate three months removed and had to hold her ground accordingly. She's a tough little thing and has a contrary streak like her mother. She will often fail to comply, not because she doesn't know how to, but simply because she can...she can be a difficult little beast.

I milked Zorra through yard work and bird introductions. Once we got to the field she tried to self-hunt and I cranked her in, which she didn't like, a lot. She then decided that she wouldn't hunt in front of me, and we have seesawed from there. The problem for her is that she likes birds and the birds are out front. She is at the end of six generations of our blood, and I have the benefit of hindsight. Our tri-colors mature more slowly and take three seasons to come around. Like Hunter, I was waiting for the light switch to go on for her.

And so we banked into the wind. We crossed wire and hit a patch of mesquite one hundred yards out. Zorra took the opportunity to get separated and ran back to the chain gang, only because she could. I whistled her from the fence line and got her back to us. Hunter waited at the fence with me, while Sara Beth disappeared out ahead, looking to turn a bird.

Three dogs: same blood, same training, same handling, three different sets of circumstances, three different personalities and temperaments, resulting in three very different individuals. Each required a different training approach and each of the three was separate and unique in his or her response to yard training and the later bird introductions. They were beyond anything I could do for them now. They knew what whoa meant and they were beyond dragging a rope, so I no long controlled their actions with any sort of hard structure. They were free agents left to follow their noses. I waited and watched for the magic to appear. I accept that much of later training is beyond my ability to control. I was given these three dogs to shape and form. I had done my required work for them. What was left for them to accomplish was beyond me.

I ran these three youngsters on this piece of grass and cactus and mesquite, waiting for the blood of their parents and grandparents to wrestle control and to shape their responses; to override adrenaline, enthusiasm, and youth.

I watch for the moment. I feel their passion and wait for the magic to happen one more time.

Bandita and puppies many years ago.

Generations

Bandita and Pepper begot Belle, Rose and Kate, who begot Emma, Jasper, Dandy, Musette and Concho, who begot Rascal, Rebel, Beryl, Sarah Beth, and Hunter, who begot Zorra...

It has been one of the blessings of my life to have lived and worked with some truly wonderful dogs. Standing alone, under a towering sky, on an expanse of open grass, I have felt more connected to them than to the majority of my own species.

Much of this book has been devoted to the nuts and bolts of gun dog training- important stuff when you need to train a dog, but there is more. Dogs are more than tools, more than friends.

I have lived with dogs for a long time. Within any generation of those dogs there have been different personalities with different evocations. Always within any group, one or two or three took it upon themselves to be my dog. By that I mean that in their mind, their job was me. Bandita was my dog. We kept three of her daughters: Belle, Rose and Kate. All three came for birds, but Belle was there to lead the dog yard, Rose was there to find birds, and Kate was my dog. It was very hard when I found her dead on the side of the highway that day. I know the other two felt it as well.

In the next generation, Concho and the Chessie, Sadie, were my dogs. Sadie, the ferocious beast that she was, held my fear and slept by my side of the bed each night, and Concho was my shadow, with a wall between us. If he was in the dog yard he would lie against the portion of the house of whatever room I was in. He followed me through osmosis. He mirrored my physical being. When I got sick with hypoglycemia, he did also. As I pushed myself and went downhill, he went ahead of me and said, "Keep going, this is what it will look like."

My will is stronger than my body. I continued working customer dogs 14 hours a day, 7 days a week. I started falling over while training and Concho said, "Here, let me take this to the next level for you." Several times I had to carry him out after he got disoriented. I hit him with glucose and protein, the same stuff I had for myself. I loved training dogs and I didn't want to stop. I went to doctors. They gave me a drug to reduce my rising insulin levels. I kept training.

I put Concho on the trailer one morning. I had to work customer dogs and he was insistent on going. I cut him loose when I got to the training area to let him run and blow off steam, something he had done untold times. He took a flyer, which is not a thing Concho did. I tried to find him and he was gone. It took a couple of hours to work dogs and towards the end he came in. He was in bad shape. I had neglected to load the dog first aid kit that morning, and I had brought nothing for myself, as well. I had no karo syrup or honey to hit him with. I got him home fast and dosed him, but the spin had already gone out of control. He started going out. We did the hour and 15 minute drive to the Vet in 50. Put him on an IV and tried to get him back. He seemed to stabilize and that evening I took him home. There was no way to know what had happened internally, whether any organs had infarcted. At home we set up a bed in the front room and waited. It's as if he said, "Let me show you how this works. Watch close because I'm only going to do it once." The convulsions started that night. It took him about 45 minutes to die.

His daughter, Rascal, took over. She watched and stayed close and became one hell of a singles dog. She also developed the same sort of sensitivities to allergies that I manage with reactive hypoglycemia. We both take pills in the morning. She's at retirement age now. She splits duty with Beryl, an orange and white youngster that bears an uncanny resemblance to our first dog, Bandita- same look, same personality, same temperament, same hunting style. Beryl is my shadow and my keeper. She has an iron will. She inspects everything before me in my line of travel. She requires my presence and I hear about it, if access is not forth coming.

Beryl forever on watch.

There are currently nine dogs living here. As I write this I am sitting in a chair by the wood stove. Most of the dogs are outside. They went through the doggy door to bask in the afternoon sun and worry the pigeons. A couple of senior dogs are lying under the dining room table snoring soundly. This leaves two: Rascal and Beryl are sleeping a few feet away, at the gate just over my shoulder, the gate that keeps dogs out of the living room and bedroom. They are piled up together and Beryl has her front paws and muzzle extended under and through the gate to be as close as possible. If I look to Beryl, the slit of her eyes open.

It has been a few years since I began this book. I don't train anymore, save Snake Safe training, and I think I'm about done guiding as well. I have been quarter time for a couple/three years now. I write, I travel and I teach people how to train dogs.

I was driving home from a trip and I stopped at a restaurant after spending the night in a motel in Kingman, AZ. The waitress was in her sixties, friendly, competent, professional. I had two dogs with me. A setter and a shorthair. We had done an International Sportmen's Show in Salt Lake and they had been serving as greeters in the booth, and trick ponies for dog arena presentations. The weather had turned snowy in Utah and I couldn't get a hotel that would allow dogs, so they had been bunking behind the jump seat in the cab of the truck. They were good kids and had been very pleasant and patient, but I'm sure they were not as comfortable as they would have preferred.

I ordered steak and eggs. The waitress brought the meal to the table and then noticed on one of her walkbys that I had cut the steak in half and then cut one of the halves in half.

"You got two friends?" she asked.

I pointed to the cab of my truck which was in a front parking space just a few feet from the window booth where I was seated. Each dog had taken a front seat. One had driver and one had shotgun. They were studying me very intently.

Business was slow and she stopped to talk. She said, "You're a dog person." Not so much a question, but as a statement of fact.

"Yes ma'am."

She told me that she had a canine best friend at home. That her daughter had shown up one day years earlier with two strays that someone had abandoned out near a windmill in the desert. The daughter had gathered them up and dropped one off at her mom's. They were in bad shape and she couldn't tend to both. Mom protested and told her daughter that she didn't want a dog. Her daughter replied that she couldn't leave them there, that her parents hadn't raised her that way. Argument won, one of the dogs stayed for tending until other arrangements could be made.

Her husband hadn't been feeling quite right and had a doctor's appointment the following day. Out of the blue, they received a diagnosis of pancreatic cancer. He was given three months to live. She told me that he lived another six months and that that dog absolutely saved her life. She said that without that dog she could not have made it. Then she told me that she was absolutely certain that that dog, the timing of his arrival, was a direct gift from God.

If you are a dog person, you will understand this. If you are not yet, I hope this book helps you to become one.

APPENDIX

Training Tools

Bark Collar

When electronic bark collars started years ago, they were cumbersome and not terribly user-friendly. They turned off and on by means of a magnetic switch, and were equipped with variable intensity plugs to control the level of stimulation they delivered to a barking dog.

Today's collars are small, slick affairs that operate with the push of a button. The vibration detection pads that sense an offending dog's vocalizations are now integrated into the body of the unit so there aren't any delicate parts to wear out with extended use.

They work very well and are the one sure short-term solution to a barking dog problem.

Top: multiple dogs means multiple collars. Bottom: previous generation Tri-tronics.

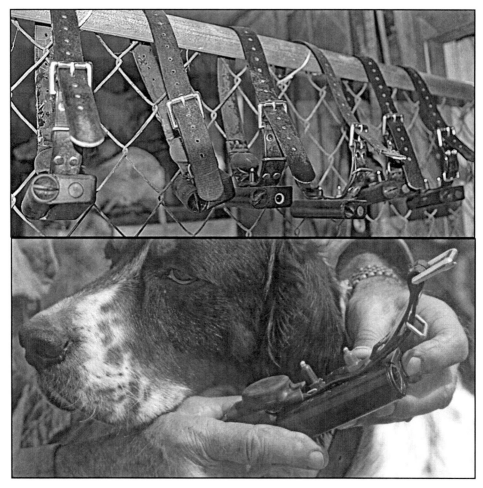

Beeper Collar

Beeper collars are locating and tracking devices that emit a beeping sound which allow a handler to monitor the location of a standing dog, or the line of travel of a moving dog. They are the modern day electrical equivalent of the dog bell, with one important exception: unlike a dog bell which falls silent when the dog goes on point, they continue to make noise when the dog stops moving.

The unit emits a steady monotone beep sound on a preselected, consistent interval of time while the dog is on the move. Once the dog ceases movement, a small switch in the collar senses the absence of motion and alters the timing and tone of the beep signal being generated by the collar unit. In this way, the handler knows the dog is now standing still.

I confess that I detest the sound of a beeper when I am running dogs. I personally think it ruins the solitude of time spent out of doors. I harbor these negative feelings right up to the point when I can't locate a dog. Then those shrill beeps in the distance sound like the voices of angels on high. The longer the dog has been missing, the more ethereal the sound of the beeper.

I use a combined e-collar with beeper units that have a remote turn-on function. To activate the beeper signal, all I have to do is press a button on the transmitter. I never release a dog in the field without one of these e-collar/beeper units strapped around the dog's neck.

The newest technology uses GPS-enabled tracking collars which will make all previous systems obsolete.

Placing a beeper collar on a GSP at the start of the hunt.

Bells

I use bells if I am releasing dogs at home to take a few laps around the house. They are the inexpensive alternative to the electric beeper collar. There is quite a long tradition of bell use, particularly with East coast grouse dogs that don't extend their search past the far line of trees. They are sold in various configurations through gun dog catalogs. I also see bells for sale in Western feed stores for hanging on goats, sheep and cattle.

I rig mine with a quick release snap so they go on and off easily. I have multiple shapes and sizes because each has a different tone and I can track individual dogs through the sound differences.

Top: close up image of two means of attaching bells to collar.
Bottom: image of various bell designs.

Note: of the two attachment methods, a clip and a snap, the clip is a more secure connection, but difficult to take on and off. The snap is easy to attach, but is also the type most frequently lost when the dog is running.

Belt Lead

I won't handle dogs without having a couple of these hanging from a snap on my belt. That way, they are easy to get to when an emergency comes up and it is critical that a dog be put under control and removed from an area.

They are not found in retail pet supply outlets, but are readily available in gun dog supply catalogs.

Bottom: lead and accompanying clip that is worn on trainer's belt.

BIRD CARRIERS
Bird Cages

Housing birds requires some infrastructure, particularly birds required for strong flight while dog training in the field. Those training a single dog may opt to purchase birds daily on an as-needed basis. Short of that, a handler can put together a pigeon loft with a minimum of space, time, and expense. Pigeons are a fairly easy keep if the numbers are kept below twenty birds. Homing pigeons also make a superior training bird because, after they are flown over the dog in training, they return back to the loft to be used for the next session.

Game birds such as bobwhite quail, chuckar, and pheasant require more space and expense. They can be housed in a call back pen or johnny house if the handler has access to a sufficient amount of open land. Housing game birds is really beyond the purview of this book and those with an interest should check the book section of the McMurray Hatchery at www.mcmurrayhatchery.com. They can be reached at: 1-800-456-3280.

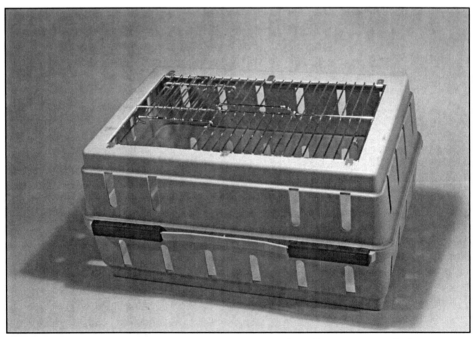

Bird carriers come in a vast range of designs, materials and costs. Pictured above is a common, inexpensive model that has served the author well for many years. These are available through feed stores or pet supply stores.

BIRD CARRIERS
Bird Bucket

It can be exasperating getting pigeons out of a cage or carrying case, and usually, there is a toll involved. Every few birds successfully caught up and transferred are balanced by the escape of a bird or two. Bird buckets are the answer for transferring and planting birds in the field. These buckets can be bought already fabricated through the dog training supply companies. However, in truth, they are very easy to make. I use a five gallon plastic bucket and modify the top to include a rubber overlapping passthrough gasket. The rubber insures that birds won't know to push through and escape. However, a trainer can easily reach into the bucket and grab a bird as needed.

A very effective bird bucket made from a five gallon plastic pail.

BIRD CARRIERS
Bird Pouches

A bird pouch is simply a means to carry birds while training. Specifically, it is used to carry birds when a handler leaves the vehicle carrying the bird crates and walks out to plant a training course or fly birds for a dog. For years, I used a pair of Indian army gas mask bags I bought in a military surplus store. They were cheap, big and roomy and had a shoulder strap. They were made out of a very loosely woven material that allowed ventilation for the birds being carried inside. The dogs in training quickly learned to love those bags.

There are commercially made bird pouches that have net ventilation panels incorporated in the design. They all work well and facilitate getting birds into the field.

A bird pouch that works well for hunting generally crosses over for training uses as well.

BIRD CARRIERS
Call Back Pens

Call back pens are also referred to as recall pens and johnny houses. These bird holding pens may be small and portable, or run up to the size of a medium sized shed.

The pens are equipped with wire hardware cloth cones leading into the pen and mounted at ground level so the the game birds that are released from the pen have a ready access route back into the enclosure and can be recovered to be released again and again. The birds on the outside hear the recall whistle of birds left inside the pen and return to join back up with the covey.

Bobwhite quail are the species most commonly used, but chuckars also will recall. The use of a recall pen helps transition dogs from planted birds to free ranging wild birds.

Three call back pens built and used for training by the author. The one on the left is constructed out of a plastic barrel and is meant to be left in place in the field. The remaining two, center and right, are portable models that were transported each morning to the training area. Through years of use the author discovered that smaller generally was better. The larger of the two was double-sided and bird releases were alternated every other day. The smaller of the two was a single compartment where a few birds were held back at release to call the liberated bird back after the close of the training session.

BIRD RELEASES
Nylon Bird Harnesses

These inexpensive harnesses are manufactured by the Scott's Dog Supply company and are sold through them and several other mail order outlets. The operative component in these designs is a velcro release strip which allows the handler to free the bird with a quick jerk or snap of the wrist. They are sold in two sizes to accommodate birds ranging from quail up through pigeons and chuckars. Scott's markets them with and without a pull cord attached. The harnesses sold without pull cords are for releasing birds by hand. Those with cords are for planting birds on the ground and releasing them while the handler is standing.

Scott's also produces a wing strap that allows a pigeon-sized bird the use of his feet alone. The harness binds one wing closed and eliminates the bird's ability to fly away. This device is particularly useful for boldening up shy dogs by providing them a mobile bird in plain sight.

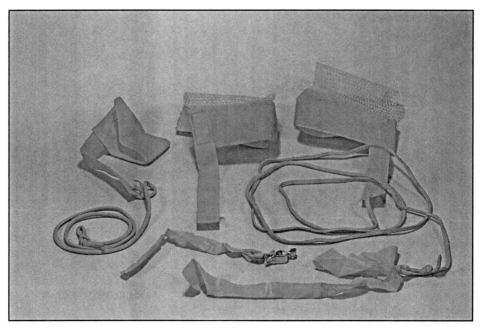

These nylon/velcro harnesses are the neatest thing since sliced bread and were used extensively by the author for many years. They are inexpensive, easily carried in the pocket of a bird pouch, and they work well without leaving much additional scent to tip off a dog that the bird is a human plant, like an electronic remote release often will.

BIRD RELEASES
Mechanical Releases

Bear in mind, not so long ago mechanical releases didn't exist and gun dogs got trained anyway. They are cumbersome and can be a real pain to load and use. A handler really needs two or three to set up a proper course. They are expensive. Having said that, they can be just the ticket for getting a dog over the hump on bird introductions.

They come in two basic flavors: those that are released manually and those with electronics that allow them to be released with the push of a button from an extended distance.

The manual releases are manufactured in several configurations. They are rigged to fly the bird when the handler pushes a lever down with the toe of his or her boot. They can all be modified to release the bird by means of a pull line attached to the travel bar on the release lever. I used cord as pull line material for a few years, but it was never really satisfactory. If there was any length to the cord it would stretch, which meant that I really had to yank it to move the release arm far enough to trip the mechanism. It was just one more thing to have to do when I also had to watch the dog with one eye and watch for the bird with the other while holding a whistle, a gun, and the button on an electric collar.

I went instead to using nylon weed-whacker cutting line for the release trip pull line. This is sold by garden suppliers in bulk spools for refilling weed-whacker cutting cord. It is heavy and stiff, and sold in bright neon colors that are easy to find laid out in the grass.

I would typically rig each release with a thirty-yard length of pull line so I had the option to handle the dog and then release the bird from a distance. If needed, I could tie in additional line to extend my working distance from the release. I would attach a neon colored flag made of surveyor's tape at the end of the pull line and work the dog in on it and then up the line and scent stream into the bird.

The addition of an electronic release mechanism allows a handler much more latitude in working the dog. It is also much more user-friendly. No tangled pull lines to contend with, no pull lines to thread through the vegetation. I mark each unit with a different colored surveyor's tape flag and then coordinate the same color to the button that releases the bird. Without this precautionary indexing, a handler may be working a dog at one trap only to press the wrong release button, and watch the bird fly away from another trap down field. The current designs allow one transmitter unit to handle multiple release traps, helping to stem the confusion of using multiple transmitters for multiple traps.

The trade off for the ease of use with electronic releases is the price tag, particularly if a handler purchases multiple units to set up a proper training course. I think the cost is warranted if a person will be training multiple dogs, over a period of years and can justify it on a per dog basis. If, on the other hand, a person is only training one or two dogs and is focused on transitioning those dogs over onto wild birds, I don't know that I would spend the money. In reality, all that a handler needs to get done can be accomplished in most cases with inexpensive nylon harness releases.

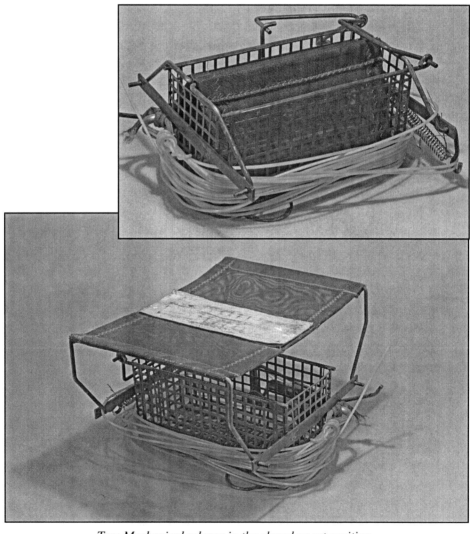

Top: Mechanical release in the closed or set position.

Bottom: Mechanical release in the open position.

Blank Pistols

Years ago, I went shopping for a blank pistol for dog training. I went to one of these general sporting goods stores that handle athletic equipment and looked at their selection of starter pistols. They had three or four models that all looked cheaply made. The prices ran from ten to twenty-five bucks. To be honest, they all looked pretty cheesy and I couldn't detect any real quality difference in the assortment of models, irrespective of the price tag. I picked up the cheapest one and asked the salesperson if at these prices they actually worked. The salesman replied with a very tired tone to his voice, "Sir, the price is reflective of the quality." I'm sure that the translation going through his mind as he uttered the words went more like, "What the hell do you think, you cheap so and so?"

I bought the cheap one, fully intending to upgrade in the near future. I put the purchase on the wish list because I figured the cheap blank gun wouldn't hold up for long. In the end, however, I actually used that gun for years; at the end it was held together with rubber bands. I think it's still buried out in the training trailer somewhere.

I did eventually upgrade to an H&R 22 caliber blank gun that ran over a hundred dollars at purchase. It goes bang just like the cheap one and I don't need rubber bands to keep it held together. I continued to use the cheap gun on shy dogs because it was quieter and, as a result, a little easier for starting gun introductions.

Each handler must gauge their intended level of use, but I would not spend a great deal of money on a blank gun unless you're training at the professional level. Also, I would stick to using 22 caliber crimped blanks, not true 22 blanks. The true blanks are too loud for most practical training uses. The loud, sharp report may do more damage than good with a sensitive dog.

A blank pistol with 22 crimps and 22 blanks.

Bumpers

The term bumper is a general term referring to something that is thrown for the dog to pick up. In the old days, they were made from short lengths of old fire hose, stuffed with buoyant material to provide floatation, and then sewn shut at both ends. A short length of stiff rope was tied to one end to act as a throwing arm.

When I was a kid they were made commercially of canvas and came in different diameters to fit the size of the dog being worked.

Today, bumpers are machine molded of a hard plastic or foam material. They come in different colors and are nearly indestructible. Bumpers are available through any dog supply outlet.

Chessie holding a bumper and waiting for the next retrieve.

Chain Gang

A chain gang is an important tool used anytime a dog has to be controlled. This can be while training, traveling on the road, or at home. It is basically a long length of chain with short drop chains spaced down its length. Each drop chain has a snap swivel to hold a dog to the chain. It is basically a dog-sized fish stringer.

I have several that I use. I have two that run 30 feet each and are so heavy I keep one on each trailer (we have two dog trailers). I haul them in rubber livestock feed buckets. The buckets are indestructible and have held up to years of chains being dragged out of them. In addition, I have two more that are left in place, attached to the ground in the dog training area near the whoa post. They are anchored to short lengths of chain protruding from cement plugs poured in the ground.

My drop lengths are not permanently attached to the main chain. Rather, I have bull snaps on both ends of the drops so I can adjust where I want the dogs to be on the chain. The drops are cut at 26 inches and, once the chain links and bull snaps are attached to each end, they measure a total length of 34 inches. This allows me to position a dog every 3 to 4 feet along the length of the main chain. Be advised that bull snaps are the only attachments I have found that will hold up with dogs bouncing the chain gang drop length.

In addition, on each end of the main chain I attach both a heavy welded ring and a chain hook. The hook allows me to wrap the chain around a ground based object and hook a loop into the end of the chain. In this way, I can readily anchor off an end to a parking lot light pole, fence post, telephone pole, etc., while I am traveling with dogs on the road. The welded ring serves as a ground attachment when I drive a spike through it and into the ground with a sledge hammer. The best spikes I have found are automobile rear axles. They will hold up to years of sledge hammer pounding and never give.

Chain gang and components

Check Cord

A check cord is essentially a length of stiff rope with a snap on one end. The snap is attached to the dog and used by the handler to control the dog's movements and to reel the dog in when necessary. They can run from ten to thirty feet in length. I keep several in varying lengths, but I find that the twenty footers get the most use.

The rope should be of 1/2 inch or 3/4 inch diameter and made of a stiff material and weave that allows the rope to snake well when being dragged by a moving dog. Limber rope tends to loop easily and will tangle and snag up with brush. The snap end has both a snap and a welded ring to allow the handler to thread the end of the rope around the dog's chest and back up through the ring at the snap. This forms an impromptu harness that centers the trailing rope high over the dog's back and out from under his feet.

I have both made my own check cords and purchased them through the Scott's Dog catalog. To make a proper check cord, a person must start with a length of stout, stiff rope. This can be hard to find and expensive when located. Feed store equine sections generally have stiff rope available. I use a high quality snap and welded ring, critical components that need to be able to withstand the stresses an enthusiastic dog will subject them to during training.

I have found that it is much more cost effective to purchase the pre-made check cords. I can't make them for the cost that Scott's sells them. Throw the new rope into a mud hole when it first arrives. Let it soak up some brown water and then dry hard. This will make it good and stiff and it will be ready to use.

Nylon webbing can also make a good check cord for limited use. It doesn't drag that well in the field, but it can be just the ticket for yard and kennel work. A handler doesn't need a snap and thereby foregoes bending down to snap and unsnap dogs being led. Take a length of strapping double the length that the cord needs to run, and double it through the dog's collar. Hang on to the doubled end when working the dog, and when finished release the dog by letting one end go and slide free of the collar. This works particularly well when shuffling dogs back and forth to their runs and while working with dogs on retrieving.

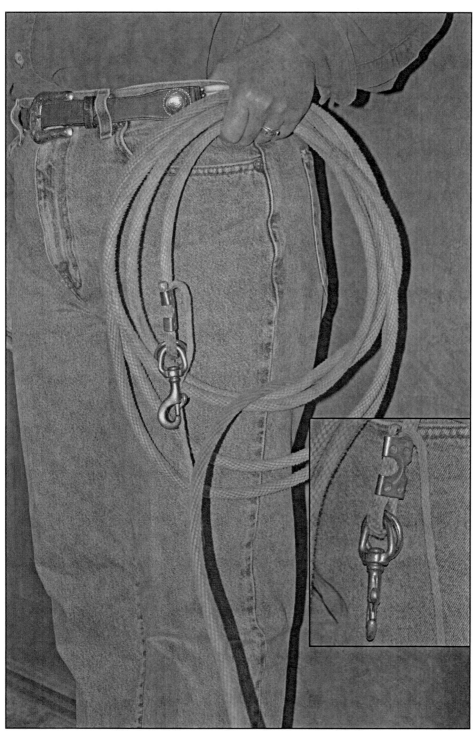
Check cord image and inset showing snap detail.

D-ring Collar

There are several different collar designs marketed today. Some are pretty trendy looking. These fancy collars work like halters on a horse; or, they are constructed with plastic snap-together latches. Don't buy these unless you need to control your toy poodle.

Instead, buy a stout, well made D-ring collar with metal buckles. I use collars made of nylon strap material because I can get them in different colors, allowing me to tell dogs apart from a distance. Also, the collars I buy are made with a clear plastic coating which cleans up a little quicker than the bare nylon web strap models.

Always rivet engraved metal tags on the collar with your current contact information. If your dog gets lost in the field, the person finding him will be able to contact you. Don't buy cheap collars, spend the money to get the best available. It will be worth it in the long run.

D-ring collar images.

Dowels/Training Bucks

Dowels and training bucks are used in structured force-breaking or modified force-breaking drills. The dowels can be cut from any sort of round stock. Old broom handles are the proper diameter. An old axe handle makes good buck stock because its flattened shape fits well in a dog's mouth. In reality, the material doesn't need to be restricted to wood. PVC plastic pipe would make a good dowel as well.

Training bucks are merely dowels with short legs attached to raise the round form above the training surface and allow the dog to more easily get it into his mouth.

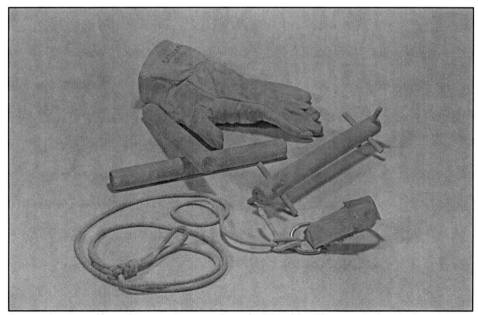

Image shows tools used in training on a force break table. These include: leather gloves (top); two styles of training bucks, with and without legs (middle); and a toe nerve hitch cord, including velcro attachment borrowed from a T. E. Scott hobble set.

Hobbles

These small training harnesses connect three of the dog's feet together and prevent the dog from moving any distance without pitching forward onto his nose. They are used in whoa breaking and in steadying a dog on birds.

The hobbles are constructed of metal D-rings, metal snaps, nylon and velcro. They are made with fluorescent orange material that is easy to spot should they get dropped or thrown while in use.

They are manufactured by the Scott's Dog Supply Company and are available through their catalog.

Illustration of a hobble set.

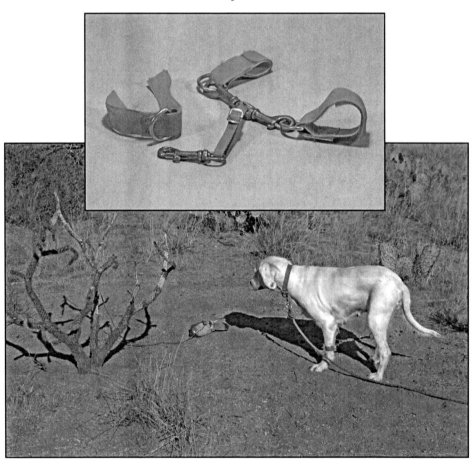

Hobbled English setter holding on a pigeon restrained in a velcro release.

Kennel Box

The most reasonably priced and user friendly kennel boxes are those made from plastic and designed to separate and spoon together for shipping or storage. They come in a broad range of graduated sizes geared to fit any dog, from chihuahua to great dane. I have used them for years and have yet to have a dog work his way out of one.

They have a removable metal door which conveniently allows you to choose the direction the door swings open (right or left).

Also available on the market are metal and fabric-composite crate designs. I imagine that the fabric composite models could be very useful with a mature dog not prone to chewing. I haven't used one, so I can't speak from personal experience. I do own a couple of collapsible metal cages, however, and have found them to be heavy and cumbersome. When they are used to travel in a vehicle, they tend to tear up and mark things that come into contact with them.

I would stick to the plastic models. They do the least damage inside a vehicle. Pick a size that offers your dog ample room to stretch out while he is stored inside. The best prices I have found on these are at Wal-Mart stores, located in the pet department.

These kennel crates come in all sizes. They fit the smallest dog to the largest. They hold up amazingly well for all the grief I have heaped on them over the years.

Leather Gloves

A good pair of gloves are a necessity when handling moving check cords. Severe rope burns are a certainty unless a layer of protection is worn on your hands. The best gloves, I have found, are made of goat skin. They are thin enough to allow a handler to feel subtle nuances through the gloves; yet, are still tough enough to keep the handler safe from injury.

Cow leather is the material most often used to make gloves, and when it is thinned down a little it can make an adequate training glove. Try the glove on and imagine manipulating a trigger and loading a shotgun while wearing it. The gloves you need will give you the flexibility for these activities, while providing protection for your hands.

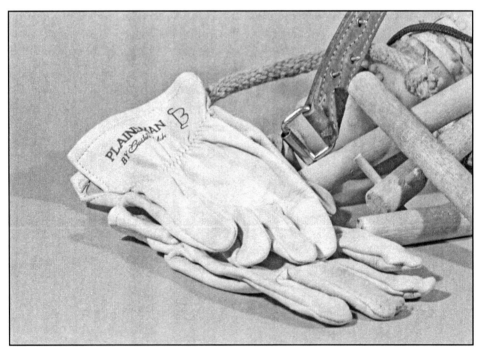

Above: glove illustration.   Opposite page: pig tie illustration.

Pig Tie

The current Scott's Dog Supply catalog calls this item "The Delmar Smith Wonder Lead." I had a past client go to a Rick Smith dog training seminar. After attending, he came out to train with me, and had an extra one of these to give me. It is just the ticket when a dog is giving a handler grief during the early stages of whoa post introductions.

The lead is made from a springy raw hide material that has just the right feel and sound when sliding to get and hold a dog's attention. They are available through some feed stores or they may be purchased via mail order.

Pinch Collar

The pinch collar is a specialized training tool designed for whoa training and obedience work. It is essentially a leather collar built with a spring steel core that returns the collar's diameter back to an open position once pulling pressure is removed. On the inside surface of the collar are inset roofing nails. The overall appearance of the collar, with the spikes and leather band, is a little ominous to those not familiar with its use.

The purpose of the spikes are to pinch the dog's skin when the collar is pulled snug around his neck. It doesn't so much hurt the dog as make him lift up on his toes. It is a necessary tool with some dogs, and the best way to get their attention and keep them on track. I would characterize it as a transitional tool used for specific problems at specific times during training.

Current catalogs list them as being available in both leather and nylon models. I have two leather ones that I have used for years. I would imagine that nylon would work as well.

Chain pinch and choke collars are also marketed. They are generally used by obedience trainers and not typically used for gun dog training.

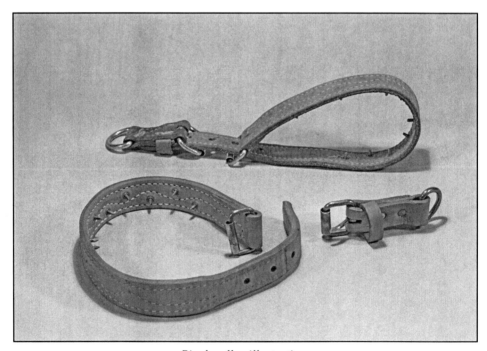

Pinch collar illustration.

Tie-Out Cable

It's always good to have a tie-out cable handy to control a dog. One end can be wrapped around a tree or clipped to the undercarriage of a vehicle. This will provide a tie-off point and keep the dog contained.

These cable setups are made of stiff cable coated with a plastic sheath and finished with a sturdy snap clip on each end. They are lighter and more portable than a length of chain, but they offer the permanence and protection that a piece of chewable rope can't.

They are available at most discount store pet departments. They come in various lengths. I would get long as opposed to short because extra length can always be wrapped into the base object. If, on the other hand, the cable is too short, there isn't a lot that can be done to make it longer, short of clipping a second length of cable to it.

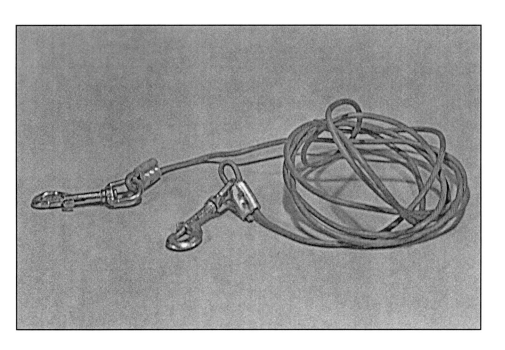

Tie-out cable illustration.

Training Shotguns

Many pros have an old, ravaged, single shot 410 hammer gun tucked away in the accumulated clutter of their training gear.

When choosing a training shotgun, a handler must remember that these poor weapons are going to see the wars. They will be dropped and cast aside in the field while training. They will be bled on and packed with feathers while the handler is attempting to quickly load shot shells into the breech. The random hard case dog is going to urinate on them from time to time. They will be the afterthought during the training process because the dog will require all the available mental focus the handler has at his disposal.

The point is, don't use a gun that will require any care or ginger handling. Get a used or inexpensive 410 and 12 gauge. Single shot or pump will work for the 410. A handler will probably want to stick to a pump for the 12 gauge because multiple bird plants will require multiple shots. The single shot is a much safer gun because, once it is discharged, it can't fire again until the handler takes the time to reload it. Of course, a handler has the option of loading a pump gun with only one shell at a time.

Synthetic stocks aren't a bad idea, either. The tough plastic stocks take tousling much better than their wooden counterparts. You may want to paint the stock fluorescent orange while you're at it, so that the gun is readily recoverable when it is laid aside in the field and left behind while you take off after a dog. I spent a little bit of time over the years looking for my gun when I needed to be dog training. Eventually, I put slings on my training guns so that I could drape them over my shoulder and keep traveling after the dog when the shooting was over.

Small, light, fast pointing shotgun used in gun dog training.

Examples of common shotgun sizes viewed from left to right: 410 caliber, 28 gauge, 20 gauge, and 12 gauge.

After training, author examines the chamber of a pump action Browning 20 gauge shotgun to make sure the chamber is empty and that the gun is safe to handle and store.

Training Tables

Please reference the photos for both the force break table, and the NAVHDA (North American Versatile Hunting Dog Association) training table. These two designs have been in use for decades in these two basic forms. The designs have held up through actual use and require no alterations. It is hard to improve on success. I covered the use of a force break table in a previous section of this book. Those individuals interested in the NAVDHA style training table should read the NAVDHA training manual, The Training and Care of the Versatile Hunting Dog, Sigbot Winterhelt and Edward D. Bailey, North American Versatile Hunting Dog Association, Puslinch, Ontario, Canada,1973. For more information contact: NAVHDA, P.O. Box 520, Arlington Hts., IL 60006 or www.navhda.org.

Top: Ed Rader whoas setter on top of a saw horse stand.

Middle: Setter positioned on top of 55 gallon barrel during whoa training session.

Bottom: Setter holding a bumper on a conventional style force break table.

Opposite page: Jay Smith works Chance, a Labrador retriever on the force break table.

Whistle

Whistles come in a vast array of designs, materials, and functions. A handler has the option of picking out the whistle that calls to him.

Different types of whistles are typically used with different types of gun dogs. The flushing dog handlers will often go for a slim-line designed two-tone whistle crafted from something exotic like Buffalo horn. Flushing dog handlers tend to be on the whistle a lot because the flush dog must work within shotgun range for the handler to put any birds in the bag.

The retriever folks want the loud and sturdy, classic whistle made out of plastic or some other synthetic substance that won't stick to their lips when they blow it during a waterfowl hunt in freezing temperatures. They also want the whistle loud to handle dogs sent on long marks.

The versatile dog people favor a two-tone design that allows a clear note for handling and a trill whistle for freezing a dog on whoa.

The bird dog guys can use an old coach's whistle. They need something that will be around through the miles of walking it takes to locate the birds.

Regardless of the design, the whistle should hang from a sturdy lanyard, around the neck. They are available from sporting goods stores and gun dog supply catalogs.

Examples of types of training whistles, both metal and plastic.

Whoa Post

The whoa post can be any post or pipe anchored firmly in the ground. The post or pipe needs to be heavy enough that it is unbendable when pulled, and it should be at least five feet high so that the whoa cable can't be pulled free from it when the cable is being pulled and under pressure. I use a collapsible post for the training area because we also park cars there. I cemented a two foot piece of pipe into the earth, with its top flush to the ground. When I wish to use the post, I insert a seven foot tall, smaller diameter pipe into the buried pipe. This leaves five feet of workable pipe extended above ground.

Over the upright post I drop a heavy gauge, welded steel ring. I then clip a ten foot, or doubled twenty foot, tie-out cable to the ring. The other end of the tie-out cable is clipped to the dog's collar. To the same D-ring I attach a check cord and the dog is ready for whoa work.

Top: English setter learning whoa on the whoa post. Note: rather than anchor this whoa post in the ground with cement, this post is moveable and weighted with a concrete platform poured from the bottom of a plastic trash can.

Whoa post and components

Emergency/First Aid Medical Box List of Contents

1) a couple of large cans of contact lens saline solution
2) Panalog--a topical antibiotic cream
3) sutures
4) medical skin staple guns
5) specialty pliers needed to remove the staples
6) collection of differently shaped stainless steel surgical scissors, forceps, long and short tweezers, sharp sterile scalpels
7) neat little pair of grabbing forceps that only move at the tip
8) welder's tweezers
9) small diameter surgical tubing for a proper tourniquet
10) disposable plastic razors
11) a spoon
12) coat brush
13) stripper
14) dog nail cutters
15) Wound powder
16) Betadine
17) an assortment of Band-Aids, sterile surgical bandage packs
18) a roll of gauze
19) vet wrap
20) lighted scope for looking into a dog's ear channel or nostril
21) little electronic thermometer
22) stethoscope
23) antibiotics: Amoxicillin for internal stuff and Tetracycline
24) Prednisone as a steroid for allergic reactions and swelling
25) Dramamine for motion sickness
26) Benadryl to calm a dog
27) a bottle of aspirin to address soreness and stiffness
28) horse doctoring stuff: Cut Heal, and Wound-Kote blue lotion
29) Orphaned socks make great covers for injured feet, tails and ears
30) Glucose related problems:
    •large, needle-less syringe and a bottle of Karo syrup
    •honey packets
    •packets of water soluble electrolyte powder

One book:
Dog Owner's Home Veterinary Handbook, Delbart G. Carlson, D.V.M., and James M. Griffin, M.D., Howell Book House, New York, N. Y., ISBN 0-87605-537-4

Joe Guirfa inspects his GSP for injury during a Utah ruffed grouse hunt.

Index

A

adrenaline 96, 103, 124, 125, 129, 143, 144, 165, 178, 235, 263
affection 82, 105, 106, 224
air scent 57, 61, 169, 170, 171, 173
anchor chain 100, 205
association/s 29, 44, 53, 75, 79, 80, 82, 83, 90, 91, 92, 96, 100, 116, 124, 129, 138, 143, 152, 153, 157, 164, 165, 178, 195, 198, 200, 204, 206, 207, 209, 210, 212, 213, 223, 253
auditory association 198

B

backing 56, 58, 61, 75, 89, 120, 138, 188, 202, 235
balk 87, 142, 262
Bandita 9, 32, 35, 264, 265
Bark 'N Spray 255
bark collar 13, 270
barking 13, 218, 249, 250, 251, 252, 254, 255, 270
barrel 75, 79, 178, 254, 277, 299
Beau 16, 17, 136, 137, 138
Becky 25, 26, 27, 28
beeper collar 100, 103, 195, 201, 202, 242, 261, 271, 272
Belle 133, 134, 208, 264
bells 197, 198, 242, 272
belt lead 13, 273
Beryl 260, 262, 264, 265, 266
Bill Tarrant 7, 8, 9, 40, 151, 166, 235, 257
bird bucket 13, 275
bird cages 13, 274
bird carriers 274, 275, 276, 277
bird pouches 13, 276
bird releases 278, 279
bird work 96, 102, 218
blank gun 96, 221, 225, 226, 281
blinking 13, 42, 226, 227, 228, 231, 232, 235
boat chain 103
bobwhite quail 116, 121, 136, 261, 274

Boo 13, 218, 219, 220
boredom 72, 78, 91, 92, 125, 217
Boyken spaniel 65
breath 31, 43
Brittanies 11, 15, 17, 47, 48, 49, 51, 53, 61, 62, 89, 126, 138, 158, 200
bumper/s 13, 34, 38, 68, 141, 142, 150, 164, 282, 299
Buster 13, 218, 219, 220

C

"Come" 12, 105, 106, 178
cable 30, 83, 90, 92, 94, 95, 96, 100, 145, 146, 152, 200, 295, 301
cage 51, 111, 117, 120, 275
call back pens 13, 277
canine culture 216
car avoidance 210
carry pouch 105, 114
carry the bird 105, 143, 159, 161
chain gang 13, 26, 27, 29, 40, 46, 283
check cord/s 12, 13, 55, 75, 79, 80, 83, 90, 91, 100, 102, 103, 104, 105, 106, 108, 113, 129, 142, 143, 152, 162, 189, 206, 211, 212, 215, 217, 235, 238, 242, 286, 292, 301
check whistle 176, 177
Chesapeake Bay Retrievers 11, 49, 67, 68, 89, 135, 144, 247, 265, 282
chuckar 116, 117, 120, 121, 157, 164, 274
click method 73
Cocker spaniel 11, 62, 65
command/s 41, 43, 74, 75, 79, 80, 82, 83, 86, 90, 91, 92, 94, 95, 104, 105, 106, 107, 108, 123, 124, 138, 141, 145, 147, 154, 155, 159, 164, 165, 177, 178, 179, 206, 207, 218, 252, 253, 254
commercially produced bird scent 141
communal dog yard 60, 143, 254
compassion 257
compliance 75, 79, 82, 86, 89, 90, 91, 92, 96, 97, 99, 106, 108, 124, 126, 130, 135, 142, 152, 154, 155, 163, 166, 177, 178, 198, 204, 206, 217, 254
Concho 247, 248, 264, 265
confidence 40, 42
continuous button 197
conventional force breaking 12, 148, 162
covey instinct 117
cower 86, 87, 89, 222
cripple/s 49, 58, 60, 138, 175
cue/s 29, 38, 43, 75, 80, 90, 91, 92, 105, 106, 123, 124, 129, 155, 156, 165, 176, 177, 178, 201, 210, 212, 226, 237, 238, 253, 254

D

D-ring collar 79, 80, 83, 93, 241, 288, 301
Dandy 264

Delmar Smith 151, 166, 293
Delmar Smith Wonder Lead 293
discharging weapons 223
distractions 82, 93, 102
dizzied bird 108, 112, 113
dog fight 247
dog handling 44
dog nail cutters 192, 304
"dogs know everything all the time" 40
dog trailer 26
dove 52, 144, 166
dowel/s 14, 147, 148, 151, 153, 155, 156, 158, 162, 163, 164, 289
drag chains 205
dragged check cord 103, 206
Drathauers 11, 59
drill/s 43, 44, 78, 82, 83, 86, 89, 90, 92, 96, 100, 103, 108, 124, 129, 134, 136, 142, 143, 155, 157, 159, 164, 225, 226, 241, 253, 289
dummy collars 200

E

ear pinch 151, 153, 156, 162, 163, 164
e-collar/electronic collar 53, 55, 57, 92, 100, 103, 138, 165, 178, 195, 198, 204, 206, 207, 238, 279
electrical stimulation 78, 124, 129, 197, 198, 200, 206, 209, 213, 228, 250, 251
electronic bark collar 250, 251, 255
electronic remote controlled launchers 108
electronic remote control releases 111
Elegant quail 173, 175, 183
Elhew pointer 244
Emma 11, 16, 31, 32, 33, 34, 35, 36, 264
enforce compliance 75, 91, 96, 99, 126, 152, 177, 198, 204
English pointer 46, 48, 50, 55, 57, 61, 89
English setter 5, 9, 37, 45, 48, 49, 53, 57, 72, 73, 78, 81, 90, 93, 97, 101, 126, 128, 133, 158, 166, 174, 218, 228, 290, 301
enthusiasm 34, 43, 102, 103, 165, 225, 249, 250, 251, 263
envy 160, 217, 223
evaporation 130
expectation 83, 124, 135, 198, 225
eye contact 47, 80, 86, 91, 106, 147, 154, 155, 177, 204, 211, 224, 225, 238

F

fetch 96, 105, 137, 159
field trial 23, 49, 50, 51, 53, 57, 78, 126, 157, 158, 232, 236
field work 12, 63, 69, 89, 96, 100, 116, 195, 226, 236
fighting 13, 246
First Aid 12, 14, 188, 304
flat of the hand 80, 86, 90, 91, 124, 159, 177

flush 35, 44, 66, 91, 96, 99, 110, 111, 112, 113, 114, 121, 123, 124, 128, 129, 130, 131, 172, 174, 176, 177, 235, 300, 301
flushing dogs 12, 64, 75, 108, 123, 124, 237, 300
fly away/ flyaway bird 96, 105, 106, 108, 113, 123, 128, 174, 278, 279
flyer 51, 100, 102, 106, 130, 204, 219, 225, 236, 239, 240, 241, 242, 243, 245, 261, 265
flying birds 12, 102
fold-down table 100
force breaking 12, 145, 148, 150, 151, 152, 156, 157, 158, 159, 160, 162, 163, 164, 165, 166
force breaking table 12, 133, 143, 144, 145, 150, 163, 289, 298, 299
foundation posts 216

G

Gambel's quail 28, 34, 174, 231
game birds 116, 274
genetics 31, 40, 49, 52, 53, 56, 58, 63, 64, 66, 69, 74, 103, 104, 125, 126, 133, 142, 144, 145, 156, 174, 220, 239
German Shorthair Pointers/GSPs/shorthairs 11, 15, 16, 17, 24, 25, 47, 48, 49, 50, 58, 59, 60, 62, 66, 74, 84, 99, 110, 122, 126, 127, 136, 160, 161, 169, 173, 176, 183, 219, 229, 230, 232, 233, 234, 235, 239, 246, 247, 248, 260, 266, 271, 305
German Wire-haired pointers/GWPs 49, 59, 60, 126, 144
Global Positioning Satellite functions 202
Golden retrievers 64, 67, 69, 169, 247
Gordon setters 53, 126
GPS unit 202
Griffons 11, 59, 60
ground scent 49, 58, 60, 169, 170
gunfire 44, 74, 75, 222, 223, 225
guns 191, 222, 253, 296, 304
gun sensitive 219, 222

H

"here" 12, 105, 106
"hold it" 154, 155, 157
hand command 82
handling in the field 105, 195
handling problems 43
hand signal 90, 91, 177, 178
hard mouth 12, 42, 143, 144, 145
harness 90, 91, 111, 112, 114, 151, 278, 280, 286
heat/heat prostration 12, 181, 182, 183, 184, 185, 188, 238
"heel" command 80
"here now!" 106
hobble/s 14, 93, 96, 103, 115, 121, 124, 126, 129, 154, 163, 187, 217, 289, 290
hoe-on 43, 82, 86, 155
hold 34, 41
"hold it" 147, 148, 155, 159

homing pigeons 31, 96, 102, 108, 110, 115, 116, 117, 131, 234
honoring another dog's point 138
hook 78, 79, 80, 83, 86, 90, 91, 92, 93, 164, 200, 241, 283
Horace Lytle 51
hot walker 83
hunting 15, 16, 17, 23, 28, 29, 32, 34, 43, 44, 49, 51, 53, 56, 57, 58, 60, 61, 62, 63, 64,
    66, 69, 73, 74, 75, 78, 79, 100, 108, 116, 123, 134, 136, 145, 158, 165, 166, 169,
    172, 173, 175, 176, 178, 182, 183, 185, 188, 189, 217, 218, 219, 220, 228, 236,
    237, 238, 239, 243, 244, 253, 258, 259, 265, 276
hunting instinct 58
hunting stock 57, 63, 64, 66
hunting style 49, 265
hup/hupped 23, 74, 75, 81, 87, 88, 90, 104, 114, 123, 124, 135

I

instinct 50, 58, 60, 61, 63, 104, 117, 125, 126, 173, 183, 235
intentionality 43

J

Jasper 34, 174, 234, 264
javelina 35, 209, 210
Jay Smith 7, 8, 94, 99, 102, 110, 146, 150, 299
jealousy 160, 217, 223, 229, 234
johnny house 120, 274, 277

K

Kate 133, 134, 264
kennel box 14, 291
kindness 29, 43, 44, 219, 224, 257

L

Labradors 11, 49, 66, 68, 255
launchers 108, 109, 123, 202
layers 23, 82, 87, 90, 96, 100, 103, 108, 123
line of travel 105, 134, 178, 265, 271
long range blast of a whistle 92
Lost Dog 239

M

"momentary" stimulation 197
magic 23, 24, 27, 28
malpai 187
manners 111, 116, 123, 125, 130, 138, 164, 177, 178, 201, 217, 232, 235, 239
Mearns' quail 26, 45, 122, 171
mechanical launcher 111
mechanical releases 13, 279

metal release cage 111
modified force breaking 12, 150, 156, 157, 158, 159, 160, 162, 164
momentary stimulation 197
Musette 5, 128, 192, 264
muzzles 246

N

natural instinct 125
neck collar 80, 83, 152
negative stimulation 151, 162
nerve hitch 136, 138, 151, 156, 162, 289
noncompliance 89
nose 24, 38, 39, 40, 41, 75, 87, 93, 104, 123, 135, 154, 169, 170, 173, 174, 175, 211, 225, 252, 290
nylon bird harnesses 13, 112, 278

O

obedience command 75
olfactory communication 38
osmosis 29
overhead cable 145, 152

P

"page" function 198
pads 12, 186
Panalog 190, 304
passion 21, 23, 24, 43
passive-aggressive 86, 89, 217, 218
patience 8, 11, 15, 16, 29, 44, 72, 216
pheasant 64, 110, 116, 117, 144, 207, 274
physical and verbal cues 29
pick-up dog 49, 52, 66, 135
pigeon 31, 94, 96, 97, 99, 101, 102, 103, 104, 106, 110, 111, 112, 113, 114, 115, 116, 117, 118, 119, 120, 123, 125, 131, 157, 158, 160, 164, 215, 217, 225, 229, 231, 232, 233, 234, 235, 266, 274, 275, 278, 290
pig tie 14, 87, 89, 91, 292, 293
pinch collar 14, 87, 89, 91, 217, 294
planted bird/s 12, 27, 108, 109, 111, 112, 115, 121, 123, 127, 128, 129, 130, 215, 223, 277
planting birds 108, 125, 275, 278
point/pointing 4, 7, 12, 24, 31, 32, 35, 41, 42, 44, 52, 53, 55, 56, 58, 60, 61, 62, 63, 66, 68, 72, 74, 75, 78, 79, 80, 82, 83, 86, 87, 88, 90, 92, 93, 96, 99, 103, 104, 105, 106, 107, 108, 110, 111, 113, 114, 120, 123, 125, 126, 128, 129, 130, 131, 134, 135, 136, 137, 138, 142, 144, 146, 152, 154, 155, 156, 157, 159, 162, 163, 164, 165, 170, 173, 174, 176, 177, 178, 179, 181, 182, 183, 197, 201, 202, 207, 209, 211, 212, 213, 215, 217, 222, 223, 224, 225, 226, 235, 236, 237, 238, 239, 241, 242, 248, 253, 258, 261, 262, 271, 295, 296

pointers 11, 24, 25, 46, 48, 49, 50, 51, 52, 53, 55, 56, 57, 58, 59, 60, 61, 89, 126, 158, 170, 182, 186, 239, 244, 245
pointing breeds 12, 66, 75, 125
pointing instinct 60, 61, 63, 104, 125
pointing labs 53
porcupines 189, 204, 209, 210
positive interaction 97
positive outcome 86
post 27, 33, 43, 44, 46, 73, 77, 79, 83, 86, 87, 89, 90, 91, 92, 93, 94, 96, 100, 103, 125, 130, 152, 154, 155, 157, 158, 163, 164, 205, 221, 225, 231, 248, 283, 293, 301, 302
prairie grouse 175
praise 82, 89, 105, 158
presenting birds to hand 142
pro-active collar use/association 204, 206, 209
professional trainers 39
proper cue 43
proximity 27, 106, 212, 216, 262
Pudle Pointers 11, 48, 59, 60, 215
puppies 28, 29, 30, 31, 32, 34, 48, 49, 50, 51, 52, 53, 57, 59, 60, 62, 64, 65, 66, 68, 71, 125, 133, 134, 136, 141, 142, 143, 174, 216, 228, 229, 231, 233, 239, 247, 251, 252, 259, 262, 263, 264

Q

quail 16, 26, 27, 28, 34, 36, 37, 45, 47, 52, 111, 116, 117, 120, 121, 122, 134, 137, 138, 139, 144, 157, 158, 164, 166, 171, 173, 174, 175, 183, 184, 231, 232, 233, 260, 274, 277, 278

R

"release" 147, 155, 157, 159
range 35, 41, 63, 92, 103, 107, 126, 138, 158, 162, 177, 178, 179, 200, 201, 203, 205, 206, 223, 225, 236, 237, 238, 249, 250, 274, 291, 300
Rascal 37, 264, 265, 266
rattlesnake/rattlesnake aversion training 7, 69, 204, 208, 209, 210, 211, 212
reactive e-collar use 13, 209
Rebel 262, 264
recall pens 117, 120, 277
rechargeable units 202
red setters 53, 126
release/release command 42, 43, 82, 86, 100, 104, 111, 118, 123, 128, 129, 130, 136, 137, 142, 147, 150, 155, 156, 157, 158, 159, 162, 164, 175, 176, 177, 195, 262, 271, 272, 277, 278, 279, 280, 286, 290
release traps 111, 128, 279
remote control launchers 123
remote control releases/traps 111, 128
repetitions 78, 86, 89, 96
respect 29, 43

restraint device 129
restraint harnesses 111, 158
retrieve/retrieves/retrieving 12, 28, 34, 50, 51, 53, 57, 58, 61, 63, 66, 67, 88, 96, 101, 105, 122, 124, 126, 130, 133, 134, 135, 136, 137, 138, 139, 141, 142, 143, 144, 149, 151, 152, 157, 158, 159, 160, 161, 162, 164, 165, 166, 169, 215, 217, 218, 225, 282, 286
Retrievers 11, 49, 56, 57, 60, 64, 66, 67, 69, 75, 81, 105, 108, 133, 138, 141, 143, 145, 151, 152, 153, 163, 166, 207, 225, 299, 300
rope 43, 44, 79, 80, 82, 83, 86, 90, 91, 103, 105, 141, 142, 186, 206, 234, 235, 248, 263, 282, 286, 292, 295
Rose 133, 134, 135, 264

S

Sadie 265
Sara Beth 262, 263, 264
scent 12, 24, 35, 49, 57, 60, 61, 74, 99, 111, 123, 125, 126, 129, 135, 136, 141, 169, 170, 171, 172, 173, 175, 176, 209, 210, 212, 213, 221, 231, 241, 278, 279
scent cone 99, 129, 169
scent stream/trail 24, 111, 123, 125, 126, 175, 212, 279
Scott's Dog Supply 93, 111, 278, 290, 293
self-hunting 56, 57, 100, 201, 218, 219, 236, 237, 239, 244, 263
sense of smell 38
Setters 5, 9, 11, 32, 34, 35, 37, 45, 48, 49, 53, 57, 58, 61, 67, 72, 73, 78, 79, 81, 84, 89, 90, 93, 94, 95, 97, 99, 101, 104, 110, 122, 126, 128, 133, 138, 158, 160, 161, 165, 166, 174, 184, 218, 228, 229, 230, 231, 232, 234, 235, 236, 239, 246, 247, 248, 258, 259, 260, 261, 262, 266, 290, 299, 301
sharptails 182
short-tied 25, 72
shot 68, 75, 96, 116, 120, 122, 124, 130, 131, 134, 135, 144, 157, 169, 177, 216, 221, 222, 226, 296
shotgun 15, 35, 100, 138, 178, 226, 261, 267, 292, 296, 297, 300
shy: gun, bird, man 13, 15, 33, 218, 219, 220, 221, 222, 223, 224, 225, 226, 228, 232, 278, 281
simultaneous touch 43
sit 23, 26, 29, 68, 74, 75, 81, 86, 87, 88, 158, 224, 225, 260
skunks 189, 209, 210
Smokie 229, 230
Snake Safe training 64, 65, 211
soft tissue wound 190
Spaniels 49, 61, 108
spiked harnesses 144
Springers 11, 64
staple gun 191
staple removal pliers 191
steady 41
stimulation 92, 124, 129, 138, 162, 165, 178, 195, 196, 197, 198, 199, 200, 204, 206, 208, 209, 211, 213, 255, 270

stimulation levels 92, 124, 196, 197, 198, 200, 204, 206, 213, 255
structure 56, 57, 73, 75, 87, 96, 124, 157, 158, 162, 210, 217, 236, 237, 251, 252, 253, 263
structured training 41, 58, 60, 75, 96, 133
surveyor's tape 115
sutures 191

T

table work 100
team player 74, 103, 116, 133, 201
telepathy 44
temperament 38, 49, 50, 53, 56, 59, 63, 64, 65, 66, 67, 68, 211, 213, 218, 265
tie-out cable 14, 83, 295, 301
tools 38, 79, 87, 96, 131, 152, 163, 188, 195, 204, 217, 223, 257, 264, 289
trailer 16, 26, 47, 48, 100, 102, 106, 120, 220, 222, 229, 230, 237, 239, 242, 245, 260, 265, 281, 283
trainer 23, 30, 39, 40, 41
training bucks 14, 289
training bumper 38
training introduction 41
training problems 13, 215
training table 14, 75, 298
transmitter 123, 198, 199, 202, 203, 208, 213, 271, 279
trill whistle blast 91, 178, 300
trust 30, 38, 44
tweezers 87, 189, 191, 192, 304

U

unencumbered planted pigeons 112
unintended consequences 139, 143
unrestrained dizzy bird 108
upland flush dog 66
upland game birds 117

V

velcro cuffs, harness, straps 93, 111, 115, 121, 154, 157, 278, 290
verbal command 43
verbal cues 29, 80, 90, 91, 92, 178
verbal release command 43
versatile breed 58
vet wrap 188, 192, 304
vibrating page feature 204
Vizslas 11, 53, 63, 126
vocalization 86
voice 42, 43, 47, 48, 80, 86, 91, 92, 100, 105, 124, 129, 177, 178, 181, 206, 238, 245, 249, 253, 254, 281

W

waist pouch 96
water 12, 25, 26, 30, 31, 35, 49, 50, 56, 57, 58, 60, 62, 64, 66, 67, 106, 133, 142, 170, 172, 176, 181, 182, 183, 184, 185, 190, 193, 219, 231, 237, 238, 241, 242, 248, 255, 259, 260, 286, 304
waterfowl dog 66
water work 50, 56, 64
Weimaraners 11, 63, 126
welder's tweezers 191, 304
wet 32, 58, 106, 182, 183, 184, 185, 255
whistle 42, 51, 75, 91, 92, 100, 104, 105, 106, 107, 108, 113, 123, 124, 129, 137, 176, 177, 178, 179, 207, 234, 237, 238, 242, 249, 252, 277, 279, 300
whoa breaking/whoa/whoaing/whoaed 11, 12, 14, 23, 27, 42, 43, 46, 53, 56, 57, 73, 74, 75, 77, 78, 79, 80, 81, 82, 83, 84, 86, 87, 88, 89, 90, 91, 92, 93, 94, 95, 96, 97, 99, 100, 102, 103, 104, 108, 113, 114, 125, 126, 128, 129, 130, 137, 145, 152, 154, 155, 159, 164, 177, 178, 201, 207, 220, 221, 225, 226, 230, 231, 232, 234, 235, 238, 260, 263, 283, 290, 293, 294, 299, 300, 301, 302
whoa/hup breaking 207
whoa barrel 75
whoa circle 83, 96
whoa hook 78, 79, 83, 91, 92, 93, 164
whoa post 27, 43, 46
wild birds 23, 24, 27, 58, 73, 78, 111, 115, 116, 120, 121, 123, 128, 131, 135, 144, 157, 158, 159, 165, 169, 174, 175, 176, 201, 220, 226, 262, 277, 280
wind direction 129
wing 31, 94, 96, 97, 112, 113, 114, 116, 118, 119, 121, 125, 131, 134, 145, 158, 225, 229, 232, 233, 234, 235, 278
wing-pulled 158, 225
wing-tied 94, 112, 158
wither's collar 79, 80, 83, 86, 154
wobbly platform 79

Y

yard session 130
yard work 23, 40, 42, 44, 74, 96, 100, 103, 108, 125, 126, 129, 130, 138, 218, 219, 221, 224, 230, 263

Z

zone of compliance 204
Zorra 262, 263, 264

Contact and Ordering Information

If you would like to order additional copies of this book or other Casa Cielo publications, want information on our training and seminar schedule, or have questions or comments please contact us at the address below:

Casa Cielo Press
P.O. Box 1296
Oracle, AZ 85623
(520)896-9555
casacielopress.com
webparton.com
birddoguniversity.com

casacielopress.com

Printed in the United States
113325LV00004B/46-102/P